CHIRON:
THE NEWEST PLANET IN ASTROLOGY

Chiron was discovered in 1977, and since then there have been few books on this exciting discovery. There has been little time for in-depth research and astrologers are just now adding it to their chart readings.

But, what does it mean? What does it rule? How can you use it in your readings?

Clow contends that Chiron rules Virgo and the sixth house. She supports this with ample evidence and over 700 charts from her personal files. Fifty-five charts are included in this book. There has long been an argument over the rulership of Chiron—Sagittarius or Virgo. After reading *Chiron*, you will *know* it is Virgo.

Included are descriptions of Chiron in the Houses, Signs, in Aspect to other planets and the Nodes, an Ephemeris so that you can locate your own Chiron natal position, *plus* a full exploration of the mythology surrounding Chiron. Clow concentrates heavily on Chiron transits as well.

The discovery of Chiron brought farsightedness into astrology because Chiron is the bridge to the outer planets Uranus, Neptune and Pluto. It orbits on a 50-51 year cycle between Saturn and Uranus. As Mercury helps you to understand the rest of the inner planets, so Chiron's alchemical gate wisdom now makes it possible to fully understand the outer planets. Chiron is alchemy, the gate to the philosopher's stone. It also rules the Tarot reader.

Saturn, Chiron, and Uranus rule the three major life transits, while Pluto is the evolutionary transit force which clears, deepens, and cleans out energy in relation to the whole life cycle. The early attempts to define this planet were the most rapid planetary research in the history of astrology. The reason for this quick action is simple; Chiron can be a healer or a killer. It rules initiation into the next level of awareness which the whole culture is entering.

Clow specializes in transformative astrology. She works mainly with New Age healers and leaders. She works with helping her clients raise the Kundalini force and with healing. She is a New Age astrologer writing about a New Age planet. In this book you will find answers to questions you never knew you had.

About the Author

BARBARA HAND CLOW is actively involved with lecturing, counseling, research, writing, and teaching astrodrama. She studied behavioral psychology in 1965 at the University of Washington, Seattle, and then began extensive reading and study of Reichian, Freudian, and Jungian therapeutic techniques. In 1969, she discovered that astrology was the most accurate and quick diagnostic technique for her, and she began exploration into esoteric and astrological teachings. As she read charts from 1973-1981, she did not believe it was possible to be obtaining the accurate results she got from any known source. In 1982-83, she earned a Master's Degree, and her thesis compared Jungian psychoanalytic techniques and past life regression therapy. During 20 regressions under hypnosis for the thesis, she experienced many past lives as an astrologer-seer, and she began research on the newly discovered planet, Chiron, during that same year. *EYE OF THE CENTAUR: A Visionary Guide into Past Lives* based on the master's thesis was published by Llewellyn Publications in 1986.

To Write to the Author

We cannot guarantee that every letter written to the author can be answered, but all will be forwarded. Both the author and the publisher appreciate hearing from readers, learning of your enjoyment and benefit from this book. Llewellyn also publishes a bi-monthly news magazine of New Age esoteric studies, and some readers' questions and comments may be answered through the *New Times'* columns if permission to do so is included in your original letter. The author participates in seminars and workshops, and dates and places may be announced in *The Llewellyn New Times*. To write to the author, or to secure a few sample copies of the *New Times*, write to:

Barbara Hand Clow
c/o THE LLEWELLYN NEW TIMES
P.O. Box 64383-Dept. 094, St. Paul, MN 55164-0383, U.S.A.

Please enclose a self-addressed, stamped envelope for reply, or $1.00 to cover expenses.

THE LLEWELLYN MODERN ASTROLOGY LIBRARY

Books for the *Leading Edge* of practical and applied astrology as we move toward the culmination of the 20th century.

This is not speculative astrology, nor astrology so esoteric as to have little practical application in meeting the needs of people in these critical times. Yet, these books go far beyond the meaning of "practicality" as seen prior to the 1980's. Our needs are spiritual as well as mundane, planetary as well as particular, evolutionary as well as progressive. Astrology grows with the times, and our times make heavy demands upon intelligence and Wisdom.

The authors are all professional astrologers drawing from their own practice and knowledge of historical persons and events, demonstrating proof of their conclusions with the horoscopes of real people in real situations.

Modern Astrology relates the individual person to the Universe in which he/she lives, not as a passive victim of alien forces but as an active participant in an environment expanded to the breadth, *and depth*, of the Cosmos. We are not alone, and our responsibilities are infinite.

The horoscope is both a measure, and a guide, to personal movement—seeing every act undertaken, every decision made, every event, as *time dynamic*: with effects that move through the many dimensions of space and levels of consciousness in fulfillment of Will and Purpose. Every act becomes an act of Will, for we extend our awareness to consequences reaching to the ends of time and space.

This is astrology supremely important to this unique period in human history, when Pluto transits through Scorpio and Neptune through Capricorn, and the books in this series are intended to provide insight into the critical needs and the critical decisions that must be made.

These books too, are "active agents," bringing to the reader knowledge which will liberate the higher forces inside each person to the end that we may fulfill that for which we were intended.

Carl Llewellyn Weschcke

OTHER BOOKS BY BARBARA HAND CLOW

Stained Glass: A Basic Manual co-authored with Gerry Clow, Little Brown, 1976

Eye of the Centaur: A Visionary Guide into Past Lives, Llewellyn, 1986.

Forthcoming Books

Heart of the Christos: A Visionary Guide Through the Age of Pisces, a sequel to *Eye of the Centaur* in the Mind Chronicles Trilogy.

CHIRON:

Rainbow Bridge Between the Inner and Outer Planets

Barbara Hand Clow

1987
LLEWELLYN PUBLICATIONS
St. Paul, Minnesota, 55164-0383, U.S.A.

International Standard Book Number: 0-87542-094-X
Library of Congress Catalog Number: 87-45244

First Edition, 1987
First Printing, 1987
Second Printing, 1987

Library of Congress Cataloging-in-Publication Data
Clow, Barbara Hand, 1943–
    Chiron: rainbow bridge between the inner and outer planets.

    (Llewellyn modern astrology library)
    Bibliography: p.
    1. Planets, Minor—(2060)—Miscellanea.   2. Astrology.
I. Title.   II. Series.
BF1724.2.C48C56   1987   133.5'3   88-45244
ISBN 0-87542-094-X

Cover Painting: David Egge
Book Design: Terry Buske

Produced by Llewellyn Publications
Typography and Art property of Chester-Kent, Inc.

Published by
LLEWELLYN PUBLICATIONS
A Division of Chester-Kent, Inc.
P.O. Box 64383
St. Paul, MN 55164-0383, U.S.A.

Printed in the United States of America

THIS BOOK IS DEDICATED TO
THE CLEAR FALCON EYE OF HORUS

ACKNOWLEDGEMENTS

I wish to acknowledge the teachings of Horus, Seti, Mena and Imhotep.

As astrologers, I wish to acknowledge Martin Schulman, Bernice Prill Grebner, Marc Robertson, Philip Sedgwick, Bil Tierney, and Ellen Backus.

As healers, I wish to acknowledge Gregory Paxson, Chris Griscom, Kurt Leland, Jessie Fleming, Randall Baer, Tom Cratslie, Brugh Joy, and Matthew Fox.

As great minds who have influenced my thought, Zecharia Sitchin, Marcion, Wilhelm Reich, Mark Lerner, Robert Graves, Bruce Cathie, Immanuel Velikovsky, Robert Temple, Christopher O'Brien, Jerry Ziegler, Brian Swimme, Peter Rogers, and Jose Arguelles.

As Chiron researchers, I wish to acknowledge Zane Stein, Richard Nolle, Ken Negus, Erminie Lantero, Philip Sedgwick, Tony Joseph, and Neil Michelsen.

I especially wish to thank Philip Sedgwick for introducing this book, Angela Werneke for the illustrations and charts, Sue Kurman, Gerry Clow, and Terry Buske for editorial assistance, and all the clients the last four years who made it possible for me to apply the Chiron archetype in readings. I am grateful to Gerry, Chris, and Elizabeth Clow for their patience within our family as I was called away for all this work. At Llewellyn I would like to thank all who assisted me, especially Terry Buske and Phyllis Galde. Without their extra work at the end, this book would not have been possible. And, I would like to thank Carl Weschcke for holding the light for all of us as we struggle to bring healing into the New Age.

Contents

Foreword

by Philip Sedgwick

Currently, as I sit at my typewriter, Jupiter slides through a few remaining degrees of Pisces having just completed an intimate square to Saturn in Sagittarius and Chiron in Gemini. Still to come remain Jupiter square Uranus and the array of Chiron oppositions to Saturn and Uranus. Within the somewhat complicated matrix of these energies lies the implication of changes in the basic philosophical structure of life—a paradigm shift in thought. Astrology is certainly not immune to this transition, and Chiron, one of the newcomers in the astrological scene, represents a significant contribution to this shift. With the duality implied in Chiron's current Gemini visitation and the blending with Saturn's passage in Sagittarius one important concept emerges from this planetary generation—undisputedly, there is more than one right answer!

Chiron by Barbara Hand Clow represents this change in collective thought processes perfectly. Claiming to be open minded and objective about new information due to personal innovations in astrology, I found my beliefs and thoughts confronted and challenged as I passed through Barbara's words, page by page. Many of the beliefs she presents are strong, insightful and provocative.

Barbara presents much solid delineative information for the novice about Chiron which will be most helpful in assisting clients, friends and selves through the straits of healing crises. The mythological background fills in many blanks in previous astrological thought and many of the other ideas . . . well, they will carry your mind to other places.

The point of these mental wanderings you may encounter as you read this work are timely and purposeful. Should you return to your previous realm of astrological thought, then you will be more certain and confident of your contentions than before. Should you adopt new ideas and concepts from these pages, then your time was now for a personal shift in belief.

For astrology to evolve into the New Age which we so fondly and frequently tout, new ideas and applications are essential. Such thought forms must be incorporated without fear, with open minds and in open hearts. All of these are ideas which Barbara Hand Clow encourages you to encounter.

The reasoning applied to Chiron's rulership fit well into the beliefs held by many, and not all, astrologers. While you may not find all parts of the book to be your Cosmic Blend of Tea, you will emerge with new or renewed perspectives to assist in your own personal astrological quest. You may even feel stirrings while reading this treatise. Some of those stirrings could feel like resistance—that may even be a part of Chiron's healing process within you.

In accord with Chiron's wishes . . . To Your Health (Physical, Mental, Emotional and Spiritual).

Philip Sedgwick
February 9, 1987
North Hollywood, CA.

Introduction

In the late 1970's, the general cultural phenomena of ESP, visionary breakthrough, and spontaneous channeling surfaced around the world.

Historically, there have always been "visionaries," people who had paranormal experiences, or received communications from other dimensions. But this planetary eruption of communications from other realms appears to be a worldwide event which is only now in the beginning stages. This eruption is coming at the end of a complex 400-year age of science, and is breaking through into an intense field of skepticism and perceptual denial. As we all know, channeling, divination, and paranormal experiences are nothing new. Such skills were the norm before the rise of Christianity, and these skills still exist in some native traditions. Many believe that ancient cultures existed, such as Atlantis, which had a high level of scientific skill and also utilized magical and divination tools. What really matters is that these forces are becoming more powerful every day in our present reality, and we all sense this change is going to alter our lives beyond recognition.

In the 1930's, waves of blackness and fear swept the Earth. Hitler, Mussolini, Stalin erupted like monsters from the deep. Scientists, mostly in America and Germany, created the early stages of the nuclear and chemical killing technology holding us hostage at this time. Some new energy was manifesting which caused a breakout of negative forces. This energy was causing changes in individuals, societies, and religions, and astrologers worldwide attributed this change to the sighting of the planet Pluto in 1930. Pluto rules the Underworld, the dark forces, and evolution. We are being taught to see that the light only exists because darkness also exists. We are learning that we will never know our divinity until we also look at our shadow.

Most astrologers practicing in the 1960's through 1980's have lived with the integration of the Pluto archetype, and have grown in their skills because of this addition of the archetype of evolution. The eruption of channeling, divination, and multi-dimensional perceptual skills is ruled by the planet Chiron. Within a few years of Chiron's sighting on Nov. 1, 1977, astrologers already had Chiron ephemerides, a journal devoted to Chiron research called *The Key,* and many felt a deep inner movement in the psyche.

From the beginning, some of us felt a deep inner stirring of hope that the bridge was being built which would help us cope with the release of the forces of the outer planets since 1781, when Uranus was sighted. Chiron rules the Chirotic point, the place between dimensions which is timeless, empty, and placeless; it is the place between dimensions which is the interface point from the inner planets to the outer planets.

Nothing has changed out there in the other dimensions. What has happened is that *we* have changed, our perceptions about reality have changed. You will find this book contains many new terms such as resonance, Chirotic, dimensional, and hologram. You will find this book redefines many old terms such as divination, magic, alchemy, occult, and dark forces. A new language is required because we are in the middle of a massive energetic reorganization which is opening new perceptual centers within ourselves. This is a critical leap phase to new consciousness which cannot succeed without new concepts, and language helps us identify the new feelings and experiences we are all having.

At this critical juncture, we are in grave danger of falling into atavism or reversion to a more primitive state of mind unless we define the new bridging energy according to our present reality instead of the distant and de-energized past. For example, if we respond to the word *occult* as the old definition—the repository of ancient, secret, hidden magical skills—then we respond by hiding ourselves and attempting to build up secret powers which we shield from all others. My new definition has to do with the technology of the eye—the ability to see into the inner beauty of the cosmos. As this book goes to press in the winter of 1987, scientists are saying that they are seeing a new supernova, and 13-billion light years from Earth they are watching seven galaxies being born. A physicist agreed with me that this goes back to the old Berkeley-Hume discussion about the tree falling in the forest. The question was, does the tree actually fall if no one is in the forest, if no one sees the tree or hears it falling? The physicist, Dr. Brian Swimme, and I believe that these cosmic happenings are *now* because we *see* them now. My definition of occult is that we can see creation if we empty ourselves of time and place boundaries. There is no such thing as secrecy once we are ready to really look. The word *occult* carries the optical sense of the point where the optical nerve interfaces with the brain and awareness is the result. That is one of the Chirotic points.

Divination was re-defined by Christianity as a magical skill of using augury or omens to read the future. If we want to be atavistic we can immerse ourselves in old ritual forms to get that power back. Or, we can redefine the energy now that the physicists have joined up with Eastern mystics and are teaching that there is no past, present, or future. We now are able to see that time is just a useful third-dimensional construct for organizing reality that we can divine through time anytime that sight is useful to us. That is how we can take a horoscope map of an incarnation in place and time and divine its meaning. We are not looking into the future or examining the past; all time exists in that horoscope as you peer into its revealing landscape.

Magic has been defined as taking and using power to compel action whether it was positive (white magic), or negative (black magic). But we live in an age where we know that matter is never destroyed, it just changes form. We are beginning to understand that the real power we have comes from alignment with natural processes that have existed in the cosmos from the beginning of time. Those vehicles and processes are so macrocosmic that our real energy comes from being in alignment or attunement with that order in the universe. We are exhausted by our obsession with control (Saturn) and we intuitively know that we will die if we do not change. The magicians of our times are the atomic scientists, and the alchemists of our days are the chemists who are altering our genetic fabric. They are recreating our hologram of life structures.

A hologram is a unifying energy structure which is exactly the same within all its parts. Recently, many of us have been able to examine holographic photography and we instantly perceived that reality is no more or no less a series of unified energy fields. And the astrological chart is a hologram, a unified energy field of consciousness which maps the energetics of the soul's formation into matter from birth to death. I use the words *holographic, resonance,* and *attunement* throughout this book as tools to help all of us begin to grasp the Chirotic point. Most of us now have been told that we are empty space inside, that the distance between one molecule and another in our bodies is from the top of the World Trade Center down to the East River in New York City. As an astrologer, I like to think about the fact that the distance from one molecule to another inside me is the distance of Mercury to Venus or Uranus to Neptune. We are empty within; we are diaphanous. Even the lead which Saturn rules is empty within.

Dimension has been understood in many fields, particularly mathematics, to mean measurement, a way to determine boundaries. But, if you can stay with the magnitude of emptiness in all matter, what has boundaries or can be measured? In fact, nothing. We have been looking at it all backwards because we did not understand that we are nothing more than unified energy fields. Dimensionality actually has to do with energy definition and with interface points between energies. We are moving away from third-dimensional consciousness and beginning to sense the actuality of the fourth dimension. The fourth dimension is the timeless and spaceless place or placeless space; it is the zone in between; it is *Chiros.*

There are many places in this book where, when at a loss for words, I have resorted to examples of the dynamics of Chiron. When we were children we were taught that we could not define a word by using an example, that we had to describe it. Therefore, all of us are accustomed to limiting instead of *expanding* perception. Chiron describes energies and not things; Chiron is like an action verb instead of a noun. Egyptian hieroglyphics are a Chirotic language, and that is why the real truth in Egyptian sacred scriptures can only be read by those who think as the Egyptians used to think. For example, a bird hieroglyph is not just a bird. It means communication from one point to another, an ability to see what is going on, the ability to know what season it is and how one should respond to weather and star patterns, and the ability to be free. The placement of Chiron in the sky and the natal chart is like that. It is an energy point, a magnetic pull into spherical time and place. It is a vehicle to employ magic and divination into what we really are.

As we move out from rigid Saturnian constructs of who we are, it is like leaving the shore and traveling in outer space. Chiron orbits between Saturn and Uranus, and before we saw the planet in 1977, it made sense not to just jump off the edge into nothingness. But now we have the bridge to teach us how to form ourselves here in matter in a way that also invites in the consciousness of the outer planets and the cosmos. We are really ready now to interface with the cosmos, and that is why astonomer Kowal saw Chiron in his telescope in the late 1970's.

Saturn is the planet which rules making structure and form in our Earth lives, and it orbits around and contains the inner planets. The inner planets are the rulers of our personal response patterns. Mercury rules the way our mind functions and is an indicator of how well we can see ourselves. Venus rules our receptivity to all that exists. Earth rules our integration of self, and is the center of our astrological hologram. The Moon screens the perceptions coming into our awareness and rules our autonomic responses to experience. Mars rules the projective power dynamism which gives us the energy to think, receive feelings, respond, and drive ourselves to become Solar, to know ourselves. Jupiter expands us as much as possible so we can contact our higher self, as Saturn takes us through experience to cause us to create a container of our energy.

Simple, you say? Yes, that part is simple. The confusion has been that we were separate from our divinity—from the energetics of the outer planets, Uranus, Neptune, and Pluto. The ancients worked with the outer planets as intuitive, unseen energies. In fact, they had no bridge to the outer planet energies—Uranus as kundalini energy; Neptune as the divine within; and Pluto as galactic evolution. So, they used magical techniques—occult technology—to contact those forces. Now, with the sighting of Chiron, each individual can walk the Rainbow Bridge. The ray pathway to the galactic exists for you to use. You can now go directly to the source, and you do not need the old teachings to get there.

Uranus rules systemic kundalini/electrical resonance with the cosmos, and Neptune rules mystical letting go into cosmos. Pluto rules the most intense clearing of our karmic Earth experience according to the overall plan of our higher self, which chooses what we are to do here. Now we have the way to get to those levels while we exist in human form. Before now, we would jump out of the body and see the divine after death. Now we can experience ecstasy, *samadhi,* rapture, bliss while in physical form. Except for a few highly trained masters in the past, this is a new dimension open to all beings since 1977. We must stretch ourselves into a whole new dynamic with a whole new language.

Chiron orbits on a 50-51 year cycle between Saturn and Uranus, bridging the inner and outer planets. As we enter into early research work on Chiron, it is useful to image Chiron in relation to the inner planetary group as somewhat like Mercury to the Sun: as Mercury helps you to understand Venus, Mars, Jupiter, Saturn, and Moon, so Chiron's alchemical gate wisdom now makes it possible to better understand Uranus, Neptune, and Pluto. The orbit of Chiron is highly elliptical, making this the planet which rules spiral forms of evolution while the other planets teach us in a circular fashion. Like the fabled Wheel of Karma, we keep on going back to the eternal beginning with the circular orbits; and Chiron is the key into the actual spiral form of the universe or spherical time.

Chiron is alchemy, the gate to the philosopher's stone. Saturn disciplines us into our form in any given lifetime, and Uranus comes behind Saturn's basic 2½-year growth pattern each seven years and breaks form. At the time of each Saturn square or growth crisis, Uranus electrifies the calcified Saturn form and shocks us into new understandings about the molds we've carefully created for our lives. Uranus is the first of the outer planets, and it continually regenerates the nervous system with electrical shocks which keep us from merely solidifying into lifeless Saturnian lead. Neptune embodies energies and beings coming from little-known realms beyond our planet, Earth. Neptune has not been fully explicated by astrologers because it was not possible to grasp the Neptunian-energy archetype without the planetary and house rulership of Chiron. That is the work of this book. We can now begin to define the Neptunian archetypal force better by using Chiron in polarity relationship to Neptune because the nature of the Virgo/Pisces polarity reveals the Neptunian energy when it is viewed in polarity with Chiron and, we can now make the bridge from Saturn form to the outer planets by utilizing Chiron in readings.

When I started research on charts using Chiron ruling Virgo and the sixth house, I was relieved to find I finally could really grasp the true Virgo archetype; and then I found a profound new understanding of Neptune in the twelfth house. Pluto deepens our consciousness by driving us into the underground for the truth. Even though Pluto is an evolutionary growth experience, Pluto is circular, and ultimately it is possible for anyone to avoid circular growth. Only spiral evolution is capable of transforming *any* energy. We know Plutonian growth as a long-term evolutionary pattern even though we only experience part of Pluto's 260-year cycle around the Sun in any one life. But Chiron is the spiral energy because its orbit is extremely elliptical. Its elliptical energy is experienced unpredictably from lifetime to lifetime, but we experience a Chiron return in almost each incarnation since its orbit around the Sun is 51 years. We experience two Saturn returns if we live past age 60, one Chiron return if we live past age 50; one Uranus opposition at mid-life; and even a Uranus return if we live a long life until age 84.

Saturn, Chiron and Uranus rule the three major life transits, while Pluto is the evolutionary transit force which deepens and clears out energy in relation to the whole life cycle. Then, when all else fails, Chiron transforms or causes death. For example, we can have our first Chiron square—or awareness—any time from ages 5½ to 23! Our first Chiron square teaches us that we can know God, because the Chirotic or galvanizing experience separates us from our ego structure and fuses our being into a divine consciousness. Illumination can't be had if we are living a dream of separation, a belief system based on an emotional need for an ego structure. Thus, many five-year olds are still merged in the cosmic energy, and they will have an early and powerful mystical experience if they have an early Chiron square. For persons in their twenties having the first Chiron square, the lesson may come that the reality they have created is their own illusion, that all they believe in exists as their own projection. It is difficult to distinguish Chiron from Pluto energetically because we have only begun to define Pluto well in the last ten years. In fact, the energies are radically different. Jeff Green's brilliant new book *Pluto: The Evolutionary Journey of the Soul* will greatly help to differentiate these two powerful forces.[1] Pluto rules evolutionary growth or transformative growth, and Chiron rules alchemical process or transmutative growth; the time when a new essence is birthed and an old energy dies. Pluto rules the journey through the Underworld, and Chiron rules the encounter with the blinding light of the divine.

Evolutionary growth is circular with Pluto, but a magic leap occurs when the evolutionary pattern is completed and the soul undertakes a radical leap. This leap is always a death, and a new birth out of nothingness; a successful initiation. Initiation is the death of an old energy so that a new form can be created. Pluto is experiential and systemic; Chiron is a desperate end which propels the system into new pathways, or kills the system. The reality structure that is our teacher is circular until we admit the possibility that the reality we have defined is a creation of our consciousness. This is moving into New Physics, but in fact the whole new consciousness movement is rapidly moving into such leaps of awareness. And without Chiron as a conscious guide into these realms, without identifying exactly what this journey is, the experimenter can quickly fall into unnecessary danger. Or to put it another way, Chiron rules wholistic thought processes which trigger a holographic change and instantly alter the whole system. Pluto is more a progressive change.

Once a planet is sighted by astronomers, its energy manifests on Earth. Chiron rules healing with the hands, crystals, initiation alchemy, actual alteration of the body in some way by the mind or spirit, by finding our guide. It rules all issues of making Saturnian form on Earth and then bringing—Uranian white light—higher consciousness and energetics into form. This energy is now present on Earth since Chiron's sighting. The only question left is how quickly we will integrate it.

It may seem too early to attempt to define planetary and house rulership of Chiron, but Chiron has completely alchemized my astrological readings, and I feel compelled to offer my results at this time. This book is based on working with 500 charts using Chiron to rule Virgo and the sixth house. Three-hundred fifty of those charts were transited and progressed and read in extreme detail for clients. I specialize in transformative astrology, especially in the Uranus opposite Uranus transit which occurs between ages 38-41 and in new methods for instructing clients on healing skills in the natal chart and how to activate them. I have always attracted many extremely "difficult" charts because of this work with New Age healers and leaders. However, even in relatively balanced and "easier" charts, often the key to the most poorly understood and traumatic times in life are remarkably resolved by working with Chiron. The more I work with Chiron, the more I know it is the gateway to the least resolved and deepest fears lurking within each one of us. It is the key to facing death with awareness. Notice that the first AIDS cases surfaced in Africa and the U.S. in 1977. But, when the fears are faced, just like integrating the Jungian shadow, the personality is remarkably illuminated. I have been especially gratified in my work with Virgos. I was always uncomfortable with Mercury ruling Virgo and the sixth house, but now my difficulties have been so thoroughly resolved that I have been able to really define the exquisitely sensitive power of Virgo. Virgos have a very highly tuned frequency which has just not been recognized by astrologers until 1977. I have become more adept at working with their stresses and helping to find their own energetics with our assistance.

Once I had defined Chiron rulership in my practice in 1983 and began to apply it to readings, a deeper understanding of all the outer planets emerged, particularly Uranus and Neptune, and a whole new form of Horary Astrology manifested which will be demonstrated in Chapter Thirteen. Uranus transits are progressive struggles to raise the kundalini force in the spine and transform the individual into higher awareness, but usually the mystical experiences which empower the individual to do the strenuous Uranian work are first triggered by Neptune and Chiron transits. Chiron defines the *time* of awakening of mysticism, and the Chiron squares attune consciousness to Neptunian receptivity. Or, a client may be in serious nervous distress because energy is misfiring and going awry in the body. Counseling on the Uranus opposite Uranus transit or on the Chiron cycle is often a lifesaver.

This is a pragmatic book, because Chiron is a pragmatic planet. Since it moves us from Saturn to the outer planets, it is the "how-to" planet for initiation timing. Chiron's mythology has already been well-covered by Erminie Lantero, Richard Nolle, Tony Joseph and Zane Stein;[2] and I would recommend their books to readers since my description of Chiron mythology is very experiential because I am trying to define the archeype in the present time. I will concentrate on rulership applications and house positions and on Chiron by transit because the transit effects are profound. Since this book is working with the energy of a new planet—an emerging archetype in our awareness at this time—I will offer many charts as examples. Readers who are not professional astrologers may wish to skip all the chart examples. I am exceedingly grateful to the many clients, associates, friends, and relatives I have been able to study these past four years. They are not identified for obvious reasons. The charts I have selected are those of healers, artists, teachers, servers, and medical professionals who are manifesting Chirotic force to an extreme degree. All individuals are potential healers, not just professionals. So, even though I concentrate on people manifesting Chiron intensely, the dynamic is important to *all*. Imagine what this planet would be if all parents, businessmen, and politicians were attuned to healing. Since I wanted to publish whole charts so that other astrologers can use this book for research I have not used charts exemplifying blocked Chirotic energy, although such cases are mentioned in the text. It is radical to publish whole charts, therefore I have mainly focused on the healing and higher energetics.

If astrologers will just experiment with putting Chiron in charts and trying my recommendations for usage, I think they will be quite amazed at the new potential levels in readings. This planet truly is a missing link between the inner planets as basic personality archetypes, and the outer planets as archetypes to help us link with our galactic selves. Chiron ephemerides are readily available and Chiron is listed in the *Michelsen American Ephemeris for the 20th Century* on each page on the lower right hand side under "Astro Data." Matrix is now including Chiron on their C/Software. For convenience I have also listed general placements for 1900-2000 with Chiron by sign in Chapter Seven. For exact placement, readers must consult an exact ephemeris. Please enjoy this journey with me to find *your* centaur within.

Barbara Hand Clow
March 1, 1987
Santa Fe, New Mexico

Chapter One

MYTHOLOGY: THE EMERGENCE
OF THE WOUNDED HEALER

When a new planet is identified in the solar system, astrologers begin observing major trends going on in the culture at the time of the planetary discovery, looking for energies in the culture which the new planetary body will rule. The discovery of Uranus in 1781, coincidental with the time of the American and French Revolutions and the discovery of electricity, signaled the relationship of Uranian energy to electricity, and personal and social transformation. Society and individuals have not been the same since. The actuality of the relationship between planetary archetypal forces and identifiable cultural trends is not a "scientific fact." However, for students who are comfortable with the Hermetic principle, the relationship of the macrocosm and microcosm, sudden radical cultural shifts cannot be explained any other way.

Pluto was sighted in 1930, twelve years before the first atom was split. Soon thereafter, the chthonic death force of Nazism boiled forth from a seemingly forgotten inner Earth. Pluto rules the solar plexus, the struggle between Thanatos and Eros, primary evolution, radical alteration of matter at the molecular level, and volcanoes which erupt with sudden force from the deep, turning rock into molten liquid. Like a husband whose solar plexus erupts in uncontrollable rage when he discovers his wife in bed with another man, the volcano suddenly erupts and destroys everything in its path. These are the Plutonian issues coming from the deep, and once Pluto was sighted the world soon found itself under the threat of barbaric forces like Hitler and World Wars, as if monsters from the deep ruled the world. The world is still sickened and traumatized by the Pluto revelations—atomic release, World Wars, and genocide—and the revelation of the grip of the death archetype has been overpowering. But Chiron bridges death (Saturn) and life (Uranus). The energy to find

1

the way back to life has emerged.

In 1977 Chiron was sighted, and the symbiotic forces signaling Chiron's archetype appeared alluringly in the culture, and identification began. We got a quick start by examining Chiron mythology. Like Pluto, the mythology is rich in Chiron information. Myths come from ancestral memory which seems to be magically awakened once the physical body—the planet—is sighted. This process is indeed fascinating. As Tony Joseph put it, "The sighting of a new planet in our solar system . . . provides a metaphorical key to crucial trends arising from within the collective psyche."[1] Richard Nolle said, "Astrology and myth go hand-in-hand, at once partaking of the same magical order of reality."[2]

The association between Chiron mythology and the state of our culture since 1977 is an uncanny one, and Chiron even rules the practice of the timing of this unfoldment! This is an essential part of this journey ruling the mythical quest. Chiron rules the synchronicity principle and the art of divination itself, because it explicitly focuses into Saturnian time higher dimensions ruled by Uranus, Neptune and Pluto. The way the story unfolds is just as important as the story itself. Later on, you will see that Chiron is the key to mastery which is ruled by Sagittarius. Therefore, many astrologers feel Chiron rules Sagittarius when in fact it rules the way, gate, or key to mastery, because it is the bridge to the outer planets. Once we have learned to use the outer planet energies, then we are capable of working with mastery. Mastery is the conscious evolution of self with magical forces. The film 2010 revealed that the masters live on Jupiter, and Chiron is the pragmatic teacher who teaches us divination, astrology, healing, sacred warrior ways, and shamnism to lead us to the masters.

In mythology, Chiron was a great astrologer-teacher who initiated healers, warriors and magicians, and therefore we began in 1977 with those identifications. If you will reflect on 1977-1979 you will notice that many New Age magical, healing and sacred warrior teachings emerged in the culture. I emphasize this issue as I begin the story of Chiron because the sighting of this planet itself signals the actual possiblility of recovering all the ancient esoteric techniques for transmutation of body and soul. It has always been a sacred teaching that the adept would learn a divination skill such as Tarot, astrology, runes, or I Ching when the adept was ready to begin the magical quest. And now the energy is present on the planet for people to activate divination skills.

According to Robert Graves in *The Greek Myths*, Cheiron (the archaic spelling) was the priest king of the Centaurs who were Pelasgians or Thracians. He was skilled at hunting, medicine, music, gymnastics, warfare, and astrology. He was the founder of the Asclepian, the ancient healing temple, and he was the teacher of Achilles, Orpheus, Jason, Hercules, Peleus, and many other ancient heroes and warriors.[3] I think the best modern representation of Chiron is Master Miyagi, the master warrior teacher of a young boy in *The Karate Kid.* The movie is a powerful example of how these new images are birthing in the culture. For those who are concerned about the nuclear dilemma, the healing warrior archetype is a profound antidote to excessive political militarism.

According to Graves, the name is the Greek derivation "Cheir," which means "hand," and Centron, "goat." One of the most secret esoteric orders is The Order of the Red Hand which is the same as the divination power of Chiron. Because it is red, the Order shows us that divination power is awakened by the adept's ability to face the chaotic force, the red force, the Sethian force. And because it is the hand, we see the Saturnian molding of time and place on Earth. More about that later, but notice that Chiron is always the master teacher or guide for the adept who then goes out on the quest.

Chiron's lineage is evidence of his extreme antiquity. His grand-parents are Uranus (sky father) and Gaia (Earth mother), his parents are Kronos (Saturn) and Rhea (Venus?), but he was born of an illicit union between Kronos, who took the form of a horse, and Phylria, a sea nymph. Therefore Chiron is half-animal and half-human, and he is of the Earth *and* the sea. The sea connection, as well as the composite horse/ man body, is more evidence of extreme pre-Noatic antiquity, as many of the great teachers before the flood were from the sea, according to Berrosus.[4] The most ancient myths, which come to us through an Appolonian screen which always distorts them somewhat, often describe couplings with sky beings and animal forms. These myths are always highly charged seeds of information about the most primordial civilizations, and it is in these seeds that the Muse lurks, revealing her initiatory secrets to those who have eyes. Chiron's sighting is a physical manifestation of the revelation of significant esoteric secrets in our time.

Chiron married a water goddess, and their daughter was Thea, which means "shining one of the moon." Thea was an exceedingly famous early seer and astrologer. Notice that sexism is at a minimum in the Chiron myths, hinting that they go back to 1500 B.C. or earlier. Around 1300 B.C., the patriarchy assumed control in the Aegean with the Mycenean ascension. Also, notice that Chiron mates with a sea god-dess, which should resonate deeply in readers who are followers of Jung. The birthing from the sea creatures brings forth the integration of the feminine in males who have the courage to pursue the path of an adept. Thea ascended to the stars and became the constellation Pegasus, and mythology teaches that Chiron went to the sky and became Sagittarius (or the horse or unicorn). This is one of the reasons some astrologers believe that Sagittarius is ruled by Chiron. Twenty-seven degrees Sagittarius is the galactic center, and that is why Chiron became Sagittarius. Notice the popularity since 1977 of the unicorn and Pegasus, and that our children know these figures are part of the magical quest.

Chiron was half-horse or unicorn, and half-man. Let this resonate in your psyche as you feel this archetypal union of the animal and human in your solar plexus. Notice that the union of the animal and man is right at the solar plexus, and the phallus is on the horse body and not the man. The symbol tells us that the struggle with good and evil powers is with Pluto, and not with sex. This powerful symbol has emerged now so that our obsession with puny sins can end, and now we can struggle with the real powers and principalities. This great teacher who was animal and human, cosmic and sea immersed, was a healer and a warrior; this archetype has the power we need to face the dark side, our seemingly endless love affair with death and evil. He is the bridge to our animal selves, and the recovery of our power and energy.

In *Eye of the Centaur*,[5] I wrote that we have the same totem animal throughout all our incarnations, just as I believe that we also have the same rising sign degree which can be read with Sabian symbols. Chiron's totem animals were the wryneck and the mountain lion, and there is much wisdom in the survival of this knowledge. I suspect that the wryneck, a sacred bird like the stork in Europe, is his celestial totem (since he was God *and* man), and therefore it is an oracular revelation. The wryneck was known as the messenger of Io that attracted Zeus, and according to Graves, oracular wheels were called "iynges," which means wryneck.[6] The secret hidden here is that you can channel if you enter your consciousness into your neck, usually the right side, and you will have a "wryneck." I suspect that the mountain lion is his Earth totem, and this indicates that Chiron was originally a teacher from Atlantis, because the double lion is the symbol of the Atlantean theocracy.

Chiron is the teacher of the Earth connection to higher planes, and the planetary sighting indicates the time has come for us to manifest our divinity. The sacred teachings on animal energy were highly developed in Egyptian wisdom, and the animal images of the Zodiac show that the earliest attempts to understand archetypal energies were with elemen-tals and animals. It is actually a first step down a long path, because your totem animal will take you to your oracle and then you can hear again. As Richard Nolle put it, "As perfect a balance of animal and human nature as ever lived, Chiron was attuned to the secrets of both instinct and intellect."[7]

Ken Negus made some exceedingly valuable observations on Chiron's energy at the annual meeting of the American Federation of Astrologers in 1981.[8] Ken did extensive early research examining the Chiron natal placements of famous ecologists, and had some fascinating reflections on projection. Ken noted that according to the Greeks, the Centaurs in general were rapists, sodomizers, and plunderers; exactly the same behavior the Christian conquerers of the Americas *projected* upon the Native Americans! Historically, the source of the justification of genocide has always been exactly this type of projection on people who are in the way, and the ability to integrate this form of destructive shadow could be within our grasp, now that Chiron has been sighted. Chiron was a model of high warrior energy, unlike the other centaurs. The low warrior energy results in rape and plunder; the high warrior energy is protection of the feminine hearth and mastery of skill. Another mani-festation of working out Chiron energy since its sighting can be seen in the sexual confusion of many modern spiritual teachers or "gurus" in America since 1977. The male and female followers of teachers have desired mastery and initiation training, and they have often gotten control and sexual exploitation.

Many committed ecologists are Chiron-prominent natally,[9] and in the sections of this book defining usage, the qualities in people who are Chiron-prominent will be looked at. At this point, it is time to say that the sighting of Chiron indicates we will find the way to stop polluting the Earth and being victimized by elemental destructive forces. In the words of Tony Joseph, "By separating ourselves from nature in our attempts to harness and control it, we have paradoxically become like the destruc-tive centaurs unable to constrain ourselves."[10]

We have all been taught that we will continue to make the same mis-takes over and over again until we learn our history; that history repeats itself. But all we see around us is ignorance of that teaching. History is at this time, "his story". women and animals are ruled out like a centaur with no horse body![11] What are we left with, then, as a method to cease repeating the same endless repetitive dynamic? The answer is mple to see, now that the planet ruling this question has been sighted. The answer is that we are to become ensouled, to bring the soul into the body and bless our bodies and the Earth existence with our full essence. We are to bring in full Uranian energy into Saturn form on Earth. How? Remember, Chiron is the way, the teacher of pragmatism who leads us to mastery. What is mastery? Mastery is complete ensoul-ment, it is conscious embodiment of our highest essence or highest octave deep into ourselves.

Chiron's pupils came to him to discover their destiny, to have Chiron show them the pragmatic way to fulfill their highest potential. He taught the essential skills leading to the highest octave which was the first part of a four-part process. He taught Jason how to undertake the quest, and he taught Achilles to be a sacred runner and to play the kithara. He taught Asclepios the art of healing, and thus Chiron is actually the father of medicine. Chiron also founded the Chironium, a healing temple on Mt. Pelius, and this temple was the second part of his four-part healing process. Chiron first identified the gift of each pupil and then integrated the gift into full consciousness. Now that the usage of Chiron is available, astrologers will be gifted with the power to identify the destiny and healing gift of their clients and initiate this into the awareness of the client. Chiron is the missing key to this work, but more on mythology first.

We know much about ancient Greek, Thracian, and Minoan healing temples from archaeological, mythological, and channeled sources. Healing of illness was done by having the sick person sleep in the temple, and the person would have a dream which would identify the sickness, and therapy followed. The temple was also used to bring the highest potential octave into the essence of the initiates, and this was done with hypnosis or light sleep techniques. To put it simply, when the initiate was ready, all of the past life knowledge and training was reaccessed into the initiate's body.[12] Then the initiate could go forward at that point and be all they were and more as they lived out their destiny. Or, a sick person could recall a past life injury or illness latent in the body, and by recognizing it, they could choose to not reawaken it.

Chiron, by transit, will often identify the maximum pressure times in a lifetime which are also the illumination times. Those times are often when the relentless pressure of Saturn can be left behind, and the electrical healing potential of Uranus released. Chiron rules crystals. Crystals can be great healing tools because crystals are frozen white light in hexagonal rigid Saturnian mineral form. If you have a past life trauma or illness some place in your body, during each lifetime your higher self will try to push through that point, that density. That is, you will get sick in that place until you clear it, until you turn that place to pure crystalline white light. The point is, this second step of being taught the way to mastery involved a systematic clearing through of negativities in the system, in the body, which involved some past life reassessment before the client could go forward successfully. If the Saturnian blocks are left uncleared, disease begins in the blocks. If one goes ahead in consciousness raising without clearing blocks, he or she will get sick. Each incarnation is a chance to clear past life blocks and become whole in this lifetime, and this was the second step of Chiron's teaching.

Then Chiron trained the pupil to undertake the destiny path in the culture. All of the myths of Chiron say he was a great healer, an astrologer, and an oracle. After healing, next was the identification of the gift to be given in this life. This was essentially an astrological skill, because the cultural gift is revealed by the eleventh house which is ruled by Uranus. The third path was oracular. Chiron was an oracle himself, which shows that the oracular or divination skills come into prominence once one is cleared of negativity, and once the skill level has become automatic. This all has to do with recapturing our animal essence which is where we started, because the oracular divination skill comes after the first two steps. We are living now in a culture which has devalued and feared oracular and divination skills; but in fact, this level of skill is simply reaching a wholistic level of integration where we act without the intervention of conscious thought. Like the silver wolf, so revered as a symbol by Chiron's culture, we *become* instinct, we stop observing ourselves, and we become energy. Or, to put it astrologically, when the Uranian *electro* and Neptunian *magnetic* energies are infused into the Saturn form, oracular and divination skills flood the consciousness. Later in this book I will develop these four paths of teaching to become a master healer by using Jason and Medea as examples. But before going into the fourth path, which is mastery of death, there is one secret to give about this level of teaching: if you let yourself *become* instinct, you will find the way of the wolf—you will know how to live without rational forms.

The Chiron mythology on death is particularly fascinating because, as you will see in my work on Jason and Medea, Chiron lived in a time like ours. He lived through much death; I'm sure it was just as hard to make sense of it then as it is now. But his true teaching is revealed in his own crises. The centaurs were drinkers and carousers, and it got to the point where Chiron was the only one left. He picked up one of the poisoned arrows of Hercules, dropped it on his foot and poisoned himself. This was a poison that Chiron had taught Hercules to make, and the parallels with modern weaponry are obvious.

There are many variations on this legend, but the most interesting one is that Chiron returned to his cave in agony[13] but could not die because he was immortal. Later Hercules made his way to the Caucasus where Prometheus was fettered with vultures tearing at him.[14] He had been imprisoned by Zeus for giving fire to the human race, and Zeus set him free in exchange for Chiron's descent into Hades.[15] To me, this is the most powerful part of the mythology, because Chiron's sighting heralds a divine reprieve is coming from the nuclear dilemma. And, a powerful teaching about AIDS will come as we better understand Chirotic energy. As humans attempt to bring *eros*—Uranian sexual life force—into Saturnian form (the body), so far, diseases have manifested. This problem will continue as long as humans fear death. Chirotic energy will teach us to let go of fear so that we can embody *eros*/Uranus and *not* generate imbalances and disease.

Chiron gave himself willingly so that the fire could be released from the Underworld by Prometheus. This was done so that humankind could continue to try to learn to use power in the right way. This is a powerful statement about letting go for the greater good of the people. We live in a time when people spend thousands of dollars and resources to prolong their lives for a little while because they are so afraid of facing what comes next. Disadvantaged young people and children often die of poor care and lack of food, while half-dead rich old people radiate their bodies, transplant organs into themselves, and then leave the hospital to smoke and drink some more. Chiron was a teacher who taught healing by means of clearing and bravery, and then letting go without fear when the time comes. The planetary energies and resources are extremely stressed by ecologically unsound medical technology utilized to keep older people alive a little longer so that they won't have to face something they can't control—Uranian energy. It is like a tree with diseased limbs which go unpruned and kill the tree itself. Chiron is a teacher of bravery, a teacher of clearing that which isn't strong and healthy. Chiron deals with Pluto willingly instead of avoiding the Underworld till the very last second. There is much to learn about death from Chiron—notice how powerful the hospice movement has become since 1977. It is hard to face Pluto without Chiron as a guide, and now we have the assistance.

The true essence of any energy can be revealed linguistically since all of the most esoteric traditions have taught that words and sounds carry the secrets or arcanum. Language, as a communicator of esoteric teaching such as sacred chanting or Hebrew tonal teaching, comes forth from the pineal gland, the densest and darkest region of the brain, where intellect or inner light fuses with outer vibration or sound. The ancient Hebrew wisdom teaching is rich in this ancient awareness, and still today Orthodox Jews learn sacred scriptures in the ancient tongue. Chiron is a being coming from shadowy antiquity, as I will show with the legend of Jason and the Argonauts, and the pre-Greek language which gives us his name is a remnant of the Atlantean theocracy.[16]

Often when the truth is obscured, linguistic resonance will yield keys to secrets as if the sound "cheiros" were only uttered yesterday. So powerful was that sound that it is still today the root word of many of the ancient healing arts first revealed by the great centaur. *Chiral* means the polarization of light from one hand to the other; *chiromancy* is reading of the hand or palmistry; *chiropracty* is healing of the joints and bones by means of manipulation; *chirothesia* is energy in the hands during sacred rites; a blessing with the hands is *chirotony*; and *chirurgery* is an ancient usage which became *surgery*. In the languages of the Americas, the root word became "mana," and this word still connotes sacred energy or power to Native Americans. *Chirography* is the art of writing, and as already said, the transmission of words and writing is always the beginning of the sacred teaching, the Order of Thoth. Magic has always relied heavily upon secret word formulas which are also written down, and the actual sighting of Chiron may hint that the power of the priesthood may be over with, that anyone can learn the sacred sounds and words to enter into the revelation of the secrets.

The magical divination form of Chiron is *chiromancy*,which is the Tarot. The Tarot is a way into understanding how Chiron rules the search for the exact place and time of awareness which then is the gateway to its opposite, Neptune or the whole cosmos. Chiron continually hints by his essence as animal/human fusion, by his continual pragmatic teaching, that the way to mysticism or Neptune is through the body. Thus, the first Tarot card is the Magician, the master of the method or way into the arcana. To quote the great anonymous new work on the Tarot, "An arcanum is a 'ferment' or an 'enzyme' whose presence stimulates the spiritual and psychic life of man."[17] The magician shows the way into concentration without effort which occurs when the will has been transcended by spiritual practice, and the result is perfect calm. Then the magician is at one in the self and at one with the spiritual world. This

is the essence of the sixth and twelfth house polarity which is only definable since Chiron's sighting. Just as the Magician, the first card, is the
beginning of the magical quest, so is Chiron our individual astrological
guidepost to the focal point of Neptune. Chiron is here now to show that
the beginning of the path is to start by playing or dancing the cosmic
energy. And, it should be noted that there is *not* a Tarot card for Chiron
because Chiron rules the Tarot reader, the chiromancer.

Richard Nolle finds interesting archetypal symbolism in the root
word "Cheir" or hand. He sees it as a wholistic union of intellect and
instinct, mind and body—just like the centaur is human and animal. In
creating a work of art, both the head and hand are essential, and something magical happens when they work together to create.[18] The hand
itself is form or Saturn, the intellect is Uranus, and it seemed that never
would the twain meet, and yet it is now resolved. The bridge—alchemy—
is manifesting, and just as the third house (integration and communication) results in the depth awareness of the fourth house, so the key to the
still misunderstood sixth house, Chiron, will yield the secret to the true
essence of the seventh house, the other.

Lately, I have become uncomfortable with Venus ruling Libra and
the seventh house, although it works ruling Taurus and the second
house. It is the same as when I became uncomfortable with Mercury
ruling Virgo and the sixth house during the late seventies. Mercury works
beautifully with Gemini and the third house. I will address the seventh
house and Libra as a speculation after I have finished defining the
rulership of Virgo and the sixth house based upon extensive research.
True alchemical work can now be accomplished on the self by using
Chiron for the sixth house. The full nature of the other, ruled by the
seventh house (Libra), can be sought as we understand the sixth house
better. Astrology is ruled by Uranus, but Chiron is the energetic gate
from form to higher awareness, Uranus. Uranus is illumination; it is
kundalini breakthrough. No one ever attains understanding of Uranus
without understanding the other (the mirror) because Uranus rules
polarity along with Mercury. Chiron, gateway to Uranus from Saturn, is
also the magical gateway to the other, Libra.

Something magical happens when the astrologer carefully draws
out the natal chart and meditates on the symbols. Suddenly a whole
energetics comes alive which makes true creative awareness possible
when this dynamic is well-communicated to the client. Astrology is
alchemical, and astrology will not move beyond Saturn and be able to
utilize the true nature of the outer planets until astrologers resonate—in

the body—with their alchemical powers. Now they must realize that astrologers have been given stellar divination so that they can initiate clients into the powers of the outer planets. Since November 1, 1977, astrologers are empowered to initiate any client who manifests for them, as long as the astrologer can find the client's true purpose in the chart. This is a great power indeed, and yet if you realize this skill has been stolen from you for thousands of years by the orthodox priesthood, and by those in control, you might be willing to take your power on. Simply use Chiron, the original master teacher of astrology. If a warrior comes to you, initiate him/her into the sacred warrior; if a person comes who can pass souls to the other side, initiate that servant; if one comes ready for marriage, give them the trust; if a child comes to you, initiate/baptize the child. We are ready for Uranus now, so connect the heart, mind, and hand in your readings, and then Chiron will show you the way to initiation.

It is all really about energy passage, moving Saturn form to Uranus electricity. If the answer for your client is not initiation, then the result may be death or the beginning of dying. The human organism continually moves through Saturn form into new reorganization until it is tired, and then death can be as easily taken in as life, if death is worked with con-sciously. Now that Chiron has been sighted, the truth is available to us: how each person *dies* is just as critical as how each person *lives*.

This issue is most clearly presented to us in the Egyptian ritual of Weighing the Heart of the Soul. The soul is instructed to go through forty-two gates by being able to utter the correct sacred word at each gate. The way to understand this ritual takes us right back to the first Tarot card, the Magician. Each one of the forty-two gates is an arcanun or enzyme which stimulates the psychic understanding of the seeker. All of the Egyptian death rituals are teachings about life, and forty-two years is the finishing of the Uranus opposite Uranus cycle of transformation and kundalini integration. When this cycle is finished at age 41, all the inner gates or electrical body circuits are open so that electrical con-sciousness can attune to a higher frequency. It is like upping your amps from 110 to 220. The Uranus opposite Uranus transit is the second major life transit after the Saturn return at thirty. The preparation for Chiron's return at age 50-51, the third major life transit, begins after the Uranus opposition at age thirty-eight to forty. We also experience Pluto square Pluto and Neptune square Neptune usually after the Uranus opposition. Also, the individual transmutation cycle of the client takes hold after age forty-two because the body is all prepared by the kundalini energy moving up the spine and clearing the chakras. Implicit in the Egyptian teaching on Weighing the Heart is the teaching of Chiron that the arcanum, the enzymes, must be taken into the body at forty-two and activated. To put it simply, at mid-life the body holds the secrets ready to be released, and the Egyptians taught mastery training at that time whereby true body resonation could be attained by passing the forty-two gates. If not, death and a return to Saturn form was next.

The pathway to the other is not accomplished by Saturn pushing the rock up the hill as Sisyphus did. Instead of pushing the rock up, let it go, or find an alchemical method for lightening it, just as the pyramid builders did. They left the pyramid behind for us as the lesson. Or, *become* the rock, become dense, take the energies into the body and know them. Tony Joseph says that the nature of Chiron's death is filled with important clues to understanding his role in the human condition.[19] And I agree. No one has yet come up with an understanding of Chiron's motivation for letting go immediately so that Prometheus could be freed from Hades. I think it is obvious: the Fire will no longer destroy us if we embrace death when its time comes. The danger we face at the present time, which is truly Promethean, is that a bunch of aging men who need to let go are busy building the weapons of destruction because they are unwilling to transform their awareness and face the other.

The ultimate irony of our times is hidden in the legend of Prometheus. Prometheus was chained and vultures ate his liver daily. The liver is the organ which holds violence and destruction, and it is also the body's controller of purification and energy. The generation which is holding the world in atomic bondage, mostly the Pluto in Cancer generation, has one of the highest rates of alcoholism ever known to mankind. They invested much of their capital in the liquor manufacturers, who created the vultures that eat their cirrhotic livers. Thus Chiron is the energy in the natal chart to be studied to help clear the planet of alcoholism and slow deliberate death. That is why the co-dependence movement—helping people to cure themselves of addictions—is so empowered at this time.

The paralyzing fear of the other side is lessening hour by hour as the younger generation, which is more comfortable with transmutation, natural healing, and clearing, comes into power. Like all actions of Chiron by transit, the outcome will be revealed in a sudden and very surprising way. For, once the fear of death is dissipated, anything is possible. That is the key to Chiron's choice to go to Pluto in the Under-world and free Prometheus from having his liver eaten eternally by vultures.

Chapter Two

GUIDE OF THE MAGICAL QUEST

The magical quest is a sacred journeywalk which reopens inner-brain centers which are the secret to survival and life itself. There was a time before 1500 B.C. when all humans were initiated and put into alignment with their brother animal spirit, which enabled them to bring their full creativity into their reality. Some were initiated into the sacred warrior, dancer, priestess, sacred maiden of the hierogamos, or as carrier of the tribal force as sacred king. Once upon a time, each individual was sacral or Chirotic, each was a nerve in the community. Now the sacred rites, the connection points between linear and sacred time, are gone. The warrior is in the Pentagon in a computer room, the dancer writhes on a video tape, the sacred marriage has been forgotten and sexuality is a dirty word, and the knowledge that the king sacrifices himself for the fruits of the field is lost. It would appear that we are lost unless we recover the ancient wisdom teaching about the force lying deep in each person, the force of the kundalini serpent.

Chiron's sudden appearance in the sky and then in the collective mind in 1977 signals the return of the initiation of each one of us which will resacralize our lives and works. Initiation is the deliberate choice to experience our work as a sacred act. *Everyone* can do it. It is important to understand that modern intimacy needs are different from the ancient ways—that we aren't talking about reinstituting the sacrifice of the sacred king, for example. One of my clients is a roofer, and he blesses the houses he roofs with his protection; another builds fireplaces and installs woodstoves, and he deliberately brings the hearth into each home; another is a cleaning lady who re-energizes and blesses the homes she works within. Chiron rules the process of work, since it rules the sixth house, and we heal ourselves with initiation into work. For

13

astrologers, Chiron's sighting signals that we are to reclaim our sacred duty, which is to analyze the energy dynamic of our clients and lead them to their initiation into their destiny. Chiron signals the end of the oppressive—mainly patriarchal—hierarchy of power in the culture, the hierocracy. It is time for each person to be special again, and then the culture will awaken from its long and deathly sleep.

The recovery of our story is the only way we can accomplish the monumental task of re-energizing each person and our planet. As I have searched for the story in many sources, over time I have become convinced that the story we need to hear again at this time is Jason's quest for the Golden Fleece because Chiron initiated Jason and his 50 Argonauts for some reason. The sighting of Chiron is so recent, our memory of this powerful primordial archetype is so deeply buried, that it is going to be hard to bring the Centaur Healer back again. The sources on Jason—a name which means "healer" in Pelasgian, a proto-Greek ancient tongue—are very difficult to work with because layers of time have been added to them and much has been lost. Often the stories have been handed down through people who had forgotten what the myths meant. But the real meaning behind Jason's voyage in search of the Golden Fleece is so significant to our modern dilemma that I'm going to try to bring it back in the last chapter of this book. Others sense this need, and a modern-day version of Jason's voyage was undertaken a few years ago and was reported in *National Geographic* in 1985. Jason's journey is important right now, because Chiron initiated Jason to go out and save his culture, to save the Minoan thessalocracy from imminent disaster. Unless we find a way to recreate this level of survival force now, we are in grave danger. Most cultural collapses have come from apathy and lack of energy. Also, the Golden Fleece represents the time when matriarchal forms of cultural protection failed and the patriarchy assumed power. In the pre-Greek world or Minoan culture, Jason's quest represented an attempt to recapture the early ways. It is probable that the worship of the Golden Calf during the wandering in the desert in Exodus is a parallel event. In a sense, Moses and Jason are parallel archetypes exhibiting opposite solutions. So, let us enter into the story which captured the imagination of the Aegean sea peoples 3600 years ago.

Any great teacher like Chiron knows that the quest is a double-edged sword—or—axe, as the Minoans would have it. The journey is a mythical quest outward into the world to find our place as inner transmutation is going on, altering our soul essence so that what we *become* also changes the outer reality. A true magical journey surrenders into itself by choosing total trust in the path because the quest seeks to alter the hologram itself. That is, with holographic reorganization, a new structural dynamic must be created which changes reality at the core so that all people, places and time evolve. The alteration of the hologram is the only adequate response to Moira, to fate, to predestination. That is, as soon as you change a part of yourself, the whole changes too. Astrologers will remain medieval soothsayers until they rid themselves of the curse of predestination, or reading the chart as if one can predict the future. The events shown in the natal chart by transit and progression only manifest if the bearer of the birth chart is evolving. And the quality of the exact event is determined by the person's level of consciousness at the time. The significant work going on with modern healers, astrologers, and teachers is the teaching that we change the planet and the future if we change ourselves: it is called the *Great Work* by alchemists. Perhaps only one more initiation will be needed before we suddenly turn from the path of death to the path of life.

Chiron initiated Jason to go on the long journey with fifty Argonauts to obtain the Golden Fleece, and the journey changed Jason. The Golden Fleece was originally a golden ram which saved Phrixius from a trip to the Underworld. Because his life was saved, Phrixius had sacrificed the ram to Zeus at Aea, which is at the eastern end of the Black Sea near the mouth of the River Phasis. The resulting fleece was the Golden Fleece. Phrixius was originally condemned because of a demand that *he* be sacrificed to Zeus. Some legends claim that the demand for his death came from the Delphic Oracle. But the story itself is peculiar regarding Zeus, and the most likely interpretation of Phrixius' dilemma is that he was a sacred king who was to be sacrificed for fertility of the fields, and his time had come.[1] Before 2000 B.C. and probably up to 1500 B.C. when the patriarchy became empowered, a sacred king was ritually sacrificed at the end of the seventh moon cycle at the Full Moon at the end of the longest day or solstice. Much later in the history of this culture, the amount of time the king could live and be the mate of the queen or her chosen nymph gradually lengthened; next a young boy took the place of the king, and then lastly the sacrifice became an animal sacrifice.

Around 1500 B.C., when I believe Jason's voyage occurred, it is likely that Phrixius' refusal was a part of the general trend by males to stop observing the Goddess rituals. As you will see, Jason's search for the fleece is really the story of the fall of the Goddess, of Medea. The dating of historical events in the Hebrew Bible has moved further back in time in recent research, making it very likely that the Golden Fleece story is a related cultural/parallel version of the tale of Moses and the Golden Calf. In the Greek legend, Jason goes on an arduous journey to gain the power of the fleece to protect his culture against disaster, but Moses and Yahweh punished the Hebrew and Canaanite people for any observance of ancient fertility rites. The Golden Calf was declared a pagan idol, while the fleece was sought for protection.

According to Lynn White and other recent Biblical scholars, the extreme repression of Earth rites by the Hebrew people as contained in their scriptures and then passed down through Christianity has resulted in the gradually intensifying ecological destruction which has now reached crisis proportions.[2] The dynamic is different in the Greek legends. The Mother Goddess cult seems to have been more developed in ancient Greece, and there is much wisdom buried deep in Jason's quest regarding ecology and feminism. The sources we have on Jason and Medea are all written after 600 B.C., but the event took place about 1500 B.C.. Just like the works of Homer, there is a 600-1000 year gap. During the gap, these legends were preserved by the oral tradition. But when they were written down, they were massively altered by the tran-scribers. If my work with the legends sounds inaccurate, please be aware that archaeologists are continually pushing dates farther back as scientific date testing becomes more advanced. But before we go more deeply into it, a few other general astrological cycles need to be examined which make it possible to look at Jason in an entirely original light, a light which I hope is very close to the actual feeling of his times.

The ancient island Calliste, known in later Greek times as Thera (today called Santorini), erupted around 1500 B.C. with a massive volcanic explosion which resulted in a collapsing caldera of monumental propor-tions and a tsunami or tidal wave which swept the shores of Greece, Asia Minor, and probably Egypt, with waves reputed by modern oceano-graphers to have been 300 feet high.[3] Based on research on the earliest Delphic Oracle site, the Lycorean Oracle, which establishes that the Oracle was moved after Deucalian's Flood, it is likely that the eruption of Calliste caused Deucalian's Flood.[4] Most of the cataclysms around 1500 B.C., such as the destruction of Crete and the rise in the Red Sea which possibly blocked the Egyptians during the Exodus, are probably tied in with the largest eruption of Thera. It is also very probable, based on archaeological and oceanographic records and legends, that the Aegean area was troubled with frequent earthquakes and climatic stresses for quite a while before the final cataclysm which we know from science devastated the geographical area of Jason's quest. From the human perspective then, as the Aegean basin was subjected to constant seismic stress, it was up to the Goddess religion to guard fertility and planetary balance. In 1500 B.C., all the religious rites that worked for thousands of years were failing as the cataclysm intensified. It is in that context that Jason's search and Chiron's initiations need to be understood.

From an astrological point of view, the planetary instability around 1500 B.C. has a critical relationship to our time because an inner memory of the 1500 B.C. cataclysm is responsible for the blind fear and excessive protectionism against disaster in our culture today. The 1500 B.C. event was gigantic, and it revived the inner memory of the earlier Atlantean destruction. If this idea seems preposterous, it is a fact that the same type of relational consciousness about contemporary stress and past catastrophes exists today within the Hopi Prophecy. The Hopis teach that they have undergone three destructions and three emergences, and that we are on the verge of another destruction caused by the white man's destruction of Earth. From my perspective as an astrologer-seer, we are now in the middle of a similar cycle for reasons to be given in a moment, and now we have the opportunity to use the energy on a much more sophisticated level. Back in 1500 B.C., from the human perspective, the Goddess got blamed for the cataclysm, and women have been persecuted for their power for the last 3500 years. If we don't take this opportunity offered by Chiron's reappearance to understand another critical cycle, the cycle of the Twelfth Planet which rules the balancing of our planet in the solar system, then this time the patriarchy will be blamed for the destruction that is upon us unless we understand the larger dynamic.

It might seem to be extraneous to bring the Twelfth Planet (named Nibiru by the ancient Sumerians) into this book on Chiron usage, but the technological healing skills being manifested due to the sighting of Chiron are being created now in order to instill a new hologram about our sense of self. Then when we face the planet that probably rules Libra, the "other," Nibiru, we will be able to greet our extraterrestrial brothers as friends. The film, *Close Encounters of a Third Kind* by Steven Spielberg is an early attempt to present this information. And during our time of the sighting and integration of Chirotic force—the conscious ability to hold higher energetics in physical form—the critical reason for also discussing Nibiru is that we are in the same place in Nibiru's cycle now as we were when Chiron was a master healer on Earth 3600 years ago. That is, this is an *astrological cyclic* question. My research on the three cycles, reflected in Greek mythology, Sumerian mythology, Egyptian mythology, Nordic mythology, and Indian Vedic texts, exactly corresponds with the Hopi Prophecy. The sighting of Nibiru in 1983 by IRAS means astrologers must begin to be open to relating this new planet to cyclic catastrophes. It is necessary to add Nibiru's cycle and some discussion of the astrological ages because the ability to investigate the larger cycles astrologically and astronomically exists since Nibiru was sighted in 1983 by the IRAS satellite.[5] Astrologers will have to wait for an ephemeris because the IRAS satellite stopped operating in 1983, and we need more data.

The main documentation on the existence and cycle of Nibiru is found in ancient Sumerian sources. The knowledge from these sources has been brought to us by Zecharia Sitchin in *The Twelfth Planet, The Stairway to Heaven,* and *Wars Between Gods and Men.*[6] Sitchin's thought is mind-boggling, his sources and level of scholarship are impeccable, and readers should consult his books for further details. The facts we need for this book are that Nibiru is on a 3500 to 3600-year orbit and was last in our solar system at its perihelion around 100 B.C. to 1 A.D.. During the previous return in 3600 B.C., Nibiru was completely chronicled in ancient Sumerian sources, and these are reproduced by Sitchin in his books. I believe much of the more bizarre material in Gnostic souces and Hebrew apocalyptic literature is about the 100 B.C. perihelion. In fact, I even believe that the Star of Bethlehem was probably Nibiru rising as Christ incarnated, since the symbol for the Star of Bethlehem—an eight-pointed star—is the same as the Sumerian symbol for Nibiru.

For the purpose of this volume, all we need is the probable timing of the orbit of Nibiru and some background on its effect on us. This is available in ancient Sumerian sources brought through to us meticulously by Sitchin, who is not himself interested in astrology or the application of planetary influences on human affairs. But now that his research has so thoroughly documented the presence of another planet and its influence on human affairs for the last 450,000 years, astrologers need to be open to his research. Nibiru is on a 3600-year orbit; it rules the balances in the solar system because it tends to unbalance various planets when it moves from Pluto into Mars, and it is the source of all our difficulties and enlightenments from "The Gods." "The Gods" are the Sumerian pantheon—Ishtar, Enki, Anu, Marduk, etc.; the Egyptian—Ra, Osiris,

Horus, Isis, etc.; the Greek—Zeus, Cronus, Prometheus, Chiron, etc.; and even the Hebraic Yahweh. They are extaterrestrial visitors who return during the perihelion cycle every 3600 years to instruct and guide humankind. Up until the return of Nibiru in 100 B.C., they also visited Earth in between the perihelion. Whether they visit between the peri-helion or not, the actual return around the Sun every 3500-3600 years is possibly the *most* critical cyclic seed point of a whole new cultural dynamic delivered by God-person teachers. Elliptical bodies such as Nibiru and comets are major "seed" forces from the galaxy. They are forces of radical change.

Unlike less scholarly sources on extraterrestrials such as Von Daniken and Velikovsky, who have also contributed a lot, Sitchin tells us exactly who the "ETs" are and exactly what they did and when. This is definitely a literal rather than allegorical approach to ancient history, but it is time to begin to recognize influences on human reality reported in all ancient myths. Others have tried, but Sitchin is the first one to describe the source of the "other place" and to chronicle its history here on Earth. And Sitchin's work is relevant to astrologers because he also explores Nibiru's relationship to Earth time, to immortality.

The allegorical versus literal view of myth and ancient history is now an issue manifesting due to the sighting of Chiron, because Chiron bridges Saturn form and Uranian insight. Uranian insight comes from careful determination of form and structure on the physical plane. Since the comprehension of the true essence of this issue is the keyhole in the psyche blocking alchemical insight and the way to Chiron's energy, this lock must be opened to even get close to Chiron's energy. What I mean specifically is that recovering our story from myth is ruled by Chiron. It is important to remember the original reason of myth for ancient people and native people now: Myth was and is the story of cyclic time carefully preserved by oral or written means to help prepare for present and future events.

Uranus can be viewed as right brain or myth, Saturn as left brain or analytic thought. If you split right and left brain, you get archaeologists digging holes (Saturn) who are unable to relate the finds to myth, and you get mythologists who can't relate the story to our place—Earth. Now with Chiron, we can bridge the realities and use both sides of the brain. *Eye of the Centaur* is an early attempt to make the bridge.[7] So, for example, we must study Jason's quest literally instead of as an arche-typal myth in the veils of time. Why bother? The answer is that we have been fooled by the patriarchal priesthood during the last two astrological

ages—Aries, 2200 B.C. to 60 B.C.; and Pisces, 60 B.C. to 2100 A.D.—and
they have stolen our energy, our power! Especially during Pisces they
have effectively blocked us from taking our story seriously by teaching
that the past is myth and not real history. We cannot know who we are
without our story, our myth, our memory—we are rootless trees—we
have no fourth house.

It would appear that this point in the Nibiru cycle, from now until
about 2150 A.D. coincides with the fall of the Goddess religion in 1450
B.C., and it is a major polarity balancing or unbalancing point. Are we
going to blame the patriarchy now and create a new matriarchy? Or will
we finally balance Mars/Venus, *anima/animus,* male/female? This is a
new turning point when we can create new repression and shadows or
try balancing polarities. My personal view based on *The Mayan Factor:
Path Beyond Technology,* my own research, and Zecharia Sitchin's
research, is that we are on the verge of an entirely new, stellar synchronization phase.[8]

The ability to use esoteric wisdom pragmatically, or actually to
make higher consciousness and magic *work,* was stolen from our
grasp by the priesthood so that we could not understand that the magical technique can be discovered, described, utilized, reinforced, and
acknowledged in consciousness and *we* can become masters of magical energy. Magical energy is the ability to be in tune with the synchronicity principle, or larger order of reality. Magic only works if the
magician lets the feminine Earth force be completely uncontrolled. The
patriarchal priesthood wanted absolute control over this energy in order
to never allow the feminine chaotic energy to flood reality again. They
stole the feminine energy for 3500 years because the inner memory
from the fall of Atlantis revived by the Aegean cataclysm of 1500 B.C.
was too threatening. The cataclysm, chaotic force, was identified with
the female force as the planet Venus. This legend exists in all ancient
traditions, and it is a priestly control factor that ended as of November 1,
1977. This force is Plutonian when repressed, like Prometheus in the
Underworld, because all repressions become Plutonian. But this force
is ideally Uranian serpent power if we each let it rise in the spine as kundalini energy.

Chiron, the gateway from control/Saturn to electricity/Uranus is
now back on the scene to lead the quest. The electromagnetic energy is
increasing in the atmosphere at this time as evidenced by the re-
energizing of megalithic stone circles and pyramid temple complexes
all over Earth, because this point in Nibiru's cycle is an unbalancing

point. Notice all the New Age teachers who are taking groups to sacred sites, especially since the late seventies. Whenever this happens we have a chance to "jump the cycle" and move to another place in the spiral of consciousness evolution. Nibiru causes weather unbalances and liberates deep Earth forces, but it also liberates Eros. During the Age of Taurus up to 1500 B.C., there seems to have been a lot of time spent doing the sacred marriage under the Tree of Life. The spark can now be liberated from the temple; the Ark has been found. The Ark is the kundalini energy in the spine of all living things. That is exactly what the great Centaur was teaching all his students, and that is exactly what astrologers can now teach clients again. We do not need to be gripped too much by Saturn and de-energized by guarding ourselves from Uranian electrical energy.

But we cannot do it unless we embrace the first principle of the magical arts: *Alchemy does alter matter.* There are guides from other places who are our teachers who will work with us if we call upon them to help us understand the non-fixed quality of matter. But ultimately, the reason for this phase in experience is to teach us spirituality. Alchemy can easily become a new level of ego control over matter or Saturn. The astrological Ages are real energy forces in our reality, and we can utilize and align ourselves with them consciously. There is a larger cycle which is unfolding, and many of us have much research now. Notice our words like "*re*search." I am making a lot of bold assertions as I struggle to bring back esoteric wisdom lost since the Age of Taurus. There is a reason for my convoluted and spiraling entry into this information. You cannot hear what is said here or even read these words unless you step aside for a moment and let youself hear that *you have 3600 years of conditioning in your brain blocking you from the magical tradition.* But now that Chiron/alchemy is energized again, you can hear! Your only problem with hearing the esoteric laws—and it is a big one—is that it all can only be understood by viewing it from the "other side." That is, you must let go and walk with the Chirotic instinct now. Travel outside the inner planets to Uranus, Neptune, Pluto and Nibiru. Freedom from fear and knowing your true essence is the reward that will help you look in the mirror, the Eye of Horus.

Nibiru is on a 3600-year orbit, now 400 years in from its aphelion as it was when Chiron lived on Earth. It rules Libra from my point of view because the ancient teaching has always been that Libra rules the balance and unbalance, but a reason has not come down to us. (See Figure 1.) It is the revelation of the ancient teaching that Libra rules the guardian of the purity of the genetic pool. The Gnostics knew about Nibiru; they may even have been Nibiruans who landed on Earth in 100 B.C.. The Pope has a dolphin on his miter because dolphins have perfect kundalini flow in their systems. His popish hat keeps his crown chakra closed. Hidden deep in this secret knowledge lies the real truth about the hierogamos which is the seventh house. Until we have an ephemeris of Nibiru, we cannot know how to work with it. But we do have an ephemeris of Chiron which will reveal the sixth house, and at last we will have the way to cross the descendant bridge and know the other side.

For those of you who know myth and are anticipating the launch of the Argo, Jason's ship, perhaps we will learn something about the feminine power force and the heirogamos when we meet Jason's priestess, Medea. In 1500 B.C., during the last cycle when Nibiru was 400 years from its aphelion during Jason's quest, Egypt, Sumeria, and the Aegean were highly destabilized. Out of the volcanic dust the Age of Aries crystallized into a worldwide plunge into warfare, and the male aggressive archetype. Before 2200 B.C. when the age of Taurus ended, there is no evidence of mass warfare anywhere on planet Earth. And then next the bloodshed, born during Aries, which was the killing of the feminine, and it was deeply obscured by Neptunian mysticism during the Age of Pisces. From 0 A.D. to now, we have tried to discover how we can know the divine and human love while we also kill. We are now in the last stages of Pisces as the equinoxes precess backwards. We are now in 1 degree to 0 degree Pisces—and we can now review the Ages of Aries and Pisces as we move backwards into Aquarius, which is a fixed sign.

The Age of Taurus (2200-4400 B.C.) was a fixed age. During the fixed ages, the cosmic planes fuse with the Earth plane, and thus Taurus was an age of great spirituality and energy, and Aquarius will be the same. But this highly elliptical orbit of Nibiru, 1800 years from perihelion to aphelion, is the potential confusion in the dynamic. The destabilization which we already feel now existed in the last cycle during Jason's voyage. This electromagnetic energy creates great potential alteration of the hologram towards creativity or destruction. As I said, we can "jump the cycle" to another point on the spiral.

To illustrate how exacting and powerful archetypal manifestation can be, the first astrologer who intuited the presence of Chiron was Maurice Wemyss in 1935. Wemyss wanted this yet undiscovered body orbiting between Saturn and Uranus to be called Jason![9] The great religious traditions have all taught that humans have free will. We actually

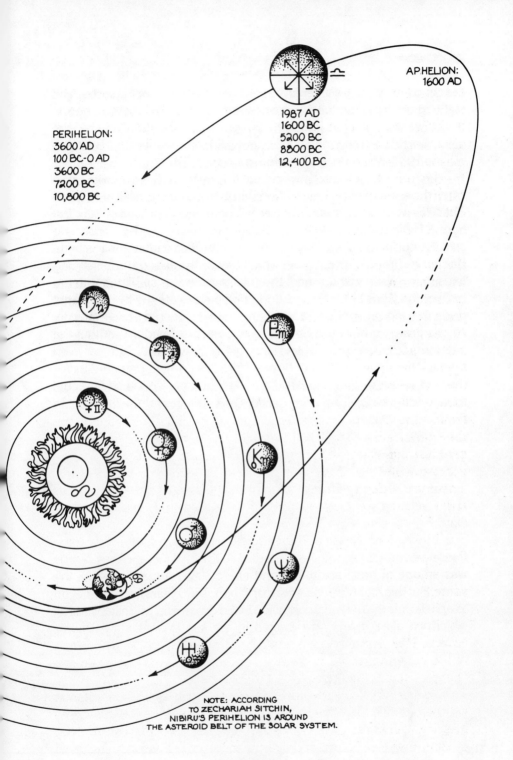

APHELION:
1600 AD

1987 AD
1600 BC
5200 BC
8800 BC
12,400 BC

PERIHELION:
3600 AD
100 BC-0 AD
3600 BC
7200 BC
10,800 BC

NOTE: ACCORDING
TO ZECHARIAH SITCHIN,
NIBIRU'S PERIHELION IS AROUND
THE ASTEROID BELT OF THE SOLAR SYSTEM.

Figure 1
The Orbital Phase of Nibiru

are choosing which it will be: an incredible Golden Age or a disaster. The sighting of Chiron tells us that the centaur is present to lead us to awareness if we will just let go, enter the 50-year cycle of Chiron, and be with Jason and Medea and the 50 Argonauts. After the work of this book, we will journey with Jason and Medea in Chapter 13.

Let me key you into how critical this cycle is: the opposite cycle when the equinoxes precessed from Virgo to Leo was the fall of Atlantis. That was when we misused our free will here and destroyed our civilization. A Nibiru return coincided with the incarnation of The Christ, who said the dominion of the Powers and Principalities ended with His birth. He said He brought a *new order* which means the extreme unbalancing caused by Nibiru was finished: the solar system was stabilized with the birth of the Christ. The Powers and Principalities are the twelfth planet gods, the gods from Nibiru, and this includes the Sacred Cow—Yahweh. At this time, we have the chance to choose our freedom without the interference of the gods. The energy of the The Christ is greater even than all the great teachers of humankind. His coming prepared us for the next return of Nibiru in 3700 A.D.. At that time, we will be on equal footing with beings from other planets and galaxies for the first time in the history of Earth.

Chapter Three

CHIRON AS GUIDE
TO THE OUTER PLANETS

Now it is time to define Chiron astronomically and astrologically. I have attempted to stretch my perception with the mythology of Chiron's times. I have attempted to really dig deeply into the archetype of this new body in our solar system because I have often reflected on the difficulty for astrologers caused by the sighting of Pluto in 1930 and astrologers' attempts to define its energy then. Much of what I present in this book may seem very amusing fifty years from now, but the only way to define Chiron's energy is to just present my findings to the astrological community as completely as I can.

Since I began to work with Chiron, my awareness about how to live has gone through a complete revolution. I present my own chart, along with Chiron's birth chart to help clarify why that occurred. Natally, Chiron is conjunct my North Node in Leo in the twelfth house within one degree, and my Sun is conjunct my South Node within 16 minutes in the Sixth house. My birth name is Hand, and I have felt marked by this new planet. As a child my father always used his name, Hand, as a symbol for his healing mark. He was a doctor. My Ascendant 29 degrees 44 minutes Leo is exactly conjunct Chiron's Saturn and Part of Fortune. That is, my soul vibration is the same as Chiron's form and way of blessing. No need to dwell on these aspects, as a reading of Chiron's discovery chart is given in Chapter Thirteen, and some may want to read Chapter Thirteen at this time. This revolution in my consciousness when I discovered Chiron needs to be explained, because that revolution is the essence of the way Chiron transmutes. And it may help readers to deal with my methodology, which is a reflection of right/left brain fusion, a rather new approach in book form. Uranus rules the right brain, Saturn the left, and we could not bridge both sides of the brain until now. Thus in the ancient

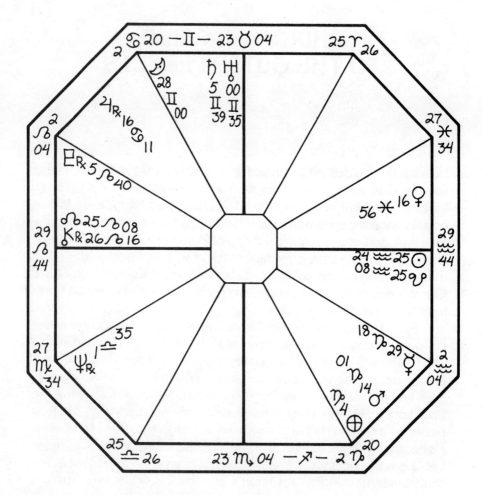

Chart Number Twenty-Eight:
Barbara Hand Clow
Koch House System

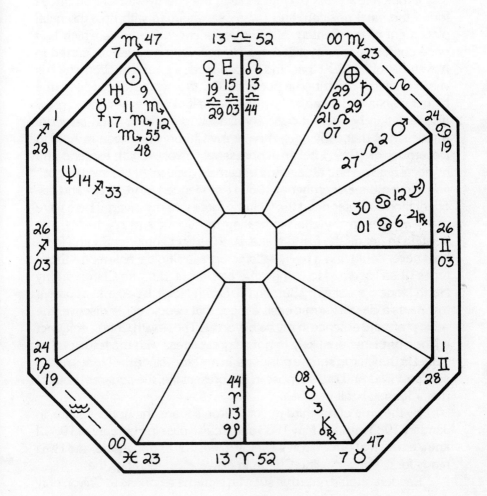

Chart Number Fifty-Three:
Birth of Chiron
Data Source: *The Key,* #16, January 10, 1981
Koch House System

days, people were too right brain oriented, believeing blindly in magic and divination; since 1600 A.D., we have been too left brian oriented. Now with Chiron's sighting, we can fuse.

It took a few years of work to align my energy with Chiron once I found the natal position, and I was overwhelmed with how the natal placement of the Centaur clarified experiences in my life which had once confused and mystified me. My first Chiron square occurred in November of 1948. At that time I experienced a transfiguration which is very completely described in *Eye of the Centaur* where I ascended to the higher planes and fused with my higher self.[1] I also experienced great disorientation because it was very difficult to adjust to such powerful mysticism at that early age. Then at my Chiron opposition in April to December of 1959, I became obsessively involved with esoteric and mystical reading and rituals, and became a recluse. At the third opposition, November-December of 1960 I experienced more stress and disorientation as I integrated the Chirotic force into my being. There were many aspects in my chart indicating mysticism and spirituality, just wanting to get off the Earth plane, such as Sun conjunct South Node, but I never could find a really satisfactory astrological answer for those times when I seemed to plunge into blackness. But with Chiron on my North Node opposite my Sun on the South Node, it became apparent that it was a classic karmic crisis aspect, that I would either discover the most profound essence in my being, or die. Those with Chiron conjunct a Node or planet are likely to notice great stress with the issue of that planet at the Chiron square positions. In my case, since the Nodes represent past lives and our purpose in the present life, the squares brought major karmic healing crises.

By the time of my third major Chiron square, the upper square, in January 1983 through May 1983 and a close pass in February of 1984, I knew enough about Chiron's energy to destroy or transmute, and I was ready for it. I began using Chiron in astrological readings then.

Readers should note that such an extreme response to Chiron only occurs when one is Chiron prominent. However, since the squares can trigger such difficulties, it would be wise to check clients to see if they are Chiron sensitive, as explained in Chapter Twelve. Possibly individual responses are more acute than normal at this time because we are living during the era of Chiron's sighting. Certainly, the Plutonic response patterns have been extreme since 1930, such as the nuclear dilemma and genocide. With the last square, the relentless energy manifested outside myself because I had reached another level of consciousness with my upper square Chiron force myself. First my dear brother died at age 42 on April 17, 1983, when Chiron was 25 degrees 25 minutes Taurus, exactly squaring my Nodes and Sun opposite Chiron. Chiron was also conjunct my brother's Uranus. He had resisted the energy of this recent Uranus opposite Uranus tranist and refused to grow. Chiron made him pay the price. Next, my father died February 17, 1984 when Chiron was making the last close pass on my upper square. How my father was my teacher and past life acquaintance was obvious to me as his Chiron was exactly conjunct to my Sun/South Node. He was undergoing his first square after his return at age 51. Then my father's only brother died eight days after my father died, another close uncle soon thereafter, and then a cousin.

I am being very frank about my own experience with Chiron to highlight the power of these squares for many people. Philip Sedgwick understood the pain caused by Chiron, and he said, "The Chiron dilemma in the horoscope seems to be one of the individual agreeing to suffer through a series of situations which induce a large amount of pain . . . One typically experiences the desire to leave the plane of existence, in this case the planet Earth."[2] Sedgwick also has found that excessive Twelfth House activity accompanies high suicide probability. Obviously, this is indicated with my North Node conjunct Chiron in the Twelfth House.

Chiron has made me a warrior, an Artemis or Inanna, and like Jason and Medea, all of my energy now is given to planetary preservation. Again noting the research of Philip Sedgwick, he has found that Chiron transiting the Saturn/Uranus midpoint resolves the Chiron dilemma.[3] I am indebted to him for this observation. This transit came after the upper square for me because my Uranus/Saturn midpoint is 2 degrees 30 minutes Gemini, right after the sensitive 26-degree Taurus upper square position. At that point my newly felt alignment with Chiron brought me into a deeper understanding about my purpose and why I had experienced various positive and negative energies up until then. And, Chiron will transit from the Saturn/Uranus midpoint through the last three houses to the return on the North Node and then to the Ascendant, indicating a very intense transmutation phase for me. I realized that nothing ever comes to me without a reason, and that I could align myself with the highest essence if I so chose. However, there is a price to pay—if you say yes to an experience or energy given to you on the synchronistic level or the level that is in cosmic attunement and you receive alignment, then you move into a zone of hearing and knowing what to do and not to do at all times. But once you align yourself a few times and you *know* that energy, you cannot say "no" when your higher self, or master, asks you to bring in something really difficult and important. If you say "no" you fall off the cutting edge, the balance is lost, and I suspect alignment is forever lost. I don't know because I have chosen to stay with the align-ment. It really has been like a new birth as a child of the universe where I no longer fear my environment in any way. So, my search for the essence of this energy is fearless and relentless because I know that planetary transmutation as well as personal work is involved. There are already too many chemicals, there is too much radiation, and there is too much confusion and hostility on the Earth for ordinary solutions. Only a radical alteration of the hologram (the basic cellular matrix of all life) and alignment of each individual with the alchemical fire can move Earth and each one of us to a finer level of attunement. The alchemical fire burns.

The asteroids orbit around the Sun between Mars and Jupiter. Chiron orbits between Saturn and Uranus. It is not an asteroid. Astronomically, it is definitely large enough to be considered a minor planet. A few astronomers refer to Chiron as a planet but most are more comfortable with minor planet. Chiron is relatively large as minor planets go, and readers are referred to works already published on Chiron which have more detail on this issue.

The important astronomical question is to try to answer *why* this little body has such an immediate and powerful impact on astrologers. I think the answer is apparent in the great interest in the asteriods during the last ten years. We are now realizing that the size of a minor planet or asteriod is not any indication of its influence—only its quality. For example, Jupiter's qualities are related to its size; that is, it expands our sense of ourselves. The latest research by astronomers is showing that Pluto is much smaller than originally thought, and yet who would deny the incredible power of Pluto? Chiron's orbit around the Sun is 49 to 51 years; when at perihelion (closest to Sun), Chiron's orbit moves inside the orbit of Saturn; and when at aphelion (farthest from Sun), its orbit is further out than the perihelion of Uranus, but it does not cross over the orbit of Uranus. Chiron bridges between Saturn and Uranus, and the inner and outer planets.

The extreme elliptical nature of Chiron's orbit causes Chiron to be in Libra for about 1¾ years and in Aries for over 8¼ years! (See Figure 2) Sedgwick notes that the Chiron crisis is "designed to get one to recognize that the soul exists in that body . . . .Often times the first realization becomes that the soul is imprisoned in the body."⁴ My experience is

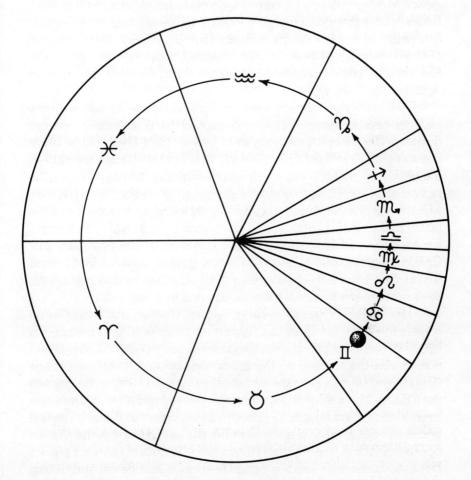

Figure 2
Chiron's Orbital Time in the Signs

similar with clients except that I would put it another way. Evolution of consciousness is growth in detachment from the personal ego and a progressive merging with the universe. The personal ego is a protection device which we require for early growth and mastery of the inner planet issues, and letting go to merge (Neptune) is always a threat and crisis. The personal ego is a structure created by our primary caretakers, and our own vision of our inner and outer needs. Dropping it can seem to be like a spider letting go of its own web, yet doing it means the universe *becomes* our own web.

The first crisis comes with the first square, although we may experience other forms of Chiron crises. And that first square can occur from age 5½, as in my case, up to as late as 23½! There will be more details on this quality of Chiron's cycle later but I would like to establish the point now that this extremely elliptical quality is what prepares the individual for receptivity to outer planet influences, particularly to Neptune which is the cosmic connection. Sensitivity to the outer planets and the ability to use outer-planet energy constructively is a level of awareness we are only now assimilating on a cultural level. The possibility that Chiron's sighting and subsequent research now signals a body/mind fusion, that it is a sign of receptivity of the Earth to realms beyond the solar system, is a force for tremendous and true optimism.

The major life transit cycle of Saturn, Uranus, and then Chiron reveals the essential truth of Chiron's rulership of Virgo because the cycles of the three planets are the gateway to Neptune. Chiron is and always was the the key to the primordial struggle between Cronos (Saturn) and Uranus. But now we can utilize the Chiron key to the cosmos from Earth. There are actually five major general growth breakthroughs beyond the individual special growth transits in the natal chart. The first one is the Saturn return about age 30, the second one is the Uranus opposition about age 39, then Pluto square Pluto and Neptune square Neptune come after Uranus opposite Uranus and before the Chiron return, and the fifth one is the Chiron return about age 50. See figure 3.

The Chiron, Uranus, Neptune, and Pluto squares are always working to push awareness, but the deepest progression in the life is seen in the three major growth points—the Saturn return, Uranus opposition, and Chiron return. This is because the three major life transits rule the growth progression of the four planes of reality which every lifetime strives to master. The planes are the physical, emotional or astral, mental and soul. These planes of existence prepare us for high spiritual awareness ruled by the outer planets. Neptune and Pluto cycles are

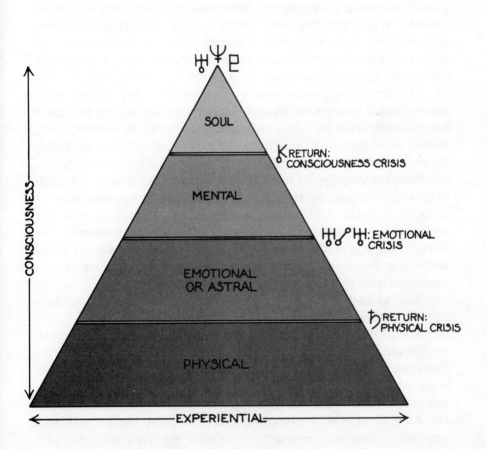

Figure 3
Major Life Changes

beyond the scope of this work, but the gateway to those energies, the cycles of Saturn/Chiron/Uranus must be clearly understood before defining Chiron rulership and the Virgo/Pisces polarity of the sixth and twelfth Houses.

At the very moment of birth, Saturn begins its plodding, inexorable growth to wisdom and maturity.[5] By house position and transit it moves around the natal chart teaching all lessons of the physical plane. For no one can aspire to emotional maturity, mental acuity, or soul intensity without learning the most essential lessons about life. Then at age 29 or 30, we each experience a crisis in work, relationships, education or finance which teaches the major lesson that is holding the soul back from moving to the next plane, the astral plane. As we move into growth, it does not matter whether we think of it as moving up higher or sinking deeper, but we need to understand that each one of the planes vibrates at a faster speed. We must experience and master the growth crisis at 30 in order to increase our level of vibration so that we can attune to the emotional growth required next. We are, of course, growing on all four levels simultaneously in many complex ways. But the trick to understanding the growth cycle of the whole life, the actual struggle between life and death, is to attune to the vibrational acceleration. Planetary transits are an opportunity to accelerate vibrations with growth. It is our cellular response to life itself, and if we manage to avoid the work of one of the transits, we begin death at that point.

People who become rigid like lead in their thirties and exhibit no emotional growth are already dying, even though they may litter the planet for many more years. When I first became an astrologer in 1968, most people did the work of their Saturn return, but very few transformed themselves at the Uranus opposition at 38 to 41. Since the sighting of Chiron in 1977, the type of tranformation required at the Uranus opposition has become a general cultural phenomenon. The mass vibrational level has increased, and people who resist their Uranus opposition are in great physical and spiritual danger at this time. The Saturn return mostly affects the lower chakras—most do the Saturn work anyway—and the physical affliction from the lower chakras are slow killers. The Uranus opposition generally affects the heart, throat, and sometimes third eye chakras. The heart can kill, as evidenced by the enormous increase in heart attacks, usually among males aged 38 to 42. Usually males experience an actual physical heart attack and women struggle with a throat chakra block. They feel unheard; they feel like they cannot speak. Their heart energy dies because they lose, in a sense, their faith that they possess existence. Both lose breath until kundalini energy balances in the body.

After the Saturn return, work is done at the next vibrational frequency, the astral, from age 30 to about 38. Now that we can work with the Chiron dynamic, a whole new level of understanding is possible about the work after the Saturn return up to the Uranus opposition. Chiron is the teacher of mastery, of doing a thing well as an end in itself. In North American culture during the 1980's, the phase of life that seems to be the most purposeless and confused is the phase from 30 to 38. Of course, we already know that Uranus teaches us by surprise and electrical energy. From age 30 to 38 is when people seem to be the most negatively affected by the culture; they seem to turn to the outside in order to avoid learning inner truths. They mistake libertarian behavior for true freedom, for freedom is mastery, a higher level of Saturn. During the phase before the Uranus opposition, at age 35 Uranus is in quincunx aspect to natal Uranus. It is pushing at consciousness to move further or drop out. As the energy intensifies up to the opposition, the real problem manifests, and it is always emotional. With Chiron in mind, clients need to be encouraged to see how their emotional problems are their teacher; they need to see that mastery of a relationship is an end in itself. Since Uranus rules electricity, the intensifying vibration which is driving the client crazy by age 38—the energy that must be mastered—is polarity, or positive and negative electricity flow.

Uranus is awareness and use of the will, and the greatest opportunity for successful astrological counseling is from age 38 to 42. The effects of Uranus at this time are systemic. I recommend *Kundalini: Psychosis or Transcendence* by Dr. Lee Sanella as a source on the medical ramifications of this phase.[6] At mid-life, Uranus is at its maximum power; it causes the kundalini or vital life force to rise in the spine, and that energy will unblock each chakra if allowed to flow. For many clients, just helping with symptoms, counseling them on letting go of useless controls, telling them when it is over, is enough. For Uranus does its work if it is not resisted. But some clients find themselves not wishing to go on without a bigger purpose. This is truly a life-and-death crisis. As with the Saturn return, death begins at Uranus opposition unless the emotional crisis can be resolved.

This transit causes the attunement to the next level of frequency, the mental plane. Our minds are not clear unless we have mastered our emotions. Without a great purpose, many find themselves unable to master emotional conflicts. We cannot master our karmic emotional

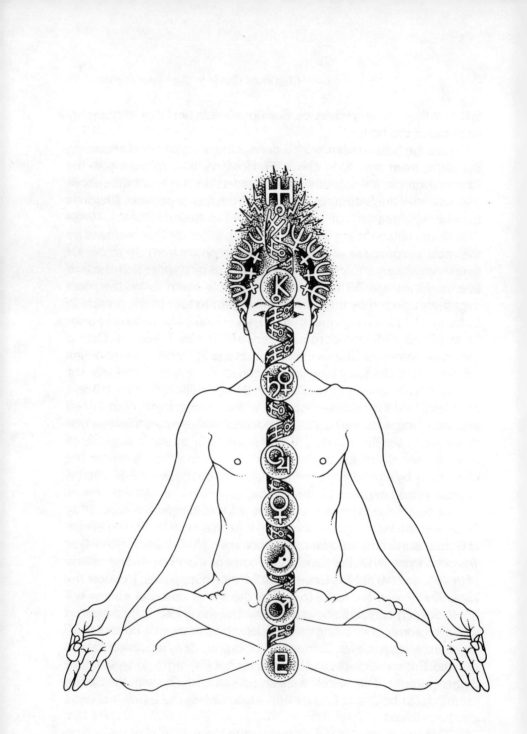

Figure 4
Planetary Energies in the Chakras

issues unless we have a purpose, and the purpose won't matter unless we are able to manifest it. And so, we need initiation into our sacred order at this time. (See Figure 4)

This is the new level that working with Chiron can bring to the astrological practice. Chiron is the key in the chart to the great big *how*. This can be clearly understood by meditating on the implications of the fact that all the planets have a major arcanum card in the Tarot except Chiron. Chiron rules the Tarot reader, the chiromancer. As you work with the technical parts of this book, you will see that Chiron analysis will show how to activate the North Node, how to use Pluto as a tool of action and will, and how to analyze the initiation cycle or *how* cycle of the natal chart. Then a deeper purpose emerges and the client has more reason to do the work of the Uranus opposition so that the work before the Chiron return can be accomplished.

If the Uranus opposition is successfully completed, a transformed human emerges with chakras open all the way up the spine, and the mind is free to perfect itself during the forties in preparation for an open crown chakra at the Chiron return. And remember, the mind is the left and right brain, and both lobes are to develop a balance between ages 40 and 50. Neptune square Neptune teaches about the subtle realms, and Pluto square Pluto teaches about proper use of energy, and forces us to clear whatever unresolved conflicts are lying deep within. But the next main work is participation in the cultural dynamic through shared ideas and purpose, the eleventh house. It is mastery of our special gift to be given to Earth. This phase is finer attunement to polarity, often expressed as left/right brain balancing, and it is mature awareness about the real meaning of our life-long emotional bonds, our web of karma. Then we are free to manifest the twelfth house, to know the soul.

Chiron returns to its natal position at age 50 and 51. The Sumerian God, Marduk, had 50 names which gave him power, and Jason had 50 Argonauts for recapturing the cosmic dynamic, sympathetic magic, the Golden Fleece. The orbit of Sirius B around Sirius A is fifty years; the Jubilee in the Roman cycle was fifty years; and economists are giving increasing weight to the fifty-year Kondratieff Wave Cycle controlling inflation/deflation worldwide. At the Jubilee, the Bible teaches that Christians should forgive all debt and start anew, and Pentecost means "the fiftieth." Imagine the freedom we could garner on the planet right now if the First World would forgive the Third World Debt! The number 50 represents attainment of a difficult task; it is an attempt to alter the circle to a spiral. When the fifty-year point is reached, if the necessary growth and work is accomplished, then a leap to the next spiral can occur. If there is not enough growth, then we go around the cycle again.

If we attain awareness at our Chiron return, then we are given the amazing fruits of experiencing the high side of Uranus, Neptune, and Pluto. High Uranus attunement is total alignment with the synchronicity principle; high Neptune consciousness is full blown mysticism; and complete Pluto transformation is freedom from poor habits and responses and the gift of clear will. As Jeff Green has so masterfully demonstrated in his Pluto book, complete transformation means mastery of the Lunar Nodes. To me that means a complete understanding our our human incarnational cycle so that we can incarnate consciously the next time. The Chiron return at 50 is true mastery of self and integration of all phases which have led up to this time. A few live until age 84 when Uranus will return; but for most, the emotional, mental and physical integration after age 50 is a great joy to look forward to if we manage to complete the work of the three major life transits: 1) Saturn return at age 29 to 30; 2) Uranus opposition at age 38 to 41; and 3) Chiron return at age 50 to 51.

Chapter Four

CHIRON RULING VIRGO
AND THE SIXTH HOUSE

Chiron energy is the exact moment, the exact place, the exact point of awareness—the Chirotic point. Christ said we would need to enter the Kingdom of Heaven through the eye of a needle. This is the perfect metaphor for the polarity of mastering the sixth house or eye of the needle to enter the Kingdom or cosmic attunement, the twelfth house.

This is the key concept of this book: *Enter totally into your body/ mind balance, in your personal life, and God is waiting on the other side.*

Christ is the most potent example we've had of Chiron-consciousness on Earth up to this time because Christ incarnated with total cosmic connection or Neptunian resonance, yet he was fully human. In case it isn't obvious, the birth of Christ occurring on Earth at the beginning of the Age of Pisces is a significant shift in energy dynamics which is a key event for all dwellers on Earth, and not just for the historical Christian church. More about the meaning of this revelation will follow in my next book, *Heart of the Christos.* Now at the end of the Age of Christ or Pisces, the planetary body ruling this consciousness has been sighted so that each individual is empowered to find this key to the Kingdom in their hearts. Chiron fuses the horse/man body at the heart place of the horse, and at the solar plexus of the man. Each one of us must discover this secret of entering totally into the present time and place, and the result of the mass of individual discovery will be atonement or at-one-ment. The virgin or Virgo is the Great Mother who births the Christos or Pisces. The sighting of Chiron symbolizes the empowerment for finishing the work of the Age of Pisces so that we can enter Aquarius with The Christ pouring the waters of Pisces out into the galactic stream.

39

The sixth house is the *way* or *method* to awareness; it is the initiation to the upper six houses and the opposite of letting go or merging of the twelfth house. Virgo itself is the perfection on the Earth plane (Saturn) required to prepare the electrical body (Uranus) for the cosmic light (Neptune). Virgos simply cannot be understood with Mercury awareness; it does not explain their high mental frequency mixed with their unusual fixed and perceptive personalities. Now the healing Centaur's mythology—his being as composite animal/human, his story of unceasingly and compulsively training and initiating planetary servers, his need to even get sick himself to learn healing skills—explains Virgo. A golden key it is indeed, and now we need Virgos to teach us how to open the gate to the Age of Aquarius. We need them to show us how to purify the Earth also. Gone are the days when the inner-driven Virgo will be criticized for his/her monomaniacal drive for perfection. They are seeking divinity, after all! Allow them all the time they need; honor their desire for perfection as their tool for mastering reality.

Virgos know the way through the needle. The fourth and sixth houses are quincunx the eleventh house: Cancerian nurturing (4th) and Virgo grounding (6th) are the key to manifesting the Aquarian Age (11th). The fourth and eighth houses sextile the sixth: Cancerian depth of the fourth and Scorpionic intensity of the eighth are required to comprehend Virgo. The grand trine to the sixth house/work/healing is the tenth house/earthly attainment, and the second house/grounding on Earth. Always the trine is the easy part, and Virgos do work and ground well. But the real key to Virgoan natural mastery exists in the sextiles of nurturing and intensity. If we can resonate now with Virgo's sextiles then we can identify Virgo's inner strength. Then if we can push further and feel the quincunxes directly to Virgo which are Aquarius (New Age awareness) and Aries (creative use of aggression) we will see how the Virgo work is the essential gate to the New Age. We cannot let the Age of Pisces go until we have completely experienced its fullness, just like we must completely experience the Full Moon each month. Chiron will repeatedly ask *how* until the quest is complete.

How does Chiron energy feel?

A meditator is in a yoga pose. The instructor walks over to the body holding the position with each limb in place. She adjusts the spine just slightly and the person is in perfect position. The breath floods the body with prana and the meditator knows illumination for just a moment, but never forgets.

A man is fishing for trout with tiny flies. He sits quietly in the boat, the gear is perfectly poised. The man watches the water reflecting the sky, intuitively connecting with the movements of the brown trout under the water. He casts the tiny fly directly over the water beast, the beast rises to strike the fly, and the man pulls back the line hard, deeply imbedding the hook into the fish's mouth.

A musician is playing Bach's *Three-Part Inventions*. Her hands are so perfectly trained that she is no longer conscious of her fingers striking the keys. Her eyes are so focused on the music that she no longer is thinking. The music comes out of her as if Bach existed in her essence.

You are casting a natal chart. You know the meaning of each planetary energy, aspect, and house so completely that you no longer think of the verbal or imagistic meanings. You feel each part of the chart in your body as your mind comprehends the meanings and is busy integrating all the parts into a whole. Suddenly your system shudders with orgasmic pleasure when you grasp the incarnational search of the soul revealed on paper in front of you.

The same can be described of the Tarot reader doing a reading. Saturn form is completed, Uranian awareness exists for a second, and then illumination manifests. The trick to really understanding Chiron energy is to validate the Neptunian illumination in consciousness, let it go, and go right to the next task of Saturn for making form.

Chiron is process. It is the way to Uranus, but just as you would not wish to hold a lightning bolt, do not try to freeze process. For process exists only while it is being experienced.

Repetition of process is jaded, it is the essence of desire, and the lighter you become with your Virgo energy, assuming you also are carefully focusing it, the more you will get the point. How? Seek the exact moment and take the pleasure then. The Hestia part of us becomes lost in the pleasure of folding laundry or polishing a floor. If our Virgo focuses only on the need for an ever-perfect floor, then a deathly no-win compulsion takes over which releases bile into the spleen and eats up everyone in the house with acid. All of us have known people with a lot of Virgo who have this problem. The same analog can function in the office with the

Virgo-driven boss who must control everyone working with him/her. But now that we can understand the energy, it is possible to focus on the constructive use of this energy and its balance to Uranus.

Chiron rules ecologists in a general sense, and we must unleash the power of Virgo perfection to the whole planet before it is too late. The key is to help make people conscious of the difference between Virgo compulsiveness and process enjoyment. If people experience enough letting go, which immediately allows the Piscean illumination to flow in, then it is easier for them to work on freeing themselves of Saturn compulsiveness. The awareness that astrology can offer about our potential choices of energy use can be a very powerful aid.

The key is in the sextiles to the sixth house, the fourth and eighth houses. Clients afflicted with Virgo compulsiveness need guidance to go deep into themselves with the fourth house and be counseled on facing their dark side by means of eighth house analysis. They need counseling on ceasing to resist Uranian neurological reorganization in the body by means of overemphasizing Saturn control. The Saturn return and Uranus opposition points need to be closely analyzed in light of transits and progressions occurring during these cycles for counseling to guide the client into helping them mature with Saturn and Uranus.

The elliptical orbit of Chiron needs to be examined for special guidance about the transmutation cycle of the client. The transmutation cycle is the individual growth process with the moments of mastering Saturn form, allowing this new understanding about the physical plane to open a window to awareness (Uranus), and then allowing the integration of Uranian awareness for the next growth process. That is, when we transmute, we change form from one essence to another. We transform ourselves by means of Saturn growth and Plutonian depth pressure. Transformation is growth from one stage to the next. Transmutation and its highest form, transfiguration, is a different kind of energy. All the planets rule various forms of growth, but Chiron rules growth from one energetics plane to another, from the inner personal planets to the outer planets that help us to resonate with all beings and things in the universe so that we can increase our vibration.

Transmutation and transfiguration are those experiences which occur when we get out of the physical body and experience the non-physical realms (such as masters and guides)—just as real as the physical realm; we simply experience them differently. In order to be capable of non-physical perceptions, we need to know how to trigger the non-physical or etheric perceptual system of our bodies. This topic is a book in itself, and it will be addressed here only to help explain the effect of the Chiron transit journey in our lives. We know a lot about the process of Saturn growth by structure and form in the life; we have been learning a great deal about how Uranus rearranges the neurological system in the body, causing greater awareness in our lives. Since Chiron is the third major life transit after Saturn and Uranus, my goal will be to describe it well enough so that its work in the life can be as clearly understood as Saturn and Uranus is now.

Chiron is the essence of pragmatism, of gaining a palpable or "hands on" awareness of ourselves so that we can metamorphose into something entirely new. This Chirotic form of transmutation is so systemic, the change so complete, the experience so intense, that most people forget it happened to them within hours. Often it can only be recognized by its effects, such as a sudden new vision, a complete path alteration in life, a feeling of being reborn.

For astrological counselors, the main objective with Chiron is in-depth examination for clients desiring maximum consciousness growth. Now that Chiron has been sighted, I am noticing a whole new level of consciousness emerging in clients who have been made conscious of Chiron natally and by transit. A major Chiron aspect is a multi-dimensional realignment. In the past, this type of experience was so far removed from normal perception that it was quickly forgotten. Now, clients can consciously align with and affirm multi-dimensional shifting. Some day, consciousness will be redefined when enough people can recognize holographic shifting.

We know from holographic research that we are all made of fundamental units which are always the same whether we divide ourselves into a million parts or one. Those units are the organizing principle of reality as we perceive it, that is the *ground of being*. If we truly ALTER CONSCIOUSNESS, the basic hologram evolves. Chiron analysis and timing is often the key to the real solution to seriously disturbed and unbalanced clients. Intense Chiron experiences are the time in our lives when we separate radically from the physical plane in order to experience other dimensions. Some have lost balance and sanity at that point and can regain touch with the Earth plane with the assistance of an astrologer who can examine transits and aspects at the time of the consciousness separation. They have lost their way, and literally need to be guided back.

The main Chiron aspects by transit are the lower square, the opposition, and the upper square. The lower square can occur any time from age 6 to 23, as shown in Figure 5. The way the energy is experienced is determined by the level of consciousness existing at the time of the aspect. This is determined by the age of the client and the supporting environment around the experience. The way all transits are experienced is heavily influenced by the surrounding environment with all planets, but with Chiron the wide differential in age causes a unique dynamic. First of all, the age when the parents experienced Chiron is usually going to differ radically from the cycle of their children. The only time there is not a big difference would be when parents and children are about 50 years apart. So, parents born in the early forties had their first square by age 6 or 7. They are the Pluto in Leo generation; they are radical transformers, and they have little patience with going slow. Their children experienced their own first square when they were in their late teens or early twenties! As the parents talked about mystical experiences or astral traveling, chances are their children thought they were half nuts. It must be added that many of these children have Pluto conjunct Uranus natally—the major transiting aspect which caused their parents to manifest radical transformation energy in the culture by means of anti-Vietnam war political activity and psychedelic drug experimentation—and these children will end up manifesting the breakthrough energy of their parents in lasting cultural and consciousness solutions.

We don't know enough yet about effects triggered by the first square. But people born in the forties were themselves raised by parents who had their first squares very late. So when the children born in the early forties had Chiron square Chiron and started seeing the light and watching the skies for spaceships, you can be sure that these parents thought their children were a group of budding schizophrenics. Notice how that older generation even created brain lobotomy rather than deal with consciousness! Although we don't know a lot about the timing effect on consciousness, two hypotheses can be offered. One would be that those experiencing Chiron squares early are open sooner to higher consciousness. The second hypothesis would be that Chiron aspects may be the reason why so many children really feel close to their grandparents on a mystical level, but feel alienated from their own parents. Grandparents are often about 50 when their grandchildren are born. If Chiron cycles trigger the generational skip, and if astrologers can teach the reality of the Chiron mystical breakthrough at the first square, parents will have a bridge to get more in touch with their children so that we can lessen generational tension.

This is the place to repeat again that as Chiron separates us tem-

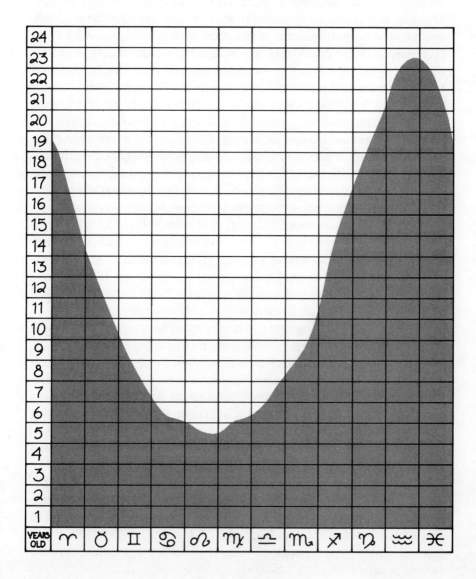

Figure 5
Age Differential of Lower Chiron Square

porarily from the Earth to create a space in our consciousness for realignment with the etheric planes or God essence, some children may respond by wishing to leave and become self-destructive or suicidal. The Chiron square or opposition also causes the child to radically separate from whatever comforts him or her the most. Make sure this child can talk to someone at this time, especially if the child has Chiron strongly aspecting a Node, or Neptune. Also, often *samadhi* experiences occur around the time of a person's death. At each Chiron square, there is a strong tendency to die, as my father did in his first Chiron square after his return at age 51. This is why death is often blissful.

Chiron rules the most intense and mystical experiences; it rules spiritual ecstasy. Whomever we share those levels with are the ones we resonate with most deeply. This lesson was driven deeply home to me by my oldest son (see Chart #24) who had his first square at age twenty-three, although I had mine at age six. I blindly experienced life with him thinking he truly understood Chirotic consciousness, probably because his natal Chiron is conjunct my Venus in Pisces. I never really knew him until I realized one day that he just didn't understand that level yet. And since this book is all about honesty, I have to admit that this Chirotic differential in our consciousness really separated me from him during his childhood. Then I began to meditate on what it might mean for him to feel Chirotic consciousness at age twenty-three for the first time. Just in time I intuited that the experience might be devastating. I called him to warn him to avoid drugs, especially during the exact square, especially crack, and he followed my advice. Crack is a very Chirotic drug because it is possible to take it, experience Neptunian ecstasy and then instantly leave the Earth. Notice that crack injures the heart chakra causing massive coronaries in some users. The day after I called my son, basketball star Len Bias, age 23, had tragically indulged in one dosage of crack and died of a heart attack. My son felt that it could have been him.

I feel that Len Bias and many other people his age experiencing the first Chiron square so late might be saved by understanding Chiron transits. Chiron transits break Saturn form and open the consciousness to the outer planets. There is a danger of Uranian neurological readjustments (potential coronary in a healthy heart), Neptunian drug confusion, and/or Plutonian possession.

Full understanding of Chiron energy lies in a deep resonance with astrological polarity. The true understanding of the energy of any planet comes only with a complete grasp of house polarity—just like light cannot exist without dark—positive energy without negative energy. The polarity of the first/seventh houses is, of course, Aries/Libra or Mars/ Nibiru. This is not the time to dwell on the rulership of Libra, but the polarity is Mars/animus/male aggression and Nibiru/the other side/ receptivity to opposite being. Thus we know our deepest selves when we experience the unknown other.

The polarity of the second/eighth House is Taurus/Scorpio or Venus/Pluto. The work of the second house is to ground our essence after it has become known through self-revelation in the first house, and the work of the eighth house is to discover the true values of life after we have grounded on the Earth plane. What would I be if all was removed? What is the most essential is a great eighth house lesson. The subtle receptivity and balancing of Venusian grounding becomes truly known when we eliminate all but what is most essential. That is Plutonian clarity, and it is found by a complete growth experience with the Lunar Nodes as Jeff Green points out.[1]

Then we move into the polarity of the third/ninth Houses with the energy of Mercury/Jupiter, Gemini/Sagittarius. The work of the third house is communication and integration on Earth, and the ninth house is integration with spiritual forces, communications with our masters and higher selves. Thus the true energy of Mercury is completed with Jupiterian expansion, and the potentially diffused energy of Mercury is focused and explicated by the Sagittarian arrow aiming for the exact point.

After knowing the self and others in the first/seventh, grounding and identifying our being in the second/eighth, we then integrate and expand our being in the third/ninth. With the journey through the first three houses and the corresponding polarity teaching of the seventh through ninth houses, we have completed the journey of discovering who we are, what our place is, and how to communicate and expand ourselves. We have moved into the energetics of the Tree of Life.

The bottom of the chart, the third and fourth houses, are best imaged as the root system of the Tree of Life. The powerful trunk of the Tree of Life grounding Earth and sky is on the line of the IC and midheaven. As we move into the fourth house, we are moving into the deepest experiences in a given incarnation. We move with all the experiences of the first three houses into the deep womb of the fourth house, and it is there that we find out who we really are. Only the silvery Earth satellite screening all perceptions outside Earth, the Moon, knows who we *really* are. As we move into the tenth house, the branches and roots of the Tree of Life reaching high into the sky, we take with us knowledge of the world from our experiences in the seventh through ninth houses. Only Saturn has the energetics to consistently lead us into form, to offer us power and creation work on Earth as the fruit of years of effort.

The Cancer/Capricorn polarity is the place to know the level of nurturing necessary for true growth; it is the place to test the depth of our root system, to gauge the power of the tree trunk in order to know just how high we can reach for the sky as we live on Earth. Once this powerful systemic dynamic has been tried and practiced, next the will is tested on the Leo/Aquarius axis.

We move on to the fifth/eleventh houses, ruling expression of the child within and the gift of the individualized expression of a being in the eleventh house. The polarity is Sun/Uranus, and there is much wisdom in this polarity, for both bodies rule free will. The highest faculty that humankind possesses is the will, that ultimately we are free if we will just take back our power. Thus we are to shine with the solar power of the fifth, and we are to create the most intense Uranian/Kundalini energetics in our consciousness so that we may manifest our greatest essence for these times. And with all that personal development and power, we move into the transition of the sixth/twelfth houses.

The astrological chart is on a wheel; it is not a straight line continuum. So, the sixth house will birth us into the seventh, the other; and the twelfth house will birth us into the first, knowing ourselves. In order to transit to the other, the seventh house, we must locate ourselves to the maximum degree here on Earth in space and time. This is only accomplished by initiation into ourselves and knowing ourselves in Saturn work, form and healing. Have you ever noticed how many people heal themselves first in their work? A total grounding is necessary before the complete letting go of the twelfth house, otherwise we are lost in Neptunian delusion.

Thus, Chiron rules the sixth house; it is the guide to the other side to the seventh house and the initiator to Neptune, to the universe. The two focusing dynamics of higher energy and consciousness are in the sixth and ninth houses, and there has been some confusion about Chiron ruling Sagittarius because of this. Chiron focuses as Sagittarius does, but Chiron focuses the subtlety and other worldliness of Neptune, and Sagittarius focuses the expansion of the self based on integration here on Earth, shooting it as an arrow to the higher self. Just as Chiron rules the astrologer and the Tarot reader as they read, Chiron rules the way to Jupiter, the home of the masters. Chiron rules the way through Pisces to the Age of Aquarius.

Chapter Five

CHIRON IN THE FIRST THROUGH SIXTH HOUSES

The individual house pattern in the natal chart is the holographic energy dynamic of consciousness. The house dynamic is a whole diagram of personality, and yet a really skilled astrologer can read the whole chart just with a complete analysis of any one house and its contents. Just like a hologram, each house reflects the whole chart. The house dynamic also shows over and over again how the soul interfaces with the galactic dynamic. It shows "our place," so to speak. In ancient esoteric astrological wisdom teaching, the soul creates the same ascendant in each lifetime and possesses the same totem animal throughout all incarnations. This is a radical teaching which few modern astrologers work with, but I have found it is very effective to work with clients to help them resonate with their ascendant Sabian symbol as a reading for their soul. With the same ascendant, we have relatively the same house cusps. Sometimes we create an interception which alters that dynamic, and interceptions are always the greatest insight into a given incarnation because the resulting shift announces a lifetime of predictable karmic breakthrough. This new and radical teaching is given in Chapter Eleven.

With the same rising sign, the house dynamic we experience is well-known. Therefore the placement of the planets, Nodes, and aspects tell us the most about the energy dynamic in a given lifetime. For example, the *natural dynamic* of the first and seventh house—Aries/who am I? what will I manifest? and Libra/what is the other in relationship to me?— is shaped into experience by the individual soul dynamic recurring throughout incarnational growth. So, for example, take an individual who always begins with Cancer/Capricorn on the first/seventh house dynamic. The parameters of Arian who am I? are always understood through manifesting Cancerian nurturance in self-expression and rigidly and wisely approaching the other. Then as the other house cusps fall into place due to geographical location and birth month, the individualized psychic structure can be ascertained. The planetary placements, Nodes, and aspects are unique to each incarnation, and this is where the astrologer must identify the energetic dynamic shaping this incarnation. It is very interesting to just map the energy dynamic *without* the house placements, because the result is an active dynamic of consciousness totally devoid of life experience.

Chiron rules the focal point in time and place of multi-dimensional consciousness on the physical plane, the ultimate trigger of compassion on the emotional plane, the exact point of insight on the mental plane, and the maximized point of mysticism on the soul plane. Therefore, all those dimensions including higher dimensions above the soul plane are focalized into the house that Chiron inhabits. All four bodies or planes are the focal point of the Chirotic healing breakthrough. The Chirotic place is the point where the absolute quintessence of cosmic fusion dynamic with incarnational existence operates. This energy becomes known in each life with Saturnian experience and Uranian neurological alteration. Gradually we get used to this energy throughout a lifetime if we do not resist it, and then this knowledge results in soul knowledge about a life and a conscious death.

As a dynamic in the natal chart, the house placement of Chiron reveals the quality of life understanding about the soul within. This is the part of one's nature that is never talked about because the individual cannot even imagine how to put it into words. Like Saturn, they just know it from experience. Therefore, the most quintessential life experience occurs with the issues of that house which contains Chiron. Now the time has come to reveal the nature of this soul growth dynamic. Chiron in the houses reveals the path of the soul, the touchstone point to multidimensional reality, and the method the native must perfect to learn how to heal.

CHIRON IN THE FIRST HOUSE

Chiron's presence in the first house signifies that the individual will play a Chirotic role in the lifetime. That is, they will embody Chirotic energy in their sense of self and how they express themselves. If their energy manifests successfully in the culture, this being is charismatic, unforgettable, and a true leader of consciousness unfoldment. When the energy is blocked, which will occur periodically in any lifetime, the individual is like a blocked dam of nervous energy. A blocked person with Chiron in the first house is still watched by everybody as if it is only a matter of time until the obvious spiritual force will actualize. I am utilizing charts of which I gave complete analytic readings; i.e., natal, transits and progressions, and significant life transits. I also know the individuals extremely well, and I have been able to validate my findings.

I selected seven charts with Chiron in the first house, and six of the seven people are major New Age teachers or professional healers. The seventh person is addicted to higher consciousness experiences, and is what I would call a "workshop junkie," and yet I just heard a report that she is suddenly manifesting a high school based on Hermetic principles. Three of the seven, the New Age teachers, are so charismatic that the room sizzles with energy when they are present. In fact, people around them have mystical breakthroughs just by being in their presence. All seven individuals find it absolutely impossible to be just ordinary, and when they are going through an ordinary phase in their lives, they almost go crazy with nervous energy. Two of the people are hands-on healers, and I have been touched by both. They both have an inordinate amount of electricity in their hands which they are able to direct into the bodies of people they heal and to rearrange their energy. One of the healers has Chiron one degree past the ascendant—it's not on the Sabian symbol—and she has a very difficult time bringing the energy in. I feel she may not find it flows until her Chiron return at age 50.

Always the most useful counseling with Chiron is to help the client become *conscious* of the energy so they can direct it better. For those with Chiron in the first house, they must ground the energy solidly, direct and intensify it. Acupuncture is extremely effective with these individuals, and they require a stable and nurturing domestic environment. Often this is hard to achieve. One of the teachers is very well-known and charismatic (see Chart #1, physicist), and he requires the balance from his family and children. In fact, just about the only soothing moments he ever has are when he is alone with his family. Outside of his small nurturing unit, the sky literally crackles with fire around him, and the elements seem to be altered. These individuals need nature and soothing music to stay centered.

The key to Chiron in the first house is that the first house always delineates the ego structure, the personality structure, the personality vehicle which expresses the individual until their known essence is mature, understood, and activated. Egotistical Chiron fixations are easy to spot because people think THEY are the healing force. As long as that idea is coveted, the energy short circuits and ungrounds them and destroys the stability they require. Careful counseling is required to help this client understand that energy flows through essence if we are not attached, that the synchronicity principle takes over one's reality when the ego structure is no longer needed for personality stability. If they can just let the energy go out from themselves freely, they will find manifestation; i.e., what they think about is what is happening. The Native American political leader of Chart #23 has this position, and he has a very "hot" effect on his constituents. He is charismatic and directed. The Jungian analyst (Chart #27) is very fiery and is sought after as a teacher. The priest of Chart #37 is one of the most charismatic speakers I have ever heard, and he leads rituals with many people. Chiron is right on the ascendant for the Jungian analyst of Chart #40, and he is a powerful healer. R.D. Laing, Chart #31, has Chiron in the first house.

CHIRON IN THE SECOND HOUSE

The second/eighth house polarity describes the life values of the client. The second house shows what is needed on the material plane to be comfortable and productive, and the eighth house shows what is most essential. The axis is very energized, grounding us into the Earth with the energy of the second house, and then increasingly driving us to purify and deepen with the eighth house. Chiron in the second house signifies extreme interest in balance here, as the second house is ruled by Venus. Richard Nolle notes a strong proselytizing urge with second house Chiron, a desire to define values in general.[1] Of course, then there is danger of belief that these values are the only correct ones. Astrologers must work especially hard with this position to help the client see that value systems are unique to the dynamic of each person. It is likely that natives with Chiron in the second house will be very sure of themselves and judgmental, and it is wise to show them that all aspects of their chart are unique to them. Astrodrama would be great for such individuals because they could actually observe the energy dynamic of another person. They need to be encouraged to enhance their values because those values actually do involve the healing of others if they are given out, but judgmentalism and fundamentalism must be watched closely.

Of the charts I selected, all but two clients are very opinionated, with a strong belief in the importance of what they have to teach. They *know*, so to speak. Two are healers of elderly people with special interest in passing people to the other side. One of these, the harpist of Chart #36, has developed a technique for healing the elderly involving slow articulation of melody. A very young New Age body healer (Chart #2) has an ability to bring in other dimensions into clients that is quickly becoming legendary. In her case, Chiron is conjunct her Sun and opposite Mars conjunct Pluto in the eighth, and her power is palpable. Her mother, also a healer (Chart #48), is a great teacher. Chart #17 is that of a teacher, a highly charismatic priest whose love of the Earth and Chirotic energy makes the energy in the room ground. People find his teaching irresistible; he has a tendency to become too opinionated, but the energy he exudes has all the power of Chiron. It is interesting to note how the energy of this teacher differs from the three New Age teachers mentioned in the discussion of Chiron in the first house. The priest adds the power of a value system; his energy is Plutonic because of the eighth house polarity to the second. The first house teacher frees the Chiron energy by embodying it into the listener; the second house preacher creates values in his listeners.

The key to the second house Chiron is to help the client better define their values. If they can, they will be energized by Pluto and find inexhaustible resources within. Other charts I chose exemplify a more quiet second house position. One client builds and caretakes orphan-ages and almost seems surprised when anybody admires him for this. He cannot imagine that everybody wouldn't do the same if they hap-pened to have the chance. Another builds roofs and makes his clients so secure that they feel healed by his roof. Chiron in the second house is a potentially very beautiful giving position, for it often manifests as un-selfconscious compassion for all beings.

Carl Jung, Chart #13, has Chiron in the second house opposite Jupiter in the eighth. This position has been a powerful vehicle for expanding into the occult and collective unconscious and then ag-gressively grounding Chiron in Aries in the second. Chart #38, teacher and writer, has Chiron in the second in Libra conjunct Jupiter and Nep-tune, and this native brings in Chirotic energy with mysticism and then strives to balance it all.

CHIRON IN THE THIRD HOUSE

Chiron's presence in the third house signifies a crisis of integration here on Earth that involves communication, agility, and personal mastery. There are usually problems with discrimination, and the native undergoes many wasteful experiences until maturation. This behavior is often accompanied by unusual teaching and communication talents which are usually utilized at a young age. This may be the position of the teacher who does not live as she/he teaches. As always with the third house, this native needs to learn by making mistakes, and the mistakes are often outlandish, as this being simultaneously manifests a lot of Chirotic force. Eventually, stubbornness mellows into great single-mindedness, and more ease with life suddenly appears when mastery of some skill is accomplished. Richard Nolle noticed that this position usually creates some kind of important experience with siblings; either that a sibling is critical to growth, or there is no sibling, causing a sense of isolation.[2] I have found this to be correct in almost every case I have observed of Chiron in the third house.

This client is often the adept who instantly seems to comprehend your reading, and/or is very blind about their own failures and discrepancies in the most mundane facets of life. Watch out or they will convince you that they are an adept. Do not let them get away with not seeing where they are failing in general, for the sooner they wake up and see they are not integrating well, the better. Under the smooth Mercurial surface is usually the small child who got picked on during recess on the playground and who ardently desired a true friend. Become the friend and advisor of these clients and subtly encourage them to realize that they can find their higher selves if they can consciously and honestly identify the ways in which they do not fit here. The connection to the ninth house higher self provides them with the brother or sister they lacked; they will stop their obsession with being alone all the time, and they will be in a postion to become great communicators. Obviously, this is often a tough position, for the Virgoan Chirotic force is hard for Gemini to master, but it is the key to the ninth house, the polarity, the way to the Masters.

Usually with Chiron in the third house there is sexual confusion which is greatly exacerbated by the power of the media in the late twentieth century. The media encourages us to get addicted to stimulation while we are all alone, and is the ideal vehicle for avoiding integrating well with other people. The media easily becomes the missed brother or sister. And, naturally, some individuals with Chiron in the third house are great media teachers who are healing with the media. Phil Donohue has Chiron in the third house, and the astrological publisher of Chart #3 has Chiron in the third. Chiron is retrograde in the publisher's third house, indicating he is a significant teacher bringing in critical teachings from past lives during this critical age. Sigmund Freud, Chart #51, has Chiron in the third house.

As an astrologer, it is important to help third house Chiron clients with lack of discrimination and emotional addictions, because low astral hooks such as sexual habits based on need or violence are the most tenacious blocks to the integration of the higher self. These clients are very stimulated by images, and they can clarify such responses with consciousness. Most of my clients with Chiron in the third house have gone through an inordinate amount of rather dangerous experimentation with drugs and sex. But I've also observed a striking ability to identify images not even visible to others. These individuals ultimately will heal the lost brother or sister they seek by integrating their lives in a striking and meaningful way. This person may turn out to be your most maddening *and* enlightening client. This is a difficult position in a child's chart for parents to handle.

The key to Chiron in the third house is that the third house is the communication and integration vehicle for the whole chart. All effort must be expended to make clients conscious of their behavior, to make them see that the ability to bring the higher self into essence is the key to their happiness, because then the third house is balanced by integration of the ninth house. The higher self, our inner teacher, will be empowered to lead this being to mastery of self-integration. Then it is possible to singlemindedly focus the special gift and effectively communicate the gift to others. Your clients will never master their chart without mastering the third house, making room for the higher self to move in. Chiron in the third signals a crisis of the highest order. And then the karmic journey moves into the root system of the Tree of Life, the consciousness rod of the natal chart, the fourth and tenth houses. See also Charts #26, #41, #43 and #47 with this position.

CHIRON IN THE FOURTH HOUSE

Chiron's presence in the fourth house signifies that the deepest healing of the self will come from a connection with roots. The experience of the first three houses—knowing who I am, finding a way to strongly connect myself, and discovering how to integrate myself—this is taken into the fourth house containing Chiron, and the individual must heal his or her deepest roots to discover *who* they are. The root connection in the Tree of Life of the natal chart relates to the healing of the planet, for we are not separate. Chiron itself rules ecology, the healing of the body/soul, and it is in the depth of the rootedness of the fourth house that the true nature of the Chiron healing seed can be sown. This signifies the most important teaching of our times, as it would seem that we are on the verge of terracide. Each person who heals him/herself heals the planet simultaneously.

Readers may want to study Chart #50, the splitting of the atom, and Chart #53, the birth chart of Chiron, for a moment. In both cases, Chiron is in the fourth house, indicating a deep wounding or healing of the roots of the Tree of Life. In the atom split chart, Chiron is exact conjunct with the North Node in late 29 degrees, indicating an intense and fracturing crisis of the will. The birth chart of Chiron shows deep Plutonic issues with all the Scorpio planets in the eleventh, and Pluto on the North Node of the Moon at the midheaven. But Chiron's Saturn and Part of Fortune, 29 degrees Leo intercepted in the eighth, shows the Chiron archetype will heal the atom split wound with discipline and joy.

Individuals with Chiron in the fourth house are intense, brooding, deep, and often nervous. What they need most is to heal themselves, because their own level of personal disturbance unnerves everyone and everything around themselves. But they are so intense that they often think spending energy on themselves is selfish. They need to be shown that their ability to heal their own wounded natures will teach them to heal many others. Or they need to see that self-healing itself is the way to universal healing. The astrologer who can resonate with the deep message of the fourth house is always a gift to the client. If the astrologer can teach the individual with Chiron in the fourth that their own healing will holographically attune the planet to healing, they should then initiate this client as an ecologist by teaching them that their sacred gift to the planet is to protect it.

The basic Chiron archetypal energy is grasped by resonation with the sense of the exact moment and place on Earth where awareness exists. The deepest understanding of this archetype is revealed through the sextiles to the Chiron ruled sixth house, the sextiles from the fourth and eighth houses. Therefore, clients with Chiron in the fourth are teachers about Chiron depth, and they are very misunderstood individuals at the present time. They are coming into their own as we begin to understand Chiron. The most striking energy revealed in my clients is resonation with suffering humanity or compassion. Obviously, Chiron in the fourth signifies a suffering early childhood which marks the psyche. These people know about pain because they have lived it intensely.

Therefore, they know when someone else is suffering. My clients with this placement who have not found a way to resonate with people in need are having a very hard time. The younger ones are studying to be healers. They are busy healing themselves and are frustrated by not being able to spend their energy helping others. The older ones, who are basically living for themselves and not giving to others, often have severe systemic neurological ailments such as Epstein Barr virus, *candida albicans,* and shingles. These charts are not included to protect their privacy.

The power of the energy is really evident in those who are living lives of compassion. One has been helping refugees from El Salvador (Chart #4), and she shines with the light of resonant Chirotic energy. She knows that the refugees are a gift in her life that enables her to connect with her essence. Essence is the dynamic which attunes us to the primeval fireball, the very beginning of the universe. This is the energy of the Sun which fills the system when we move out of Saturn to Uranus; it is the actual fuel of consciousness. Comfortable resonance with Chiron attunes us to the universal fire energy.

Another client has given her life to counseling people in prison. She is a nun, and at age sixty, she gave herself sexually to a young prisoner who was separating from reality. A personal crisis within her whole life of moral values, the Chirotic force, took her to the next level of the needs of the life force. Chiron in the fourth house is the revelation of the root system, the root chakra. Our resonation with the primordial life force is galactic, systemic, and beyond rational definition. It is Eros, the life force. That is why the never-ending struggle between Eros (Uranus) and Thanatos (Saturn) exists in the fourth house in Chiron's nativity and in the atom split chart.

CHIRON IN THE FIFTH HOUSE

Chiron's presence in the fifth house always creates a powerful sense of the child within, and this child can be a monster, demanding first place, or a powerful generator of creative force. The work of the fourth—intense depth analysis—is complete, and now it is time to express the root dynamic pushing from deep within. The parts of the natal chart expressing Leo or fifth house dynamics always involve ego issues. The ego attachment cathexisized by Chiron in the fifth is an erotic and creative dynamic which can only be released by experience. Chiron is experiential; the fifth house is experiential, and the effect is doubled.

Therefore, the sexual behavior patterns are unusual, and like all Chiron placements natally, this is the behavioral issue that is kept most secretly hidden. John Kennedy had Chiron in the fifth, and his sexual activities were exposed after his untimely death. Clients with this position need very special counseling, as the necessary sexual experimentation that comes with this position also can activate too much Uranian or Kundalini energy too soon. And often they experience *like a child,* with little mature understanding, and they deny what they are doing. The fifth house is a powerful electrical grounding dynamic in the chart which will release the person to give their gift to the culture, the eleventh house, if they can just find a way to express the energy of the fifth house. With Chiron so placed, this energy becomes alchemized; it keeps changing force until the being reaches essence of gold.

Those with Chiron in the fifth almost always create a murky and demanding sexual dynamic themselves, or they create experiences with others for sexual experimentation which will teach them what they need to know. Of two people with Chiron in the fifth exactly conjunct the North Node that I've worked with extensively, one is celibate and is working with spiritual initiation. The other, Chart #5, guru, is an experimenter with rituals for kundalini energization. Three more are gay; of these, two are very promiscuous—their charts are confidential. They simply don't seem to comprehend that enough is enough. Others have been unable to establish long-term relationships which are really fulfilling.

Almost all are very creative, and a very striking example of Chiron in the fifth is the writer, Henry Miller, as is John Kennedy, already mentioned. For those readers who love the power of Miller's prose but wonder why there is a sexual encounter every fourth page, this is a super example of how people with Chiron in the fifth must learn by experience. The guru, #5, is very creative, and his ritual work is his life work because Chiron is conjunct the North Node.

The goal with clients who have Chiron in the fifth house is to get them to talk about the hidden side, to help them see that they are learning by their behavior, and to always emphasize the importance of sexual love. I wish I could offer more examples, but confidentiality prevents it. Affirm their need and then try to counsel them on sensitivity about their partners. Help them to calm down the demanding child within, for their ability to experience mature sexuality connected to the Leo heart chakra, love will be a gift to all they encounter. This is a tough position until we get used to Chiron, and sexual issues are confusing generally for most people at this time. Counseling to help them attain conscious expression of their sexuality is very helpful.

The key to Chiron in the fifth house is that the fifth house is the release of the child within, of creativity. Creative expression, teaching children, and conscious sexuality are the mature expressions of this position. Counseling on the nature of Chiron, how it can only be known experientially, about how the energy changes form until it suddenly alchemizes into gold—this sharing of a deep secretive part of life will open doors to conscious delight in life. The key is to move the monster, demanding child to become truly aware of playmates, and that one's lover also has karma.

CHIRON IN THE SIXTH HOUSE

Chiron in the sixth house creates a significant connection with medicine and/or healing. This person is at first the essence of Saturn; very serious, pessimistic, hypochondriacal, disciplined, devoted, and wisdom comes with time. Unless there is something to lighten the energy, such as Chiron in Gemini or Aquarius, this individual doggedly works toward becoming healthy, and then unceasingly searches for the secret to health in general. Once the person has acquired enough experience with Chirotic energy, the energy shifts, and s/he becomes an adept at sensing and identifying energy in the body. These people begin to realize that how we feel often is a function of what we think about or choose to do with the body energetics. Then they stop trying to control health by means of Saturn control, and they shift to Uranian attunement. These people are highly sensitized to the electrical nervous system one way or another, and they are intuitive about what is going on in the body.

The body/mind balance is critical to those who have Chiron in the sixth house because Chiron's rulership of this house is the prime example of how we must know Chiron by experience. Thus, our actual experiences in work and our search for a meaningful goal in life are our healers. The issue of being healed is focused into the sixth house where we must materialize or bring into form all the knowledge attained in the first five houses so we can enter into the experiences with others in the upper houses. This house teaches that the solutions we find in work ultimately lead the way toward integrating into the adult life. The work of the sixth house is very much like the Saturn return, and with Chiron in the sixth doubling the influence, the ability to release power of the sixth house involves knowing one's individual form in matter. What am I? The body/mind balance is critical because Chiron bridges Body/Saturn balance to Mind/Uranus. Those with Chiron in the sixth vacillate between Saturnian guarding/enclosure/inner obsession and Uranian/kundalini electrical integration. They need counseling on learning to sense the electrical body energy as it flows first in themselves, and on letting the Uranian energy flow without resistance.

The delicate balance of the sixth house is a great revelation of the essence of Chirotic energy, which is a new word I have been using repeatedly. I first heard it used by Jean Houston, and it will exist strongly in our language as soon as the energy it represents is better understood. Body energy integration results from careful creation of Saturn form in a life, the careful building of experiences, relationships, and values which do not block self-expression. When the Saturn work is complete, the greater levels of integration represented by Uranus have a form prepared for reorganization on a higher vibration frequency which permits more awareness and sensation. Saturn growth timetables must be respected; the sixth house is the regulator of this dynamic. This dynamic operates through work and health. If you move too fast, such as using Eastern meditation techniques to force kundalini flow at a young age, then the Saturn structural building is subverted. But one must also encourage Uranus to prod Saturn into methodical progress, fine tuning the Saturn vehicle to make it capable of expansion and transformation. Chiron in the sixth house symbolizes the working out of transformation energy in form as a karmic issue. And astrologers should take a close look at natal charts with retrograde Chiron in the sixth. Almost all of us have been healers on some level in past lives. Those with retrograde Chiron in the sixth can reactivate past life healing skills in this lifetime.

The examination of natal charts with Chiron in the sixth revealed that all are very meticulous and hard working individuals. For almost all these people, work is salvation, and except for those who are professional healers or medical doctors, all showed hypochondriacal tendencies. Of the healers, one is a superb yoga teacher (Chart #20), one a yoga mystic who teaches, one a doctor of internal medicine (Chart #21) who is working with kundalini energy in the body to develop new healing technologies, one a superb and exacting medical astrologer, and one runs a center distributing New Age healing therapies and products. Nostradamus (Chart #34) is an ideal example of Chiron in the sixth. As for the hypochondriacal tendencies I have observed, these are the clients whom you sense would get better if they would just see the sickness is in the head. They do better if they shift their energy even more into work. Contrary to the usual advice on workaholism, these individuals are better off working, forgetting their aches and pains, and it helps them to study healing and medicine. They are less likely to hold illness in their essence (Saturn in the sixth) if they encourage more awareness (Uranus).

The key to resolving Chiron in the sixth house is understanding that work itself is healing therapy. And we can heal ourselves and others by observing the healing process in the body and imaging a better flow of healing electricity. Chiron is experiential, and the more we can facilitate in the body awareness of healing processes and energetics, the more effective they become. Yoga is excellent therapy for those with Chiron in the sixth house. Ultimately these individuals are meant to serve in some way. They usually drive themselves toward perfection very hard while they are perfecting the Saturn vehicle. During early life they may seem to be selfish and insensitive as they perfect themselves, sensing that Uranus is next. Then when they begin to bring Uranian energy into the body, they begin to feel boundless, unlimited, and wise. At that point, if they give their knowledge to whomever needs it, they will be rewarded with cosmic attunement. They will begin to manifest the twelfth house, which is feeling the greatest essence in consciousness. The work of the first six houses of knowing the self and the subconscious mind is complete; the soul is ready to journey to the other in the seventh house.

Chart #6 is our example, and this is a young woman who healed herself of the wounded healer syndrome. She was involved in a car accident which occurred at her first Chiron square. She was crippled. (Astrologers should note that leg injuries are often Chiron connected.) She had many operations but was still unable to walk. She had her last operation when Chiron transited her South Node, and she felt she helped in reconnecting the muscles and bones. She had conquered a strong past life complex. Notice Chiron is retrograde opposite the Moon. She also taught herself how to be a healer as she suffered.

Rising past the dynamic of the lower houses which represent personal and inner psychic experience, the journey through the night, we emerge into a journey of knowing ourselves in the mirror. What happens to us is that our environment mirrors who we are deep within essence. Therefore, every experience with another, every experience in the outside world, is our teacher. Chris Griscom of Galisteo says we direct our own movie, that what we are inside creates what happens in our reality.[3] The upper six houses of the natal chart are our own special movie, and we are the directors.

Chapter Six

CHIRON IN THE SEVENTH THROUGH TWELFTH HOUSES

CHIRON IN THE SEVENTH HOUSE

Chiron's presence in the seventh house signifies a dynamic of knowing the self through significant relationships on the personal level, and strongly affecting other people on a mass scale. This position is the essence of charisma; these individuals have enormous potential to express the collective unconsciousness of their times, and they have an uncanny ability to mirror the self-image of other people. This is a voracious placement: the presence of Chiron encourages the native to crave the adoration and adulation of others, and more than any other position of Chiron, identification of this energy is a revelation to the native. They need to understand how they are affecting people around themselves, or the intensifying adulation will attach to the personal ego and destroy them. Janis Joplin, Bob Dylan, Fidel Castro, and Richard Nixon have Chiron in the seventh house, and all are excellent examples of the power or confusion inherent in this placement. Opposite the house of the self, the first house, is the place of maximum distortion about who we are, the seventh house. Who we are will always be distorted in the perceptions of the self by others until we master polarity. The truth is, each end of the polarity is the same: *I am you and you are me.* This is the essential teaching that natives with Chiron in the seventh must master.

Mastery of the other side, true comprehension of polarities, only comes with deep wisdom about life. Natives with Chiron in the seventh have a crisis about knowing who they are in relation to the other side. Relationships are the big teacher for all of us, and that is why we work so hard at them. For those with Chiron in the seventh, the hardest issue, relationship, must be learned in the hardest way, with a Chiron crisis about who we are in this place, Earth. The only way the learning can occur is in a relationship, so the astrologer must gather more informa-tion on significant relationships than usual. Chiron in the seventh is also very involved with mass consciousness, and often some really valuable work is going on in that area. The degree to which the client is con-scious of this work is critically important, for their concrete awareness of the effect they have on others will release their inner gift. This is an essen-tial teaching about this position because the difficulties over interper-sonal relationships are usually so potent and distracting that this individual is more blinded to the mirror source of knowledge than most of us. They literally cannot see the forest for the trees, so they need powerful and sympathetic help with the difficulties they are having inter-personally. They need encouragement to become more conscious of the potent effect they have on others so they can know that the response from others to them is their teacher. And they need to become more conscious about the gift that the culture sees within them.

The highest octave of awareness about this position would be a complete mastery of the fact that others react to us as we see ourselves, that what goes on around us is caused by our own thought forms. This is not the book to work out the true rulership of the seventh house because we do not know enough yet, but we *can* be open to the idea that the seventh house rules our connection to extraterrestrials as well as others in general. It is time to comment that what we think about them will affect who they are to us. For example, if we project upon ETs that they are as dangerous and warlike as we are, then it is obvious what the outcome of their upcoming manifestation for us will be. What matters at this time is to understand that individuals with Chiron in the seventh house will be our teachers about how to respond to the other, the galactic plane as it relates to Earth. And as the time of extraterrestrial encounter draws closer, these individuals will resonate with a special frequency.

As for my clients, I studied ten examples of Chiron in the seventh very carefully, because this is such a difficult position to explicate. All ten of them have absolutely critical relationship dilemmas. This is where the most intense learning is going on, and extra respect for it must be offered by the astrologer. Often clients are wasting a lot of time and energy mucking around in time-consuming and futile relationships, and it is our job to help them become conscious of this. It is an entirely different story with Chiron in the seventh. Here is where I have really learned from my clients and have recently had some success with this difficult dynamic. One is a great weaver (Chart #7) who has had a suc-cession of Chirotic relationships that have taken much of her energy. I knew her years before I started working with Chiron. Imagine how different her chart is without Chiron in the seventh quincunx Venus/Uranus! Once we had Chiron, I began to understand that she was a sacred weaver, birthing Chirotic symbols into the culture, and I initiated her into becoming a sacred weaver by aligning her sense of self with her higher purpose—weaving symbols for transformation. Her powerful symbolic gifts are astonishing; she is guiding people, and her relationship stress has calmed down considerably. Another is my daughter, and I have been gently teaching her the potent effect she has on others so that she can center herself better. She will probably become an actress because of this position and because of other dynamics in her chart.

Another is a significant New Age publisher, Chart #39, who has launched a project that focuses on a significant relationship which I cannot describe for reasons of privacy. The only way I could help him was to help ease him out of torturous relationship stress and encourage him to see how he is benefiting the culture with his publishing work. Chart #42 belongs to the priest who left the priesthood when he realized he had to find himself through a relationship.

The key to Chiron in the seventh house is to carefully analyze relationships, identify what the inherent teachings are, and then help free the native from the astral grip while also identifying the palpable gifts to the culture which are occurring. In the old mastery schools, awareness only came with concrete identification of actual magical acts such as moving stones with the third eye or levitating. This principle is very helpful for work on Chiron in the seventh house. These natives do not see the power of what they are doing; they are not conscious of the effect they have on other people. If made conscious, they get control over their lives and they are tremendously empowered to give their gift. They often feel bad about the long line of complex and seemingly disastrous emotional encounters. Help them to see the teaching in each experience, advise them that they need more experience here than most people, and convince them that their moral axiom is to become conscious of the effect they are having on others. Doubling of this position, that is Chiron in Libra itself or Chiron in its rulership, Virgo, creates such massive confusion that long-term counseling is a virtual necessity.

CHIRON IN THE EIGHTH HOUSE

Chiron's presence in the eighth house signifies a titanic struggle with the earthly desires: sex, money, power, and immortality. This is the relative that every family remembers for generations, the one who grabbed everyone's rightful inheritance and could not be trusted. My files were particularly low on clients with the position because they are very secretive. They often spend their whole lives conniving to control others and take away their money, and they don't talk about it to anyone, especially astrologers.

Chiron in the eighth creates a gigantic karmic crisis over Plutonian issues (sex/death/money/power), and since Chiron learning is always experiential, the results are murky and very traumatic for everyone around the native. One way or another, true power needs to be experienced in order to confront the unconscious desire for absolute control and immortality. These individuals are the most dangerous to self and others when they have no power of their own, and the astrologer must first ascertain just how much power is available to them for their own experience and growth. If the native is powerless, then violence or cancer from inner rage will ultimately win out. This is the classic position of the conniving woman at home who poisons her husband. The resolved and high side of this position is an absolute mastery over desire resulting in a deep and essential knowing about the motives of others. This would be a great position for a highly conscious detective. This individual has a penetrating mind, a great facility for exacting research, and an intense understanding of primal life forces.

Sooner or later, a highly evolved native with Chiron in the eighth will be drawn to the occult, but there they face a special danger because they may tend to misuse power, or allow themselves to become the tool of a teacher. This is the classic position of the neophyte who gives his or her will to a teacher because the neophyte has not resolved all the guilt from early manipulative and destructive experiences. The point is, these natives have much potential as powerful occultists, but they must never give their power away. It is essential with this position to attain power, gradually master the individual desires involved in this power, and then to evolve the psyche to a new level of consciousness about the need for Pluto clarity. This native has valuable gifts to offer if desires are mastered. Extra work needs to be done by astrologers and counselors on clearing pain and confusion from early childhood trauma. Then there needs to be careful probing about use of power in the native's life. It is critical to get under the skin of the client and get them to be honest. Much karma is to be cleared by a native who has chosen Chiron in the eighth natally.

The four clients with Chiron in the eighth that I know extremely well happen to be women. I have not yet had a male client with Chiron in the eighth, probably because the highly secretive nature of this position combines with the common male difficulty with seeking counseling. The material regarding one of the clients is of a criminai nature; privacy is necessary on the nature of her experience, but her criminal behavior resulted from a deep sense of powerlessness which she created out of her manipulative approach. This woman is a Scorpio native, and nega- tive Pluto tendencies affected her balance. She believed her ability to live, her financial and sexual reality, were controlled by other people because she resisted self-knowledge available to her by means of mas- tering Chiron in the eighth house. So she manifested the raging inner Plutonic force by striking out at the people she believed controlled her life.

Another client who is also powerless because she was never able to express her creativity has almost driven her whole family over the brink by her incessant control and manipulation, and has suffered three bouts with cancer. She is obsessed with a fear of sin, and she has absolutely refused to seek in-depth therapy which she badly needs. A third client, a financial consultant of high brilliance, has been very cautious and hon- est in her growth. Her Chiron position in the eighth is doubled because it is in Scorpio. She was blocked sexually when she first came to me. I advised her to focus on creating the fullest and most intense sexual life possible by finding a lover who really brought out her passion. She has found full sexuality, still in her cautious way, and she is learning about the deep sexuality of the eighth house and feels much more complete.

The final example, Chart #8, a Hermetic teacher, is the most interesting one to me. Chiron in the eighth is first about Saturn/Pluto, then Uranus/Pluto energy. This client has Chiron in Capricorn, and thus is attempting to master Saturn/Pluto. Chiron in the eighth is in a grand square with Mercury, Uranus, and Saturn retrograde with Chiron op- posite Uranus in the second. Thus she has created a full blown karmic crisis with all the Chirotic power of Chiron opposite Uranus. She is a physical healer, a Hermetic teacher, and she has fallen under the com- plete control of a very powerful master teacher. She has given her will away, has therefore lost touch with experience, and has become an occult robot. Naturally, she has great power, and this is an excellent example of the need to maintain control over our own experience.

The key to Chiron in the eighth is to carefully examine the client's progress with Saturn. Have they created power in their lives? Do they have self-control? A person who is manipulating everyone else has no self-control because their consciousness is immersed in controlling someone else. In this case, self-control means deliberately choosing not to indulge in manipulation and control over others. Then, how are they doing with Pluto/Uranus? Are they able to transform their conscious-ness with powerful depth, or are they in the middle of constant crazy scenes which involve misplaced occultism and potential violence? Only the highest value sense will help clients with conflicts due to Chiron in the eighth house. They need help developing their free will, which will enable them to deal with their intense desires in the midst of a solid value system. Their most important counseling need is for advice against ever turning over their will to another individual. It is always a step backwards for anyone to surrender their will, but it is a tragedy for natives with Chiron in the eighth.

The sextiles to the sixth house are from the depth of the chart in the fourth house and from the search for significant values of the eighth house: sex, money, death, and power. The fourth house reveals the deep unconscious nature of the search for multidimensional Chirotic bridg-ing, and the eighth house is the key to power mastery. Since the Chiron point is the moment in space and time when and where multidimen-sional reality interfaces, the eighth house shows us the nature of the struggle with Eros/Thanatos, the ability to have clear values over sex and money, and the ability to consciously develop our own power. The depth of the fourth house and the intensity of the eighth reveal the energy of the healing Centaur. This is a very difficult dynamic to describe with literal left brain writing. The description of Jason and Medea, whom Chiron commissioned to save the race (fourth house), resulted in a classic ending of negative Pluto unleashed. Readers may wish to read it for full understanding of the revelation inherent in the fourth and now eighth house sextiles to the house Chiron rules, the sixth.

CHIRON IN THE NINTH HOUSE

Chiron's presence in the ninth house signifies the crisis of connect-ing with the higher self in this incarnation. The higher self is the wisdom energy that is the integrating spiritual force of each lifetime. Some call it the *soul*. Each individual lifetime is a journey of ensoulment, of activat-ing, embodying, and radiating out of the higher self. These natives are naturally interested in philosophy and spirituality. Often they also teach these values. They understand the natural law intuitively, and they possess an unusual ability to find ways to express essential universal values. They nervously search for meaning; they tend to feel driven to know ultimate truths and convey them to others. They love to travel and experience the energy of temples and spiritual centers on the planet. But have they connected with the higher self and learned to embody the higher self in everyday life?

Chiron is pragmatism, the how-to principle in the chart, and because Chiron is experiential, careful probing will reveal what is going on with Chirotic energy in the ninth. Like the third house natives, ninth house natives appear to be the adept. They naturally embody spirituality, wisdom about the natural law, but their crisis is always over resonation with the higher self. The astrologer who can help them look at their level of connection with the higher self has the opportunity to guide them with their most closely held secret—that they actually are not in touch with the higher self themselves. This is the adept who teaches everyone else to know the soul, who longs intensely for ensoulment. Meditation connecting the higher self and work with body healers who can help bring in the God force is highly recommended. The Sabian symbol for the ascendant is a reading of the higher self, since we have the same ascendant degree in each incarnation. Special work counseling your clients with Chiron in the ninth to resonate with the ascendant energy will help them find the higher self.

The T-square to the sixth house is the third/ninth house polarity. Squares are awareness; thus, the third/ninth house polarity can teach us awareness about the sixth house. The third house is the work of integration and successful communication skills in life, and the square to the sixth house reveals the pragmatic and experiential side of Chiron. This aspect teaches us that the more well-integrated we are about resonating with our highest faculties, the more we will embody our essential humanity. How many times more do we need to hear that we use only 10% of our brain? The ability to manifast Chirotic awareness is the light we will shine into the darkest part of our brain, the pineal gland. New research on the function of the pineal gland reveals the possibility of using all our faculties by allowing ourselves the full energy of the Mercury/Chiron square, the square from the third to the sixth house. The ninth house is the work of bringing the highest octave of consciousness into life; it is the union of body and soul metaphorically expressed by the horse/man body of Chiron.

So now with Chiron as master of the tarot reading, with Chiron as initiator of the astrological reading, we can pragmatically and experientially find higher awareness. The age of despair, of extentialism, is over. The revelation of the Chiron upper square is that we know the way to our higher self. The revelation of the T-square is that full integration here on Earth (third) and the deliberate choice to bring in the highest octave of resonance (ninth) will result in divination and healing skills.

My files are bulging with clients with Chiron in the ninth house, and I selected ten for close analysis—five men and five women. All of them are unusually intense and follow the characteristics described about Chiron in the ninth. Chart #9, an artist, is one of the most interesting experiences I've had with studying Chiron. He was excruciatingly sensitive to transiting Chiron squaring his natal Chiron, probably because his Chiron is in Virgo, and because his Uranus/Mars is close to his upper square position. As his third Chiron square approached, he became paralyzed by depression. He was literally unable to move a great deal of the time for a few months. At the exact time of the first square, he was riding his bike and became paralyzed. He fell off the bike and was very frightened by the experience. Even though he was hard to communicate with because of his gripping depression, he was unusually open to hearing about Chiron because it was the first explanation he'd gotten for his problem that made sense. Naturally, he understands Chiron intuitively because of the Virgo emphasis. Chiron was literally exploding his nervous system and pushing him to greater awareness because of its transit to Mars/Uranus near the square. I gave him dates on the next two squares, and when the same effect manifested, although not as extremely, he handled the problem better and began to allow the energy to flow. The aspect is finished, he feels better, and he is bringing in great work as an artist.

Quite a few of my clients with Chiron in the ninth also have it placed in Scorpio which is an exacting and empowered placement. These individuals are excellent examples of a high degree of mastery of Chirotic energy. Chart #46 is that of a renowned healer, another client is a brilliant therapist, and Chart #52 is an architect. Another group has Chiron in Aquarius in the ninth and the energy seems to be too intense for them. They are prone to drug taking and nervous difficulties. The power of Uranus seems to push Chiron too fast, and these clients required counseling on the stabilizing qualities of Saturn. But prone to depression, they avoid the long and careful lessons of Saturn. Counseling on Uranian imbalances was helpful. More later on planetary positions, but with all clients with Chiron in the ninth, imbalances are pronounced.

The key to ninth house Chiron is to first ascertain the degree of higher self connection and then to assist natives in higher resonance with their rising sign energy by helping them interpret their Sabian symbol. Then seek balance in their lives and the natal chart. Now it is time to leave the three houses of integration with the other, the seventh through ninth, and emerge into the tenth to find our power.

CHIRON IN THE TENTH HOUSE

The angular houses of the zodiac represent the four directions on Earth, expressing vertical reach energy, which connects higher planes to Earth, crossed in the middle by horizontal spread power. We are pulled out by Aries/Libra to know the self and to encounter the other. The vertical reach of Cancer/Capricorn is the individualized Tree of Life of our natal system causing it to spread downward in the third and fourth houses, and the energy of the ninth and tenth houses reaches incessantly upward, testing our desire to ascend to the sky. These are the cardinal houses where all activity is initiated. The tenth house is the gateway to the last quadrant of the zodiac, the tenth through twelfth houses where we give to the outside world all we have gathered in the first nine houses. In the tenth, we give our power and work; in the eleventh, we give our utmost creativity; and in the twelfth, we manifest our Chirotic force into the cosmos.

Chiron's presence in the tenth house signals a crisis about manifesting true purpose on the Earth plane. The energy of the tenth house is Saturnian; the energy of the eleventh house is Uranian, thus the natural growth progression of the tenth and eleventh houses is the most specific expression we have of the bridging energy from Saturn to Uranus by Chiron. The tenth house is pragmatic, and is the essence of bringing matter into form. The eleventh house is idealistic and limitless and is the essence of stretching ourselves to the highest potential gifting. The tenth house trines the house of Chiron (the sixth). The trines to the sixth from the second and tenth houses express the full essence of the being of the Centaur. This master warrior force wants power at the highest levels of the tenth house, and he can only sustain it with the perfect grounding force of the second house. Then the warrior force moves from the power of the tenth to the prodding driving quincunx of the eleventh house. The tenth house will always be a driven house because that is where we get the planetary juice, but it only becomes a sacred power if we are prepared to give it all away in the eleventh. The native with Chiron in the tenth house is not seeking power for power's sake; he or she is seeking power for release to Uranus. But what does that mean?

In the fourth house, deepest connection and roots were sought. Our most primal lessons with roots come from our own family. Chiron in the tenth is always connected to fourth house lessons in one way or another. Chiron is quixotic here. The native often rejects the positive side of the power of the tenth house, and often family issues are heavily intertwined in the dilemma. This particular dilemma is especially confusing in the late eighties because we are switching from the dynamic of patriarchal power over life to matriarchal emphasis on survival. We will manifest nothing more on this planet if we resist this essential switch which will empower men and women. The essence of the new energy here is the master warrior who protects the hearth, and this is the essence of highly evolved Saturn in preparation for Uranian kundalini awareness. And this will happen because the centaur is present now.

You will notice it is impossible to discuss the tenth house without also discussing history and culture. The gifts that are mastered in the tenth are the food of culture and the events of history. Individuals with Chiron in the tenth have authority, although they may be trying not to take it on. They possess power, although it may stir conflicts in their being, and they have been projected upon first by their parents and later by their teachers because of all their intense energy so radically exposed. They wear the "mantle" of power, and the only solution for them is to accept their power. Now that culture is evolving and the New Age models of power favor mastery, they will find out that life makes sense. During the height of patriarchal power they were miserable.

My records on Chiron in the tenth are simply extraordinary. I decided to utilize sixteen charts I know well. Four are male and twelve are female. Of the women, eight are nuns (!), one woman is an Episcopal priest, another is a psychologist for Catholic colleges, and the last two women are contemporary New Age priestesses! The spiritual, artistic, and healing gifts of all these women are extraordinary, but the fields they have chosen are what is interesting. Literally all of them sought power in religious orders. I have seen fourteen nuns since starting this project in 1982, and eight have Chiron in the tenth house. Of the men, two are priests, one is an alchemist, and one (Chart #10) is a Catholic publisher! This selection certainly reflects my own heavy work in Catholic orders, but still the almost magnetic gravitation of these individuals to the Catholic Church during the last days of the Age of Pisces is most interesting.

Many of my clients with Chiron in the tenth were very confused about using power until their Saturn return. Many of their difficulties with Chiron in the tenth start resolving at the Saturn return. Their confusions were mostly caused by projections from childhood coming from people who had a personal interest in this child getting power. In most cases, the men had been heavily projected upon by their mothers and felt extreme aversion to success. Most of the nuns adored their fathers, who were very powerful individuals. I suspect they avoided having a power struggle with men by going into the convent. The women who are not nuns are so strong that they have found it very difficult to relate to men. The more all of these individuals identified their own power expression and lived it out, the better they felt. See Chart #14, artist and nun; #15, priest; #18, yoga teacher; #30, alchemist jeweler; and #33, channeler of Atlantean symbols.

The key to Chiron in the tenth house is the mastery of power as a sacred gift. These individuals must accept their birthright of much needed leadership with sensitivity. These individuals will begin to manifest wonderful New Age work when many of the outer planets move into Capricorn in the late 1980s. Astrologers should especially try to assist these individuals around the time of their Uranus opposition. It is hard for them to let go of Saturn control because they seem to feel the power of Uranus very intensely. These individuals become increasingly electric in their mid-thirties, and they need guidance to keep from becoming confused. Shirley MacLaine and Marilyn Monroe both have Chiron in the tenth. Marilyn Monroe could not handle her own power, and Shirley MacLaine is a model of assuming her power.

CHIRON IN THE ELEVENTH HOUSE

The presence of Chiron in the eleventh house signals a crisis over the possibility of playing a unique role in culture. The eleventh house is the place of opportunity for each one of us to give our creative gift during our lifetime. So, what if one is an impressionistic painter and arrives in New York City in 1965 ready to sell his or her paintings when the only acceptable genre is abstract expressionism? We live during an age when media-induced fame is the key to personal value. What if one simply loves being a gardener when menial work is reviled? Each one of us needs to give our creative gift, and Chiron in the eleventh is a sign of a serious crisis over creativity and idealism.

Chiron in the eleventh stimulates Uranus to create an outlet for the works of the tenth. We need to give our gift and have it be graciously received. Since the polarity is from the fifth to the eleventh house or Sun/Uranus, if the power of Uranus is not released, the individual has no vehicle of self-expression (Sun), and is tragically isolated from the will axis (Sun/Uranus). Astrologers are meant to be master teachers of enhancement of free will. Knowing one's natal chart is the opportunity to open blocking energies and bring through the gift of self, the Sun self. There are many blocks in contemporary mass consciousness culture to eleventh house gifting. We must recreate the love of individual unique-ness and learn again to appreciate the gift of each person. The eleventh house needs to be carefully examined for each reading to try to deter-mine what the natal gift might be. Then a way to give it must be found.

Consulting nine charts, the most noticeable trait of Chiron in the eleventh is eccentricity on the part of the native. They have a strong inner feeling of a great destiny which may be impossible to attain or even express. The degree to which they are ego-invested will reveal how close they are to having a gift they can give. And the extent to which they have been able to manifest the tenth house is an indication of what they may be able to give at all. If they are attached to their ability to make their goal, first of all they will not attain it, and secondly they will get sick from the struggle. They require a lot of counseling to carefully identify the goal, detach themselves from needing to make it or not, and then they will find they are closer to their goal than they think. The highest level of aware-ness for them is the realization that the energy really flows when they just channel it.

Of the nine natives, six are therapists or astrologers. My files are loaded with therapists and astrologers, but this was still a high percent-age. One male client also has Chiron in Virgo and he is a very high manifestation of the eleventh house. He is extremely detached from suc-cess although he does very well, and he is exceedingly giving to other people but seems to not be aware of how much people appreciate him. He is a very peaceful man and makes peace around himself. An older physician (Chart #11) has not done well in finding a way to give his gift. He was a doctor but also desired a great deal of power as a medical re-searcher, which he in fact did possess throughout much of his life. But his research gifts were ignored by governmental bureaucracy. Ironically, he manifested a crippling neurological disease which has never been diagnosed. In his old age, he is a delightful person but very frustrated with himself. He is angry and feels a compulsive need to express his inner rage. The futurist writer, Chart #16, has managed to bring in his vision, and he is a great genius of our time. Also see Chart #22.

The key to resolution of Chiron in the eleventh is to counsel detachment and letting go. Often clients are much further along on manifesting their gift than they realize, and their over-inflated ego is keeping them from seeing how great they already are. Astrology is helpful to them because they are often infected with fatalism and defeatism. The Hermetic principle, "As above, so below" teaches them that each action here on Earth has a purpose and is power itself. Help with the monster dragon ego helps them to gain perspective. The more knowledge you can give them about their natal dynamic, the more they will be able to activate free will and idealistic purpose.

CHIRON IN THE TWELFTH HOUSE

The presence of Chiron in the twelfth house signifies the potential to actuate cosmic immersion, to enter deeply into mysticism. This Chirotic thought potential becomes real when the native learns to use the pragmatic gifts of the sixth house to develop the acute awareness of the exact place and time of this dimension in relation to others. How?

The development of a divination skill is required in order to release consciousness from left-brain linear time thought processes so that holographic brain functions materialize.

The twelfth house is ruled by Neptune, and the only way to resonate with the Neptunian galactic vibration is to find a way to attune consciousness here on Earth with mysticism. Being a mystic is a choice; it involves free will, and it is a possibility in life after the native has mastered the will axis of the fifth/eleventh houses. There were once mystical orders such as the Eleusinian mysteries which taught the initiate the way of mysticism. Chiron was the great initiator of the pre-Mycenean Aegean culture, and he taught pragmatism. He was reputed to be a great astrologer (possibly the first astrologer), and he taught that the natal chart was the road map of mysticism. Knowing this psychic labyrinth is a need for individuals with Chiron in the twelfth house.

In *Earth Ascending,* Jose Arguelles said about holonomics or holistic thought processes,

"Holonomics depends upon a self-reflective consciousness, a clarity of perception, and an ability to account for and create order—a process culminating in the intuitive apprehension and expression of the whole system of order of which one is a member."[1]

If this "clarity of expression" is the sixth house exactitude of Chiron, then immediately the mind-reach is Neptunian, i.e., it is capable of multidimensional relational thought processes. The Age of Rationalism is over; as Aquarius comes in, this is what human thought will be.

Neptunian intuition is the forte of these natives, and the greatest service they can do for those around themselves is to cultivate inner knowing. They usually tend to be intensely curious and probing, and they tend to deep study, which has not been much appreciated at this time in the late twentieth century. However, they will be coming into their own as the Aquarian Age progresses because these natives are a gold mine of past-life esoteric knowledge. The goal in counseling should be to help them attune completely with intuitive or right brain function and then search for the pragmatic ways they can sharpen left brain skill. A native with Chiron in the twelfth will almost always have a highly developed right brain, but often will be handicapped by underdeveloped left brain function. This is where the comprehension of Chiron as a Saturnian experiential function will really help to awaken the possibility of manifesting Neptune in the world or being a mystic. Simply put, the sixth/twelfth house axis is the left/right brain polarity.

Individuals who have Chiron in the twelfth house are prone to giving their free will to teachers because their highly attuned early awareness is out of tune with the real world. These natives maintain Neptunian isolation so that they can hear the music of the spheres, and a highly trained esoteric teacher will attract them greatly. The astrologer's job is to point out that they are not supposed to be following *anybody*, that *free will* is the highest human faculty, and that they are to learn from teachers but never follow. If they can master this teaching, then *they* will become the master teacher who initiates followers directly into their own way of wisdom.

The crisis of mastering Neptune is the final test. Neptune can attune us to our highest potential, or confuse the will just when the real essence of a person is ready to become embodied. Neptune affects the astral or emotional body powerfully. Chris Griscom teaches that the emotional body functions at the lowest vibratory rate[2] because the mind and physical realms are very much attuned at the end of this long phase of rationalism.[2] She is correct, because we are in the last phases of the Age of Pisces, and all the issues of the past having to do with ancient initiatory teachings are surfacing at this time. These ancient teachings are rich with wisdom, loaded with esoteric juice, but they are the past. They are the last "hook," so to speak; they will actually pull you backwards if you're not careful, and the biggest danger sign is emotional heaviness. The vibration rate is increasing greatly as we move into Aquarius, and this emotional heaviness is very dangerous. It can attract disease and imbalance.

The Age of Aquarius will be a time of natural mystical attunement because kundalini energy blocks will dissipate. At this time, kundalini energy is intensifying as the vibration rate increases. Natives with Chiron in the twelfth house are responding intensely to this dynamic. They will be the gate openers of the coming Age, so they must be assisted to open their own gates and not dance to the tune of anyone else. In order to truly find this energy, they must hold to the highest essence of the free will axis of the fifth/eleventh and then the polarity power of the sixth/twelfth will energize by means of Chirotic pragmatism.

My files yielded thirteen examples of Chiron in the twelfth. Six of these natives are very much in the dark about their potential, although I pointed it out strongly, and seven of the natives have developed esoteric skills which can be charcterized as stupendous. With all thirteen there is a marked tendency to get mixed up with teachers and gurus, and in four-cases, the results have been very negative. Chart #19, a healer, has three planetary pairs and a stellium with Chiron, Jupiter, and Neptune in the twelfth. He is willful, self-contained, has esoteric skills not seen on this-planet since the Age of Rationalism temporarily devalued the right brain, but he is heavily influenced by a teacher. I have Chiron in the twelfth and have struggled for years to trust my own inner vision. The guided imagery healer (Chart #44) has also worked hard to trust her own great intuition.

The key to resolution of the twelfth house Chiron is a careful examination of the sixth house to determine the potential highest octave of the native. The goal is to figure out which esoteric order they have worked with for many lifetimes. And be ready for anything. One of my most highly developed twelfth house Chiron natives, Chart #12, actually works in the order protecting the sacred blood of Christ as well described in *Holy Blood, Holy Grail.*[3]

Once the mystical connection is identified, focus on the difficult aspects in the chart. These natives have come to fulfill a high purpose, and they usually have chosen a whole series of squares, conjunctions, and quincunxes which will push them faster than usual. The astrologer who can see that their clients have chosen this difficult path because their goal is very high will be in the position of unraveling confusions. Once Neptune is guided by Chirotic pragmatism, once the veil of astral confusion is lifted, the gates of Aquarius will be ready to swing open.

Chapter Seven

CHIRON IN THE SIGNS

Definition of Chiron by sign is a highly controversial and complex issue in contemporary astrology. Chiron is extremely elliptical and by distribution is located heavily in the eastern signs (Aquarius through Taurus) for thirty years, and lightly in the western signs (Leo through Scorpio) for eight years. Thus, many more people have Chiron in Aquarius through Taurus than in Leo through Scorpio, (See Figure 2) and the historical phases at this time have a heavier influence from the vibration of Chiron in Aquarius through Taurus. But individuals with Chiron in Leo through Scorpio probably play a stronger role in breakthrough consciousness because their Chirotic perceptual base is less attuned to the cultural vibration. They are radical movers and shakers instead of being at ease with convention. We have much observation ahead of us on questions such as these. Also, due to the precession of the equinoxes over time, the signs which contain Chiron change for longer or shorter periods of time.

The definition of Chiron by sign is highly controversial because this is the first book defining Chiron rulership as Virgo. Richard Nolle has been a trailblazer in Chiron research, and I am exceedingly indebted to his work in *Chiron: The New Planet in Your Horoscope* and his lectures. However, I am forced to respectfully disagree with him regarding his comments on planetary rulership. Nolle notes that the obvious importance of asteriods, especially the main ones, Ceres, Pallas, Juno, and Vesta, indicates that the system of planetary rulership developed by Ptolemy in the Second Century is an "artificial scheme which has certainly outlived its usefulness."[1] He also notes its usefulness and natural-

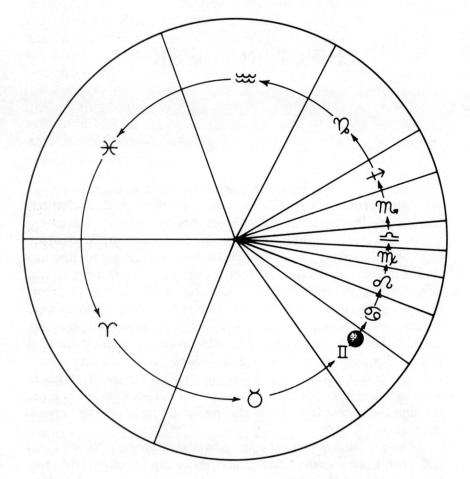

Figure 2.
Chiron's Orbital Time in the Signs

ness due to affinities between certain signs and planets.

This book is evidence of the power of working with planetary sign affinities. Also, I do not think Ptolemy "developed" his system of planetary rulership. I believe he *recorded* the teachings of the Babylonian and Egyptian Astrologers who in turn had received their information from the Atlanteans. At any rate, until the human brain evolves to greater integration with galactic synchronization, we still need analogical reasoning. Until more is revealed of the true nature of reality, we require the Hermetic system of correspondences to relate Earth experience to planetary energetics. But this disagreement is a both/and question, and not an either/or one. Just like utilizing both logical and analogical paradigms, when one ceases to rely strictly on rationalistic thought processes—that something is either this or that—then the both/and mentality is productive. For example, in the Ptolemaic system, seven planets are used to read the Zodiac. Nolle comments that, "The Ptolemaic system of rulership began to break down with the discovery of new planets starting with Uranus in 1781."[2] No one agrees with that point of view more than I do—my work questioning the rulership of Libra is proof of it. But many Indian astrologers read brilliantly with only seven planets! Astrology is a divination skill, and divination is ruled by the master initiator, Chiron, not by the particular system the diviner employs. In *Eye of the Centaur,*[3] astrologer Aspasia of Thrace in 1550 BC was using the inner planets to rule everyday events, and the outer planets (unseen) to rule psychic influences. The inner planets could be observed, the outer planets were intuited, and she also utilized the stars.

Western rationalism has taught that Uranus was first sighted in 1781, but ancient astrologers were using the outer planets. Zecharia Sitchin proved it in *Stairway to Heaven.*[4] And, why were the ancient Minoan deities such as Saturn/Kronos, Uranus/Sky Father, Neptune, and Chiron so significant if astrologers were not aware of the outer planets? The myth that the outer planets were first sighted beginning in 1781 is as outrageous as the myth that Columbus discovered America. The grip of the Western rationalistic mythos is breaking down, and the power of ancient wisdom or Hermetic correspondences is emerging.

The obvious significance of the asteroids is a major issue. We have lost Tony Joseph, but we have his work.[5] Joseph dedicated his life to "re-mythologizing astrology" or reawakening holonomic thought processes, from my point of view. Holonomic thought processes are the ability to perceive the *whole* in a single event. For example, a person might see that many American politicians in the 1980s are reincarnated

Saturnian Romans, and then the possibility of viewing their behavior as a repeating myth is available. It is a return to a very ancient way of thought which sees the Earth and its stories as alive in the middle of a vital universe. Western rationalism has come very close to destroying our ecosystem and the planet itself, and holonomic thought processes will predominate with the sighting of Chiron as a signal for hope again. Joseph works with a family of images for Virgo with Ceres, Persephone, and Vesta, which have a special affinity with Virgo.

For Joseph, the Ceres archetype is clearly expressed in the life of Demeter, the Earth Mother who guards the fields. This was ritualized in the Eleusinian mysteries which were based on the eternal life of the community which was dependent upon the power of the harvest. This is, of course, an ancient form of ecology which has obvious affinity to Virgo. Then Demeter loses her daughter Persephone to the Underworld, and this introduces the complexity of the subconscious mind into the simple cycles of nature. Possibly the myth of Demeter and Persephone is a feminine counterpart to the story of Chiron, as well as being very Plutonic. Both Chiron and Demeter go to the Underworld of Pluto, and the Persephone myth in itself is very Plutonian. And Vesta, the hearth goddess, *feels* very Venusian, very much the archetype of the second house. As with Chiron, identification of sign and house rulership along with application work on many charts will reveal the real energy of the asteroids. The point being made here is that the probability that Ceres also rules the sixth house and Virgo does not diminish the power of Chiron's rulership of Virgo. Possibly the asteroids and other minor bodies add nuances to the houses, but the planetary rulerships define the dynamics of house polarity energy and the essence of house mode.

Each sign of the zodiac is ruled by a planet which defines its energetics. Aries is ruled by Mars/aggression/*animus*/power, and Martian issues have to do with use of force for desired goals. Taurus is ruled by Venus/receptivity/anima/attraction, and Venusian issues have to do with use of attraction for drawing to us what we need. Gemini is ruled by Mercury/mind/integration/communication, and Mercurial issues have to do with how well our mind helps us integrate and communicate on Earth. Cancer is ruled by the Moon/subconscious mind/response/ reaction, and lunar issues have to do with how we screen all perceptions coming to us and how we learn to respond. Leo is ruled by the Sun/me/ will/shining, and the solar issue is becoming all that we are so we shine on Earth. Virgo is ruled by Chiron/alchemy/transmutation/initiation; and Chirotic issues involve learning the method to connect Earth mind with galactic cosmic awareness. Libra is ruled by Nibiru or another outer planet cycle/the other/the mirror/the balance; and Nibiruan issues involve learning to mirror our true self in the other side so that our view is polarized instead of being inside ourselves *or* located in the other. Scorpio is ruled by Pluto/Underworld/evolution/eruptive change; and Plutonian issues are the journeys into the Underworld to get the most powerful source of energy. Sagittarius is ruled by Jupiter/expansion/comfort/higher self; and Jupiterian issues are learning to make ourselves bigger so we can get in touch with the higher self. Capricorn is ruled by Saturn/control/father/responsibility; and Saturnian issues are mastering the Earth plane. Aquarius is ruled by Uranus/electricity/idealism/galactic resonation; and the idealistic test is to galvanize human will into universal serving. Pisces is ruled by Neptune/divine mother/ecstasy/holonomics; and the Neptunian ecstasy is the attainment of galactic mysticism.

What happens when Chiron rules each of these signs?

CHIRON IN ARIES

04/01/1918	—	10/22/1918
01/29/1919	—	05/24/1926
10/21/1926	—	03/25/1927
04/01/1968	—	10/18/1968
01/31/1969	—	05/28/1976
10/14/1976	—	03/28/1977

When Chiron is in Aries, the search for identity predominates. Who am I? Why am I here? What do they all want of me? That level of questioning becomes Chirotic, or a life and death issue, and until there is a satisfactory answer, the native is restless. But an answer will come with time, because Chiron's natural form as a warrior initiate is very attuned to Mars. When these natives were born during the last two most recent Chiron cycles, 1918-1926 and 1968-1977, the atmosphere in general was very spirited and pioneering. The parents of this generation were living through the Roaring Twenties and the Me Generation of the Seventies. These children will feel an urge to carry through the energies of their parents, and Chiron natally in Aries will offer them the means.

My clients who have Chiron in Aries are all trailblazers; they are known as courageous people. This position causes quick action to breakthrough Saturn barriers and act idealistically with Uranus. But unless there are other factors in the chart which foster mysticism, these natives may not activate the subtlety of Chiron. The *warrior energy* is the most powerful manifestation for these natives. They need to be encouraged to systematically develop a *discipline* which will enable them to empower Chiron and get in touch with the potential power of the etheric plane. Good examples of such discipline are Carlos Castenada, Carl Jung, Jack Anderson, and Aleister Crowley. All four of these men have created great power in their disciplines and made great impact on their times. A deliberate development of initiate warrior power by these natives will cause Chiron to become a very great tool for bringing their greatest essence into being. Generally these natives are frustrated unless they are extremely active, and an analysis of the house position of Chiron in Aries will reveal the area of life where they can initiate progress. Limitation will drive them crazy.

The women born from 1918-1926 have experienced extremely difficult lives unless they found a way to take on power. If not, the incidence of cancer in this group is very high. The men tend to be very powerful and Saturnian, and unreceptive to Uranian higher consciousness. Many of these men are present-day political leaders who are blocking Aquarian energy with great force. Chart #13 belongs to Carl Jung, psychoanalyst, who is a great example of the potential energy of Chiron in Aries.

A wonderful esoteric resonance with Chiron is available from the contemplation of the astrological energetics of Mars to Venus. Mars rules the first house, and is the first planet beyond Earth. It rules the *animus* because it is the first orbital plane beyond Earth to the universe. Venus rules the second house and is the first planet within Earth orbit to the Sun, symbolizing the primary need for us to ground on our planet Earth. It rules the *anima* because it is the first orbital plane with Earth to our center, the Sun. At the time of Chiron's sighting November 1, 1977, the human polarity dynamic, Mars/Venus, *animus/anima,* had intensified to an orgasmic level of Earth vibration to galactic resonance. This can be seen by the appearance of initiation, crystal, and body/mind healing therapies in 1977. The higher planes *really have* been grounding on Earth. Chiron transited out of Mars' vibration of Aries—the intense drive for self-identification within this larger cyclical time of alchemical resonance—and it moved into Venus' vibration of Taurus in 1977. This sighting signaled a coming age of receptivity toward a new level of will power to balance Venus/Mars. The children born since

November 1, 1977 are free of the fear of Chirotic energy, and they will teach the grandparents who were born from 1918-26 to let go of their death wish. Last cycle, before 1500 B.C., Chiron was Mars dominated because it was the Age of Aries. In this cycle, Chiron was born in Venus' vibration to energize material values/Earth Gaia. All of reality is in resonance, and we can again use divination to know our place in the cycle of Gaia. See the birth chart of Chiron (#53) to reawaken divination memories in essence. What I see is that Chiron was sighted when it was in Taurus to signal that the Age of Aquarius will rebirth many of the temple and healing technologies that were used during the Age of Taurus—2200-4400 B.C..

CHIRON IN TAURUS

05/25/1926	—	10/20/1926
03/26/1927	—	06/06/1933
12/23/1933	—	03/23/1934
05/29/1976	—	10/13/1976
03/29/1977	—	06/19/1983
11/30/1983	—	04/11/1984

When Chiron is in Taurus, a search for values on the material plane predominates. This position takes the question of material values to a very critical level: what is right or wrong, permanent or not, becomes a crisis. These natives rarely bring something new into reality, but they are manifestors of material from other people whom they believe in. They want to preserve the values they see in something which already exists. The house position of Chiron reveals the nature of the values they are interested in. The historical period they were born within was characterized by a search for value, and these natives are equipped natally to respond to the needs that were the concern of their parents who came out of the Great Depression. These individuals are adept at coping well with few financial resources.

My clients with Chiron in Taurus are all heavily influenced by a morality system which they value greatly. It is important to analyze these clients to see if they are stuck in the value system to the exclusion of creativity. Free will and the ability to act for justice is blocked without creativity. This system is valuable if it is being actively utilized, otherwise it functions as an opportunity to block Chirotic energy. The *house position* of Chiron in Taurus is the key. First, examine the house position to see if the value system of that house is active in the life of the client by questioning the client about it. For example, someone with Chiron in Taurus in the tenth house would show evidences of marked valuing of power and activity in the outside world. R.D. Laing, Chart #31, has Chiron in Taurus in the first, and his life work has been defining the ego structure of schizophrenics.

Often, natives with Chiron in Taurus have bizarre sexual habits because of the strong influence of Chiron with Venusian energy making them receptive to kundalini energy. Is the sexual behavior pattern disturbing the normal pattern of the tenth house Chiron natives making their mark? Three of the nuns who have Chiron in the tenth house have Chiron in Taurus, indicating they have been able to transmute the Chirotic force into religious careers. All three have a very mystical prayer life. Another is a priest (Chart #15) who has been functioning as a bridge, working with Catholicism and Native American ritual. His Chiron is in a stellium in the tenth house with Jupiter/Mars. His fusion of the Native American/Catholic value system has had a major impact on contemporary spirituality.

The publisher of Chart #3 is an excellent example of Chiron in Taurus in the third house of communications. He has been a prominent leader in reintroducing the values of Earth religions and pagan values into culture. He was born during the Depression when many people suffered from energy loss, and now the power of magic and power over one's own reality is brought through as a solution by him. Earth religions and pagan spiritualities value powerful kundalini flow.

It is important to acknowledge and reinforce the wonderful gifts that those with Chiron in Taurus are giving to culture. Often these individuals are great contributors who feel guilty about not making their own mark with something they have invented themselves. These individuals are *preservers of values,* and not creators unless some other aspects in the chart indicate great innovation. Chiron is in Taurus in Chiron's own natal chart, #50.

CHIRON IN GEMINI

06/07/1933	—	12/22/1933
03/24/1934	—	08/28/1937
11/24/1937	—	05/28/1938
06/20/1983	—	11/29/1983
04/12/1984	—	06/21/1988

When Chiron is in Gemini there is a personal crisis about integration here on Earth which affects balance and the nervous system greatly. These natives are highly attuned to the consciousness of individuals around themselves, and to mass awareness. They were mostly born between 1933 and 1938 during Nazism and atomic experimentation as Pluto manifested again on Earth. Their crisis is to find new ways of perception and integration here. This group will become very important to the human race as they wake up and realize they possess the natal tool—Chiron in Gemini—to understand and communicate about the crises their parents suffered with. Thus, astrologers must work hard with these clients to guide them into their natural role as *teachers and communicators*. Their birth placement of Chiron means they will experience their Chiron returns between June 1983 and June 1988 when the culture needs their awareness for its very survival. Natives will learn not to be so "heavy". Gemini always loves to be in the middle of everything, so this awakening will be pleasurable for those with Chiron in Gemini. This Chiron return will be intense because transiting Uranus in Sagittarius will oppose transiting Chiron often during 1983-1988.

As Richard Nolle put it, "Awareness is the keynote for persons born under this Chiron sign, whose prime existential mission is to understand the way we think in order to effect changes in our mental realities."[6] Thus, these individuals are meant to learn that the way we think creates the reality we live in, and that we can change it if we believe that. These natives will believe it when they experience it, and their very awareness will alter the hologram if they can become conscious that *how they think* alters reality at their Chiron return.

Some of my most remarkable clients have Chiron in Gemini. In a general sense, they are very plugged in to mass consciousness and are deliberately using their attunement to manifest changes they feel strongly about. Four are therapists working in the newest areas of body/mind research, and they seem to be able to feel where electrical energy is flowing in the body. Chart #14 belongs to a famous author, who is also a nun, with Chiron in the tenth. She has brought the power of God as mother back to us again with beautiful, feminine paintings. Since Chiron is the bridge from Saturn to Uranus, individuals with Chiron in Gemini galvanize their awareness into form/Saturn, then Uranus manifests easily for them because Uranus is the high mental form of Mercury. Balance only comes in to individuals with Chiron in Gemini when Saturn form has been mastered and the energy of Uranus is brought forth.

CHIRON IN CANCER

08/29/1937	—	11/23/1937
05/29/1938	—	09/30/1940
01/01/1940	—	06/17/1941
06/22/1988	—	07/21/1991

When Chiron is in Cancer the native has a crisis over cultural roots and/or a crisis of personal protection. This native sees his or her own ability to feel safe and secure on the planet as a personal and cultural dynamic, and the ecological power of Chiron usually predominates over the personal crisis. No one has mentioned it so far, but Chiron in Cancer is a very difficult position because the native is *tied to the past* and VERY threatened by the present Earth crisis. These individuals were born in the depths of World War II to parents who feared for their own survival, and this has created a profound dilemma for the security-seeking Cancer type. Most of these natives also have Uranus in Taurus, and some have Saturn in Taurus. They have been deeply shaken, and out of the power of Cancer will come a healing of the Earth when these natives experience their Chiron return in 1988-91, after the Chiron in Gemini group have *identified* the crises in 1983-88. In the meantime, these natives have an intense *insecurity dynamic* operating which astrologers can attempt to heal. Also, this critical Earth healing cycle is exaggerated only during the virgin cycle of Chiron, from 1977-2028, just as the virgin cycle of Pluto, approximately 1930-2170, is very intense. As we are all aware, these are apocalyptical times. The apocalyspe is *now* as we experience the rebirth of powerful solar system dynamics evident since the sighting of Uranus.

The struggle to break Saturn control and let go to Uranus electricity is a very tough battle for those with Chiron in Cancer. They need help to see that influences occuring from Saturn on this planet are also forming because of the Uranian dynamic; that what we think about creates our reality. We are actually much more free to act than most individuals with Chiron in Cancer comprehend, and if they can recognize their own power as manifestors, they will be at the forefront of manifesting true security for Earth. Natives with Chiron in Cancer will either be desperately seeking a means for real security or they will have the crab shell around themselves and be hiding.

A few exceptional clients will be at the very forefront of the Earth crisis. One of my clients, the futurist writer-ecologist of Chart #16, has an awareness of the aliveness of the Earth and its relationship to the galactic cycle that is mind-boggling. But he also became an alcoholic during his struggle to break through to his free will/Uranus. He also has Moon/ Jupiter in Pisces. I have observed from clients that natives with Chiron in Cancer often have a great struggle with alcohol because alcohol inhibits Saturn control in the short run. At all costs these natives need to resonate with the power of their own will power. They need help manifesting their fifth house, for the only real power is the power of creativity. Newer forms of astrological counseling which teach the natal chart as a dynamic for increasing free will will help tremendously. These natives are meant to be leaders in the battle to alchemize the Earth. They will break the hold of the conservative Pluto in Cancer generation, those born from 1913-1939. The house position of Chiron will reveal the way in which these natives feel the security crisis.

The house position reveals the Chirotic dynamic. First of all, the house shows where the native is seeking *release* from Saturn control. It shows where the experimentation is occurring. Those experiences ruled by the house position which have to do with control and letting go must be examined. Aspects must be carefully analyzed. The writer-ecologist who also had an alcoholic crisis has Chiron *exactly* trine Jupiter in Pisces in the seventh. Work as an ecologist has saved him from the horror of alcoholism; he has chosen life over death—the Chirotic crisis. Clients with twelfth house Chiron in Cancer have exhibited a life and death struggle with occultism. One has sold his soul to develop the Star Wars system. Chart #44, with Chiron in the twelfth house, belongs to a healer who is working with addictions and is intensely involved in work with dolphin ecology. *Thanatos* or *Eros,* love of death-love of life, is the essence of this position. Understand the house dynamic in relation to the security struggle of Saturn/Uranus, and the inner struggle of natives with Chiron in Cancer will be revealed. And, notice that the Chiron in Leo group coming next often have Saturn conjunct Uranus natally. Many of them have been at the forefront of developing Chirotic healing technologies. They can offer counseling help to those with Chiron in Cancer.

CHIRON IN LEO

08/31/1880	—	02/14/1891
05/18/1891	—	10/11/1891

03/02/1893 — 06/18/1893
10/01/1940 — 12/31/1940
06/18/1941 — 07/27/1943
07/22/1991 — 09/04/1993

When Chiron is in Leo, a great crisis over the ego exists which will gradually refine the native into mastering the will. Leo/Aquarius is the polarity of the will. The lesson of Chiron is to *break Saturn form* so that the native can move into Uranian dimensions, and Chiron in Leo signals a life/death struggle to develop the higher will. The higher will has great affinity with the higher self. The higher self represents the form of our soul, the essential being working through a series of incarnations. The higher will represents the ability to choose to resonate with the higher self, to choose to bring the higher self into life during any incarnation. The higher self will not manifest in the body unless the crisis of the fifth house is resolved. The fifth house represents empowerment/shining. The power comes from creativity, co-creating the Universe, and Chiron in Leo actualizes the Royal Person or soul being in the body.

Natives with Chiron in Leo feel something special about them-selves which attaches itself to the ego in the early stages. For most peo-ple, the way to break the ego hold is to minimize oneself, to identify with a purpose larger than the self so that the self takes on proper importance. For natives with Chiron in Leo, a different dynamic prevails. They must *become* the ego. Their life and death struggle is preservation of the ego as long as it is required for survival. The key is that they cannot let go of the ego until they have matured enough to handle Uranian energy. They are in danger of being overwhelmed by Uranus until they are very secure and mature. Thus, the ego structure is maintained longer, but suddenly dissipates. While it is being maintained these natives are strung out; they seem desperate, and they are involved in activities which attract a lot of attention. Generally speaking, they cannot drop the ego structure until they have experienced Uranus opposite Uranus, and they usually experi-ence a very difficult Saturn return because the ego structure is so large and empowered. Then the structure becomes Uranian and carries the higher will.

When they are ready to let the ego go and release their gift through creativity, they fuse with the higher will or Uranian dynamic. Any iden-tification of purpose is very helpful to them, and resonation with their struggle relieves their anxiety. Identification of their gift enables the astrologer to counsel patience. Their time will come; worrying won't help at all, and any work these clients do to learn to *ground* and *relax* will help. But telling them to ground and relax won't help at all, because they will have no idea what you mean. If you hear their anxiety about their desire to make and give their gift, it will speed the process. The creative process must be honored. A person who creates a beautiful garden or family is just as creative as a great painter.

Natives with Chiron in Leo were born from 1941 to 1943. They experienced their Uranus returns in 1981-84, and they have been really bringing through their gifts. In my files there are three clients with Chiron in Leo in the second house. One is a body healer, one is a well-known theologian (Chart #17) and another (Chart #36) is a famous musician. All three clients are confusing to other people because recently they have become egoless. Their professions are their gift; they are not attached. Another client has Chiron in Leo in the sixth, and she is a great healer; Chart #33 has Chiron in the tenth, and this native is manifesting esoteric symbols for the New Age. These natives are the manifestation of high use of will power, and they are a gift to their Age when they move beyond their own ego structure. Nostradamus, Chart #34, has Chiron in Leo. See also Charts #26, #28, #39, #48. Since the atom split (Chart #50) occurred in 1942, Chiron is in Leo in the horary chart cast for the split—the birth of splitting matter.

CHIRON IN VIRGO

10/12/1891	—	03/01/1893
06/19/1893	—	10/10/1894
07/28/1943	—	11/18/1944
03/25/1945	—	07/22/1945
09/05/1993	—	09/08/1995

Chiron reveals its true essence in Virgo, the sign which the Centaur rules. At this time, Chiron is in Virgo and Libra for only twenty months every fifty years! Therefore, the Virgo dynamic was felt for twenty months during 1943-45, and will return in 1993-1995 for a short visit. Natives with Chiron in Virgo are our greatest souce on this dynamic because the historical documentation is small. *Subtlety* and *exactitude* characterize these individuals, who are coming into their own due to the sighting of their planet. As we struggle to describe the healing Centaur, we create a new definition of Virgo.

The low form of the Virgo dynamic is compulsive and Saturnian.

Saturn control is being used to hold the greatly feared Uranian energy in check. Men with low Virgo tendencies often are compulsive workaholics who express Uranus with kinky sexual behavior. Chiron was in Virgo 1891-93 when the Plutocrats were born. The women tend to hold absolute power in the office or home, and then lose their control at parties. The energy of Uranus is avoided and feared, and aging is Saturnian instead of Uranian transformative growth. The high energetics of Virgo develops a keen understanding of the positive use of Saturn which is to bring matter into form, but not to hold it. The ability to allow Uranian transformation matures with time and evolves into a deep intuition about perfect timing.

One of my clients who taught me about high Virgo energy made it possible for me to write this book. She is an outstanding yoga teacher (Chart #18) with Mars, Mercury, Chiron, Venus, and Jupiter in a stellium in Virgo in the tenth and eleventh houses. She has mastered the ability to form Saturn in yoga postures and move it right into Uranus awareness so that electricity moves freely in the body and chakras. Another client who is a priest taught me a lot about lower-form Virgo dynamics. This client takes his religious training (Saturn) too seriously, is scared to death of Uranus, and is afraid of any thought outside the realm of doctrine. Reality is frozen in a Saturnian time frame which blocks normal evolution.

As already stated, Chiron rules the exact time and place where transformative energy (Uranus) interfaces with form (Saturn). The house which contains Chiron in Virgo expresses the way in which this native is working on locating transformation energies on Earth. The priest just described has Chiron in the second and is very stuck in the Saturn form. He is also creating new Catholic ritual forms in the Orient. He *feels* Uranus, but blocks his power. Another client builds roofs (previously described with Chiron in the second house), and he actually loves giving Saturn form assistance to home owners. Generally speaking, Chiron in Virgo in the second, fourth, and seventh houses causes problems with Saturn fixation. Chiron in Virgo in the third, fifth, ninth, tenth, and eleventh favors comfort with Uranian transformation.

All people with Chiron in Virgo require counseling because the past definition of Mercury ruling Virgo has created a great negative illusion. The incorrect Mercury rulership helped explain the *mental* (Uranian) qualities of Virgo, but where was all the *compulsion* coming from? There has been a damaging tendency to define the Saturn side of Virgo negatively as if somehow Virgo just created this compulsiveness out of thin air. Even work, which is ruled by the sixth house, has been treated negatively. The healing power of the sixth house and work has not been understood deeply enough, and poor Virgos have just been left to somehow deal with it themselves. But Chiron ruling Virgo demonstrates that the Virgo dynamic is to teach perfection of form on Earth so that the bridge to the higher dynamics can be built. Virgo can be the essence of love of Earth-healing combined with joy in higher consciousness.

The spirituality of Virgo has been shown to me by one client with Chiron in Virgo in the ninth, and another with Chiron in Virgo in the eleventh. Both clients came alive before my very eyes when their inner dynamic was given outer form by coming to know the warrior healer within. The client with Chiron in the eleventh in a stellium squaring the Lunar Nodes realigned his consciousness, and his access to Neptune is actually palpable. He is Christlike. The client with Chiron in Virgo in the ninth, Chart #9, was on the verge of destroying his nervous system with excessive Saturnian control. He has put his Saturn energy into karate and his Uranian powers into photography. He does nature photography, and the unseen creatures, the devas, are triggered in the subconscious mind of the viewer.

We have much work to do on this critical archetype. This is the healing archetype because only total passionate love of Saturn form on Earth and letting go into Uranian power will bring Neptune bliss and compassion back to all who live on Earth.

CHIRON IN LIBRA

10/11/1894	—	10/07/1896
11/19/1944	—	03/24/1945
07/23/1945	—	11/10/1946
09/09/1995	—	12/29/1996
04/06/1997	—	09/03/1997

When Chiron is in Libra, the native is balancing the self in relationship to the other side. Understanding of self is garnered by looking at oneself in the mirror which is offered by other people. These natives are trying to balance elements, to make order out of chaos, and they only know themselves by the degree of harmony they observe in others. No matter how much this native claims to be on his or her own, in reality this person is *measuring him or herself by others' responses almost constantly.* On the low side, the sense of self is undeveloped, and the individual craves constant new experience. On the high side, this individual has a truly remarkable understanding of him or herself that has come from observing others. Consequently, this native may possess great artistic skill.

As with Virgo, Chiron is only in Libra for twenty months during this precessional phase, and the faculty for knowing oneself in others is not well understood. In fact, these natives require strong relationships with plenty of feedback to get in touch with who they are. The first to seventh house polarity involves trying to stretch the self, and the self in relationship to others, as far as possible. Just as Chiron in the seventh house favors Saturn control over Uranian transformation because relating to the other side is so complex at this time, so does Chiron in Libra cause Saturn fixation. In fact, my clients have demonstrated strong fixations on the ruling parent from childhood.

The power of Saturn over those who have Chiron in Libra can be observed physiologically, and often these natives seem very old for their years. Often they require relationships just to exist, yet the relationships bind them until they experience kundalini release at their Uranus opposition. As I studied thirteen charts with Chiron in Libra and visualized each client, I felt constriction in my shoulders and air loss in my lungs. Thinking about their lives thus far, I saw their pathways of struggling to *be,* to breathe as they were smothered in relationships which would not let go until they had grown. And then I have seen them smile.

Zane Stein said about those with Chiron in Libra that, "One major lesson these people must learn is how to really tell when something is fair or just. They have a personal imperative to discover which side is correct, and a hatred of injustice—it must end NOW."[7] With my clients, they are either heavily involved in work which involves compassion and justice, and/or they are still working hard on their own relationship lessons or past karma. There is some blindness about who they are within karmic situations as they relate to others. Knowing and feeling who they really are comes with knowing who they are in relation to others. So, figuring out how they are doing involves carefully noticing how they are doing with others.

The house position of Chiron in Libra reveals the nature of this native's journey into finding the other side. One client with Chiron in the first in Libra confused all her relationships and became an alcoholic until she married a man she could find herself with. Together they built a compassionate relationship, and now they are healing others. Another couple, both with Chiron in Libra, is an interesting example. The woman (Chart #4) has Chiron in Libra in the fourth house, and she has been helping refugees from El Salvador. His Chiron in Libra is in the ninth, and his own spiritual search is connected with her search to find homes for El Salvadorians (See Chart #52 which is also a horary reading). Together they have created a marriage which serves the community on many levels. Another client (Chart #19) is a therapist who has Chiron in Libra in the twelfth, and he has given his life to helping other people balance their own karma, but he has difficulty hearing feedback from others. He is missing the mirror dimension for the most part. An ex-priest (if there is such a thing) has Chiron in the tenth at the top of a T-Square with the Sun in the second and Saturn in the eighth. He is a composer, bringing in the harmony of Libran Chiron balancing Sun and Saturn, but his primary relationship is very difficult.

There are many more examples, but relating to others is the primary form of learning for these natives. My clients seem to be involved in more karmic situations than would be expected statistically. Chiron in Libra seems to point to individuals who are *immersed in burning old karma off* or *creating new debts*. Out of twenty in my files with Chiron in Libra, four are homosexuals. These natives can be assisted if you try to figure out how conscious they are of justice in all human relations. Those who are involved in taking advantage of other people are in grave danger at this time when each one of us is given the opportunity to intensify our connection with the cosmos and heal the Earth as we heal ourselves. Negative karmic involvements will spin those out of time who choose to misuse energy just like the Fallen Angels. Misuse of sexuality is especially dangerous now. Past life therapy can be very helpful for those indulging in negative karmic relationships, because seeing *why* they are involved as they are can free spirit. At any rate, effort needs to be made to help make these individuals conscious of their actions with others.

CHIRON IN SCORPIO

10/08/1896	—	10/29/1898
11/11/1946	—	11/28/1948
09/04/1997	—	01/07/1999
06/02/1999	—	09/22/1999

When Chiron is in Scorpio, the transformative and evolutionary energy of Pluto becomes the personal quest. The energy for the evolution is Chirotic; that is, it focuses Plutonian depth and process directly into space and time. This is like the power of the multi-dimensional energy felt in integrated cultures during the Age of Leo/Atlantis about 13000 to 11000 B.C., during the Age of Taurus 4400 to 2200 B.C., and which will be known again during the coming Age of Aquarius. Right now, individuals with Chiron in Scorpio feel a deep memory of the time when Plutonic force was acceptable to the culture, but at this time they think no one can imagine how they feel inside. It causes the struggle between Saturn and Uranus to be volcanic, and these natives are either extraordinary in their personal evolution, or they have not found an avenue to express this increasing power within. They also may be expressing low Pluto by searching for power and pleasure at the cost of all others.

The evolutionary force of Pluto will express itself as a learning through death/Saturn or kundalini life force/Uranus. Experience is Plutonian or evolutionary, and the process of the psyche at any given moment is death or life oriented. Chiron is focus in space and time, and Pluto is unceasing evolutionary movement. Work must be done to see if the client is already dying, and behavior must be examined to see if this native is manifesting low or high Pluto attributes.

Those born with Chiron in Scorpio face a *death crisis* or a *significant choice to live* relating to the issues of the *house* containing Chiron. Many in my files have Chiron in Scorpio in the ninth house, meaning they cannot feel alive until they bring in the higher self with strong kundalini energy flow. That is probably why they went to an astrologer in the first place. They were born between late 1946 to late 1948, and I do not have a client born late 1896 to 1898. So far, natives with Chiron in Scorpio in the ninth are not very expressive. In fact, they are markedly subdued as a group. They may just be watchers of people, and they may prefer to remain silent. One client (Chart #25) has Chiron in the ninth in a grand trine with the Moon and Mars, and she is a major artist. Chiron in Scorpio encourages occult sensitivity, and this artist really brought her work together when she began to work with spiritual material.

Another client has Chiron in Scorpio in the eighth squaring a Pluto/Venus conjunction in the sixth. When she came she was very repressed; she had a gravely diminished vital force. Usually, I avoid counseling clients on raising kundalini energy because it rises naturally at Uranus opposite Uranus. There is substantial evidence that triggering it early may trigger unnecessary neurological consequences. With this client, I advised that she just get a great lover and forcefully bring in sexual/ kundalini energy because she evidenced high Pluto energy but was terribly repressed by Saturn. She found a lover and her vital force is releasing her from the deathly side of Chiron in Scorpio. Sometimes it is better to blow off a volcano before the seismic level becomes too intense.

Chart #20 has Chiron in Scorpio in the sixth house squaring Saturn and Pluto. This native is very interesting because the Scorpio Chiron is placed in the house *ruled* by the Centaur. He is a great yoga teacher and very adept at focusing the Saturn form in yoga posture. He has a wonderful balance between Saturn and Uranus because he is exceedingly disciplined in his yoga work, and he also is doing important work on neurological effects of foods in the body. He exemplifies Chiron in its ruling house, and the effects can be easily seen through the power of high Scorpio. A last example is a weaver, (Chart #7) with Chiron in the seventh house. She is bringing in powerful magical symbols right from the depths of her being, and her primary issues have been worked out in relationships.

The dynamic with Chiron in Scorpio is to notice whether the client appears to be repressed or not. Do they have a feeling for their own power? Is the issue ruled by the house position of Chiron empowered? Is the value system of that house understood? Is there any evidence of evolution there? Natives who have not had their Uranus oppostion yet and who also seem repressed need chart examination for major blocks. Aspects to Pluto, Saturn, and Uranus are critical. Many born in July-September 1947 and March-June 1948 have Saturn conjunct Pluto along with Chiron in Scorpio. These natives seem repressed, but the power of Saturn will loosen with the Uranus opposition. Some of these natives had a death crisis with themselves or someone close to them around the time of their Saturn return triggered by the Saturn/Pluto conjunction, and the Saturn loosening will be difficult. Ultimately these natives will emerge as teachers about Chiron and death. At this point, what matters is to assist them with the grip of Saturn.

CHIRON IN SAGITTARIUS

10/30/1898	—	01/12/1901
08/10/1901	—	09/29/1901
11/29/1948	—	02/09/1951
06/19/1951	—	11/04/1951

When Chiron is in Sagittarius, there is a crisis about integration of the higher self into one's consciousness. These natives are on a quest to become ensouled, to bring the highest essence into their own form so they can connect with the central organizing principle of all their incarnations. This connection is blocked until the higher self is embodied. Jupiter is the home of the masters, the beings who love us and care about our progress on Earth. People born with Chiron in Sagittarius are instinctually in tune with these teachers. Until they begin to bring the higher self in and become ensouled, they will go on many quests and explore many religions. Once they comprehend that they are the *bridgers* in their own bodies between essence/Uranus and Saturn/Earth, then they *become electrical conduits.*

It is no accident that those born with Chiron in Sagittarius late 1948 to 1951 will experience their Uranus oppositions during 1987-89 as Chiron also opposes Uranus by transit, and Saturn conjuncts Uranus by transit. That is, many with Chiron in Sagittarius will have transiting Uranus conjunct Saturn opposite Uranus conjuct transiting Chiron. This group will ensoul at that point; they are going to be the teachers of the Chirotic force; they will be the prophets of the Age of Aquarius. And Sagittarius is such a focusing arrow in consciousness that many of them are already in power positions so they can play their role in the upcoming difficult transition.

Many astrologers believe that Chiron rules Sagittarius. As already mentioned, this confusion arose partly because Chiron rules the method of the quest; but Sagittarius *is* the quest. The ninth house is where we connect with the higher self. The masters who live on Jupiter are calling us, and the Sagittarian focus is the way to ensoul. But, just as Chiron rules the Tarot reader, Chiron rules the initiation process. Sagittarius is the focus and direction, and Virgo is the battle between Saturn/form and Uranian/energetics that creates the pragmatic solution to make it to Jupiterian expansion. Thus, the Centaur's body is placed in the ninth house to symbolize all individuals who go on the quest to unite body and soul, human and animal self. The proof of this question is shown by the fact that mythological Chiron *stayed* in his house of healing, Mt. Pelion, and he sent out the *questers* he had initiated to go on the journey. Because Chiron has been sighted, astrologers now will find it possible to *be* Chiron in a reading, and determine the sacred skill of clients and initiate them into their quest. This teaching will empower clients to activate the ninth house, the Sagittarian focus, into awareness.

My files of those with Chiron in Sagittarius contain more individuals with high consciousness at an early age than is statistically probable. Literally each one of nineteen clients is very mystical and searching. One is a brilliant physicist, Chart #1, whose first book has changed the lives of many readers. Others include a priest, (Chart #37) who is creating transformative rituals, and a jeweler, (Chart #30) working with the resonation factors in gems. A client with Chiron in Sagittarius on the ascendant is the key person in the middle of a New Age teaching movement; another, Chart #12, is working on the question of sacred energy in blood and DNA. Chart #10 belongs to a publisher working on books to heal the Earth. Often when I feel discouraged by the density and struggle of the late eighties, I think of this group as a beacon of hope for the future.

Individuals with Chiron in Sagittarius require counseling if the natural acquisition of high consciousness has been blocked. Most individuals born 1949 through 1951 have Chiron squaring Saturn in Virgo ruled by Chiron. Therefore the father blocks the ability to bring in the higher self, and Saturn will hold their energy until Uranus opposite Uranus. Then, the mature energy of the square will become *awareness.* As already mentioned, cosmic synchronicity has it arranged that these natives will experience Chiron opposite Uranus during their Uranus oppositions, that transiting Chiron will be on natal Uranus as it is opposed by transiting Uranus. The Saturn father hold will break with tremendous Chirotic neurological force, and these natives will do beautifully if they understand this—or they will have mental problems. It is predictable that accidents and violence will intensify during 1987-89 because of these aspects. These natives will cause a new awareness about kundalini energy as a healing force.

The higher self cannot become embodied without kundalini integration, and natives with Chiron in Sagittarius will experience this crisis personally. The Chirotic neurological system is the inner body pathway of systems which hold energy in the body (Saturn) and the energetics which cause kundalini energy to flow which are electrical and ruled by Uranus. It is the balance within the Saturn bone, muscle, and blood systems which makes possible positive and negative polarity energization or Uranian charging in the nerves, the spine, the brain. The in-between place is the Arachnoid Membrane, which is a thin membrane of the brain and spinal column between the *pia* (internal) *mater* (mother) which reaches into the body and the *dura* (external) *mater* which protects the central nervous cords. Excuse the complication, but this is an incredibly powerful image of the way Chiron works between Saturn as an external force, or *dura*, encrusting our response, and *pia* as the inner place allowing entry of the soul or Higher Self into the body. Also, this membrane corresponds to the Van Allen Belt, the force field around Earth which mediates between Earth atmosphere and the solar system. Physical images are the most powerful forms of meditation. The Arachnoid Membrane is where Chiron is in your body as the bridge between inner matter and outside communications, and the Van Allen Belt is the galactic resonator to Earth. Natives with Chiron in Sagittarius will teach us how the Arachnoid Membrane and the Van Allen Belt are spider webs of interconnectivity and outer wholism. The native of Chart #43 is an energy healer who has developed a triangulation technique which he visualizes in the aura for healing.

CHIRON IN CAPRICORN

01/13/1901	—	08/09/1901
09/30/1901	—	04/22/1904
05/22/1904	—	01/11/1905
02/10/1951	—	06/18/1951
11/05/1951	—	01/28/1955

When Chiron is in Capricorn, there is a karmic crisis about succeeding in one's quest and balance in life between success and nurturance. This is a complex position because the natives are personally invested in their own success while they are still relatively unevolved. They have great difficulty being open to any path outside of their own. This path is understood to be a path of the higher self as well as the normal desire for success and power; thus the individual invests this quest with spiritual significance. The result is a great difficulty hearing or seeing the way of other people, resulting in the loss of the mirror or sight offered by feedback from others. This position is the essence of the Capricorn goat on the top of the mountain. These natives possess great power and energy because they hold Uranian force in the Saturn body and are adept at manifesting it. I imagine Alexander the Great had Chiron in Capricorn.

Richard Nolle noted that these natives even "desire to conquer time." But the time they wish to conquer is the Grim Reaper; Saturn always wins over those who are unable to let go. *Patience* is the key word for those with Chiron in Capricorn, for they never stop believing they will get what they want. In fact, they *do* get what they want. They usually get it all, but when they wake up from their endless sleep of entrapment on the physical plane, they are all alone.

The most important lesson for these natives is to *listen*. They must pay for readings because they will not listen unless they value the lessons being offered. The real dilemma for natives with Chiron in Capricorn is, first of all, to be able to hear other people in order to get feedback, and then to find a way to desire the freedom of Uranus. They hold Uranus in the body and use it as a power tool against others, but they do not know the experience of Uranian kundalini ecstasy as personal joy. Taurus and Capricorn are the trines to Virgo, and the natives with Chiron in Taurus and Capricorn are prone to missing the bridge from Saturn to Uranus because they are at ease with Saturn. Missing the point is most likely with those with Chiron in Capricorn due to the Saturnian rulership of Capricorn. The secret in reaching them is to examine the Part of Fortune and the fifth house very carefully. Those born with Chiron in Capricorn aren't having any fun; the seriousness *must* break down or the quest will be an iron-fisted search for control over everything, even the passage of time. Richard Nolle has a marvelous example of Chiron in Capricorn's control over time in *Chiron: The New Planet in Your Horoscope*. To show Chiron in Capricorn, he presents the chart and analysis of Karen Ann Quinlan who had such control over time that she even managed to keep on living until recently after her respirator was removed in 1976.[8]

The clients in my files with Chiron in Capricorn are almost all early achievers and very proud of it. The clients who have not succeeded at a young age are the ones who may do better in the long run. The primary characteristic of these natives who have manifested early success is some blindness toward others mixed with remarkable skill. Chart #8 belongs to a great teacher of manifestation; the native of Chart #21 is an MD who is developing a scientific method for measuring kundalini power in the body. Another chart belongs to a cancer healer, and another to an astrologer (Chart #22). But they aren't having any fun! The deadly serious quality of their work will backfire eventually unless they learn to listen to others. The extreme knowledge these natives possess about electrical energy in the body is striking, and is evidence they know a lot about Uranus. All of my clients with this position are only between 31 and 35 years old. I suspect the other levels of Uranus will come to them with Uranus opposite Uranus, but attunement with the Part of Fortune or how to feel good and work on the fifth house will help. The one client I have who was born during the earlier phase in 1901 is well-balanced and very good at having a lot of fun—and he feels that success is the most important goal in life.

Natives with Chiron in Capricorn who are not especially successful need special help in defining their true purpose. They are sensitive to other people because life has not been easy for them. Other people have hurt them a lot; they feel under-appreciated because they are tense about not meeting impossibly high standards they've set for themselves. They need to know there is *plenty of time*. The fact that they haven't given everything to the goal may help them because they are more patient. And conversely, with natives who have really made it, perspective about the many facets in life they've missed may help them. With either one, the need for Cancerian nurturing, for the small seeds in life, will have to be balanced at Uranus opposite Uranus. With Capricorn/Cancer polarity, imbalance is usually common, but Chiron in Capricorn signals that this dynamic must be resolved. It is interesting that so many in my files with this position are electrical healers. They are great at it. But no healing is possible in the long run without nurturance, comfort with the Earth, and a sense of humor. And, the Centaur Chiron's greatest dilemma was his inability to die. He finally gave up his immortality.

CHIRON IN AQUARIUS

04/23/1904	—	05/21/1904
01/12/1905	—	03/19/1910
08/30/1910	—	01/15/1911
01/29/1955	—	03/26/1960
08/20/1960	—	01/20/1961

When Chiron is in Aquarius, there is a *crisis over being grounded,* over existing on Earth in a balanced way. This is the opposite dynamic of Chiron in Capricorn, and an understanding of these two placements yields an understanding about Chiron as the bridge between Saturn and Uranus. Higher consciousness (Uranus) has no place to exist without a body (Saturn), and as we move into Aquarius we are being taught about bridging by the ecological crisis. Chiron the Centaur embodies the issue with his horse/man body; we have to have animal/human, Earth/sky, body/soul, or we perish.

Those born with Chiron in Aquarius are electrical, not grounded; they are "air-heads." These natives are meant to manifest idealism, to bring great gifts to the culture in areas ruled by the house location, but they must carefully connect deep into the Earth and become realistic. They possess great potential *if* they can balance and connect. Those born from 1955-61 are also slated to move into power positions and experience their return around 2000 to 2010 A.D., and they will greet our extraterrestrial brothers when the communion time comes. Therefore, on top of their natural difficulty getting grounded, they also are *resonating with a galactic vibrational attunement.*

My files yielded only four individuals born during the 1904-1910 phase of Chiron in Aquarius. Three died by age 70 which is young these days, and those three had a very hard time connecting here. When I knew them in their more mature years, they were isolationists. All three felt let down by life—their early idealism squashed by the two World Wars and the Depression. When they experienced typical old-age trauma, they just checked out. The fourth one is still living. She is a poet, and she has managed to keep her ideals alive. She still is ungrounded at age 79, but she was protected by a family cocoon, and she is a Taurus.

It is difficult to say a lot about those born between 1955-61 yet because they are just starting to come for readings and they have only just begun experiencing their Saturn return, but a few traits already stand out. First of all, of nine clients, all are noticeably ungrounded except for one. He is the Native American political leader of Chart #23, and his *culture* has grounded him. He is also an occultist. With Chiron in the first, his charisma is a striking spectacle to observe. Although he is also Aquarius rising with four planets in Aquarius, he still is grounded because of his Native American upbringing. This indicates that people can learn to be grounded with Chiron in Aquarius, just as those with Chiron in Capricorn can learn to let go of control. Either way, natives with Chiron in Capricorn and Aquarius are powerful teachers about the potential Chirotic force if we are to build the Rainbow Bridge. The Rainbow Bridge is the connection between Saturn form and Uranian electrical integration. The point is that astrology is all about free will; we can identify the areas in our lives where special discipline is required and *make choices* about becoming holistic people.

The other eight born between 1955-61 who are still ungrounded came for a reading around the time of their Saturn return. This is a generalization requiring more work to back it up, but there was an unusual tendency to try to avoid the consequences of the Saturn return, to experience difficulties but to refuse to learn from the experience. However, most reported that their reading was very powerful for them, but most people who have readings at Saturn return *are* strongly affected. They say they got their lesson, but so far their behavior doesn't correspond. Much more observation is needed, but it would seem that Saturn lessons are harder for these natives to get than is usual. At any rate, counsel on grounding, on bridging, on balancing, and on valuing experiential learning is helpful.

CHIRON IN PISCES

03/20/1910	—	08/29/1910
01/16/1911	—	03/31/1918
10/23/1918	—	01/28/1919
03/27/1960	—	08/19/1960
01/21/1961	—	03/31/1968
10/19/1968	—	01/30/1969

When Chiron is in Pisces, there is a *crisis over connecting with the God force,* the universal oneness. This native is hearing the siren call from across the sea, seeing the Will-O-the-Wisp in the swamp, is hearing the flute of Pan or Kokopelli—he/she hears different music than most of us. This is a fascinating position because we now possess the experiential tool, the analysis of Chiron in the chart, to gain a truly palpable grasp of Neptune. For humans, nothing can really be completely understood unless we have a material, emotional, mental, and spiritual grasp of it. The Chiron focus in space and time is the key to the materiality of Neptune. Remember, visualize Chiron as the focal point of a vortex with Neptunian resonance as the wide rim. Individuals with Chiron in Pisces are the *manifestors* of this subtle force, the Chirotic force, but they are way out on the wide rim of the spiral.

This teaching about Chiron in Pisces is the most obtuse in this book. That is because it is about the astral plane. We are only now beginning to understand how astral energy affects us on this planet because we could not get a grip on its energy until the sighting of Chiron. But, working with astral energy is part of the process of clearing that we need in order to manifest high Neptunian energies—being in touch with the divine.

I will explain the qualities of Neptunian manifestation as clearly as I can at this time. Naturally, Neptune is hard to understand because of its great subtlety, but *seeing* the way Neptune manifests here on Earth is the way to know it. Neptune is the only planet which exists in the form of etheric material on Earth; that is, we experience Neptune here by means of Neptunian matter. It can be grasped, but we don't realize it because we have not had the conceptual tools to grasp it until now. One way in which you already know this is by means of the tradition of personal experiences with demons, ghosts, and astral invasion forces which have existed as an attempt to key people into the reality of this disturbing and real force. These essences have been described by many as wispy, sticky, grey, net-like interferences. This is, in fact, how Neptune invades your mental or physical reality. Before you shy away from considering this material, please take note that the more you know about this reality—the better you can *identify* it—the less it can control or affect you. And, most importantly, *no force in the universe is good or bad;* it is only used well or poorly.

For example, the way I really *saw* Neptunian sticky stuff was in a movie called *Fantastic Voyage* which came out in the late 1960s. In this movie a group of scientists are reduced to microbe size, and they journey into a man's body. The man has congested lungs from smoking, and the sacs around his lungs are filled with sticky reticular fibers. The people in the ship get all stuck in the fibers in the sacs (which originally had formed to screen out smoke in his lungs.) That is, the stickiness is a *defense* against some invasive force. It will develop in you until you stop assaulting your body and/or mind with negativity. Until you identify this dynamic and respect its potential power, you may be weakened by it; it can suck your energy. You can clear it with visualization techniques if you can identify it for yourself. As long as it exists in you as a protection against something, you will lose energy to it. According to what you do with your consciousness, this energy can invade your aura. What needs to be understood is that it is real, it is palpable, it can be known, identified, and you have free will about it. Until the discovery of Chiron, humans did not have the *means* to identify this potential possession. We had to rely on exorcists, shamans, and medicine people when it invaded us. No more! Now we have the power to clear these energies and manifest high Neptune, which is ecstatic mysticism, emptiness instead of stickiness, oneness with the cosmos, and resonation with one's greatest potential. The point is, higher awareness draws from emptiness. It can't come if we are already filled with protective stuff.

The teachings on astral interference or this Neptunian stuff are extensive. Recently, some have found it effective to deal with it by means of deflection, with shields, or by means of Pluto purification. It is true: one can become so emotionally pure that one is not affected. You can seek an exorcist, a shaman. Both of these techniques work very well, but at what loss? Shields move us into a defensive position and imply separa-tion, and too much Pluto purification often destroys Eros. Shields and purification rituals require energy. It can be energy well spent, because otherwise astral interference can suck your power; they can de-energize you. But now, because we can visualize and comprehend the materiality of Neptune, we can utilize Chiron to identify the *Chirotic point,* that exact place waiting for Neptune. We can simply choose to see the interferen-ces caused by our own lack of awareness or deliberate manipulation by others. I am talking about "seeing" the astral realm. Once you see this and understand it, your will and power are free to be clear. Shields and purification techniques are very good, but they use energy that could be expended in cosmic merging. You can feel the heart of the universe; it never stops beating. Only *fear of the unknown* allows the astral to invade your reality and thus you build up shields and protection.

Individuals with Chiron in Pisces are trying intuitively to grasp the teaching I have just put forward. With the sighting of Chiron came the missing link; we just did not have the tool of Chiron until 1977. One is not given the vision just offered without deserving it. But this vision is a sense of living which will soon come to many. The only way for anyone to get it is to learn to heal. That is, natives with Chiron in Pisces must be helped to comprehend the concept just delineated. They must be taught about the healing attributes of the house containing Chiron in Pisces. Then they must be instructed on how to activate the sixth house. And, the level of Pluto natally needs to be studied according to the techniques offered by Jeff Green in *Pluto: The Evolutionary Journey of the Soul.*[9]

Healing teaches the opening of the heart and the way to use Chiron. One must learn Chirotic focus, the deliberate bringing down into body of the higher will and higher self. We are ready now to heal this Earth, our children, our mother and our father. With this power of bridging Saturn and Uranus comes the clear crystal pathway to Neptune. The only reason Neptune has sticky astral essence is because *we* have sticky astral essence. It is clearing with our awareness. The materiality of Nep-tune is now known, and the way to reach it is to manifest with its newly identified polarity. Chiron opposite Pisces is the Rainbow Bridge of the polarities. Neptunian ecstasy and mysticism will flood consciousness once Chiron is mastered as a tool.

The most fascinating synchronicity in this whole *astrological evo-lution* exists in the fact that the group born between 1961-68 with Chiron in Pisces almost all have Pluto in Virgo opposite Chiron in Pisces. This means that this group of future healers will walk the rainbow path in their lifetimes because their sense of Pluto is as an evolutionary force to be used for *total* clarity. Already out of nine in my files, four are healers. One is the young New Age healer shown in Chart #2. Another began spontaneously speaking master teachings to everyone around himself when he was under twenty (Chart #24). Already known to be an occult master of formidable powers, the native of Chart #41 is only seventeen. Another is a Native American priestess who is seen as a visionary for her tribe.

We are only beginning to see the powers available, because those with Chiron in Pisces experience their first square very late. High levels of consciousness seem to be spontaneous, and the other five who have not shown their potential yet are using drugs. The high drug usage of this group is probably an attempt to avoid manifesting who they are. I watched them as they experienced their first Chiron square, and their individual integrations of Saturn form and Uranian energy were quite amazing. The teacher came fully into form with his first sexual initiation at the square, and he broke through his greatest difficulty, polarization. The healer has brought electricity into form in her hands. The Native American priestess saw the ugly reality of the Anglo world of ecocide with clear eyes, and she made a full pledge to ecological publishing. The occultist has not experienced his square yet.

I have four clients who were born when Chiron was in Pisces 1911-1918. Richard Nolle says those with Chiron in Pisces "may be totally alien from the perspective of prevailing cultural norms."[10] Of my older clients, this is definitely true. They all show great difficulty bringing in the vision they carry of the cosmic Earth harmony. The remarkable behavior of my younger clients would indicate that the world we live in now is more receptive to ecological wisdom and higher consciousness. And the more the world reality shifts, the more the younger ones will be able to manifest a world of balance and safety.

Above all, natives with Chiron in Pisces need *encouragement* to manifest their powers, and to be given *acknowledgement* about their gifts. They especially need help with the Chiron/Pluto opposition by means of house analysis. They need to be carefully watched and guided when they experience the first Chiron square, or they may try to check out with drugs. Many contemporary astrologers experienced the first Chiron square at a much younger age and are more comfortable with the Chirotic force. Those who experience it late so far have demonstrated a strange tendency: because Chiron is in Pisces, they think they know about the other worlds and the interface from this place to the other side, but they do not know this bridge until they experience the first square. They feel left out by spiritual forces which they intuitively know about. Help them. They will be our teachers about the essence that materializes from the planet Neptune. They will experience Chiron opposite Chiron when Chiron is in Virgo September 1993 to September 1995, just as Chiron is also conjuncting natal Pluto in Virgo. This is the period just before the ultimate stress point of the potential apocalypse of 1996-98. These individuals will be many of the guides who will help us synchronize the energy to a higher level of vibration instead of bringing destruction into manifestation.

Chapter Eight

THE CHIRON ASPECT STRUCTURE

The aspects between planets in the natal chart are the faceting of consciousness. Like a diamond found in the rough and then expertly cut to reveal inner light, the energetic resonance of the aspects reveals the fiber of the incarnated soul, its micromolecular signature. The planet in aspect is the quality of the energy, the house position is the mode of expression, and the aspects are the energy resonators connecting the planet into the natal hologram. Holograms show that each point in a structure contains the model of the whole structure. Because of this structural energy resonance within each natal chart, aspects must be *vibrated* in the body of the reader or astrologer to be understood. How? Experience again: we must master the basic concept of an aspect, combine it with its quality of expression (the planets involved) and its mode of expression (house position) which is the Saturnian/structure/form level. Then we must vibrate this concept in consciousness to attain its personal energy resonance or the Uranian/electrical energy resonance level.

Ideally, a good astrologer vibrates with the resonances in a client's chart as he or she is doing the reading. This creates a Chirotic bridge between the astrologer and the client's consciousness so the subtle realms can be felt in the native. Thus, all aspects are Chirotic, bridging form to energy inherently, as they connect one planetary energy to another. And the aspects to Chiron reveal the resonances of Chiron itself in the natal chart; they reveal the Chirotic impact on the natal map as a dynamic. Aspects must always be understood in relation, and reading them correctly is an art.

The old days of cookbook astrology are over. Astrology is moving into a new age of creativity with the teaching of concepts, paradigms, and energetics, instead of explicit and limiting definitions. Chiron in aspect will be explored with work on the basic dynamic of the aspecting cycle of 360 degrees, and the quality of energy between Chiron and any other planet. The secret to understanding aspects is to learn to feel them in the body, to get your clients to feel them with you, and keys for visualization of energy and acting out aspects will be given to assist this process. Memorizing formulas will limit aspect sensitivity. I have learned a lot from astrodrama, and since Chiron rules the dance of experiential astrology, much new work is coming forth in this area.

In general, the *number of aspects* between Chiron and the other planets indicates the degree of healing power and natural alchemical response patterns within the native. This also applies to the number of aspects to Neptune. The *house position* of Chiron or Neptune draws the energy from the aspecting planets, and the healing force of that house is strongly affected by the related planets. When an individual wishes to learn to heal, their greatest concern is how to work with energy. The *planets* aspecting Chiron to house position will yield many clues to help the individual learn how to create energy which works. We will let Neptune go at this point. If Chiron is retrograde and/or is located in the twelfth or sixth house, and/or if the aspecting planets are retrograde or in the sixth or twelfth houses, a healer trained in past lives has manifested. Since planetary survival depends upon recovering the ancient healing technology, this native needs special guidance. Chiron is a surprising centaur, and he has a strong tendency to appear when ancient healers have returned and are seeking guidance. He is again happy to be chiromancer and lead the dance to wisdom. Just listen and *feel* the animal self in your body. Your body knows a lot. Visualization and acting-out techniques are particularly powerful with Chiron, because that is the ancient way of wisdom.

A strongly aspected Chiron also is the pathway to healing the self. Often powerful squares and oppositions from Chiron to the inner planets are driving the native to a great inner healing. Squares and oppositions always create great energy in the dynamic, but how each person reacts is unique. Thus, Chiron opposite Venus will mean that love relationships are always healing the inner psyche. One native will experience some very difficult, but healing, love affairs, and another will have absolutely beautiful love experiences that will be like being with the Goddess. The level of soul vibration in this incarnation will strongly affect the native's response to the Chirotic force. And, in general, astrologers must always test levels of soul vibration to determine the quality of aspects.

This is a fascinating time in the growth of consciousness because we are on the verge of recovering the ancient teaching of the effects of past life experience on present incarnational consciousness. As soon as Chiron was sighted, the recovery of past life healing therapy was inevitable. Past life healing therapy is based on the principle of the evolution of the soul. Pluto is the planet which reveals the present state of evolution, and the tools for determining this astrologically are all available in *Pluto: The Evolutionary Journal of the Soul* by Jeff Green. Chiron is the tool for getting the entry into the past life contents, so that all negative and positive contents that are relevant to this life can be viewed and transmuted. In my opinion, recovery of this information must be done with a trained guide because going into past lives involves travel in the astral realm. The problems with Neptune and the astral level can be very difficult as already discussed in the last chapter. But the manifestation of Chiron is the beacon that establishes the necessity of this work. To put it bluntly, you cannot evolve until you have assimilated your earlier progress. You will always be in first grade, and you can just come back later and go back into first grade again. Or you can bring what you already know directly back into your consciousness and work from that point of awareness. Then the Chirotic point is accessed, the fusion place of past/present/future is revealed, and you are born completely new at the pinnacle of all you have already been, ready to be a new creation.

The planets in aspect to Chiron are the nerve endings into consciousness which access the fusion point. That is, Moon sextile Chiron creates an emotional nature which intuitively understands healing and desires attunement to the specific place and time for alchemical fusion. The level this is working on must be examined in light of the whole chart, but regardless, what a powerful piece of news for the native! This native may be the nurse who automatically soothes the patient, the mother who calms her child.

The Sun opposite Chiron creates a being who will not develop until they access healing energy. They will atrophy and feel sickened by their environment until they are given the chance to know thier own power to heal. Now that Chiron is sighted, the issue goes to the critical level: people will find they cannot exist without the healing dimension in their lives. As Chiron kills or transmutes, they will just check out or become healers of themselves and others. There will be many teachers of this issue. AIDS is one of the first.

Jeff Green notes that Pluto is an "essentially unconscious process" which originates in the subconscious.[1] Chiron feels different than energy from the subconscious because it is the access point to superconscious/the higher self. Instead of constantly bubbling up from deep within, it *zaps* you with a ray of white light which may blind you and be instantly forgotten. Or you can learn to accept the cosmic light seed, decipher it, and next you will walk the Rainbow Bridge. Chiron is potentially an instant holographic complete systemic attunement to a new level of being.

Alignment with this energy is absolutely phenomenal, because everything is instantly new if one can allow the process to work. On that note, crystals greatly facilitate the process because, like the aspects, they are faceted, and like sextiles, crystals access the Star of David. As we go into the way aspects work, there will be many tips on holographic attunement, but crystals are ruled by Chiron and they mirror the Chirotic force. Crystals are a means to grasp the hologram because the basic micromolecular parts are all the same, and each crystal is unique—just as each person is unique. For example, the melanin in the pineal gland is made of quartz crystal molecular structure.[2] It sounds fantastic, but it is possible for *anyone* to reattune to a new level if they just know it is possible. We are not limited in any way; we are only limited by the restrictions we ourselves put on our consciousness.

Aspects are best understood as a continuum beginning at the 0 degree combust point and waxing up for the opposition back to the 0 degree point. There are many books on aspects, and I especially recommend Bil Tierney's *Dynamics of Aspect Analysis*.[3] I will explain the concept briefly, attempting to mention things that have not already been covered and to comment on dynamics of the concepts which are especially relevant in relation to Chiron. (See figure 6)

0 TO 5 DEGREES: COMBUST AND CONJUNCTION
The 0 degree point is the new seed energy and is best felt in the body by resonating with the exact moment of the New Moon. For a few seconds at the New Moon, all the galactic planes are completely open to the Earth plane. At the exact moment a *new seed* is born which will wax and wane during the lunar month. Attunement to that point will fuse consciousness completely with the lunar cycle. Therefore, any planet combust Chiron will manifest on a totally Chirotic level during the incarnation. The Sun combust Chiron would indicate that the native could not know him or herself except by alchemical interaction with environment. As the planets move away from combust through conjunction up to 5 or 6 degrees, the energies feel fused, but the planet pulling away is the leader which will teach by its energy the working of the conjunctive energies. In my experience, planets in combust cannot be separated in

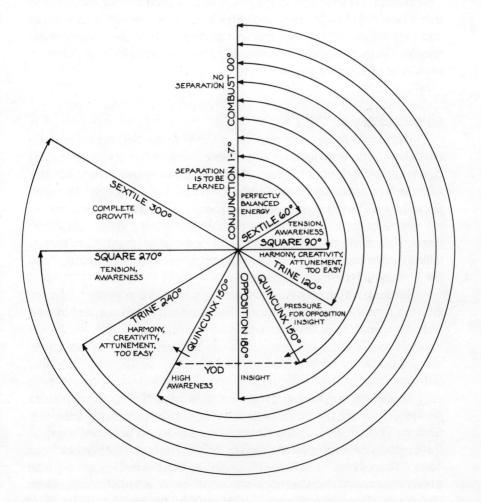

Figure 6
Aspect Structure

consciousness. The native needs to immerse perception in the fusion of the two energies. This native is critically open to the subtle planes through this combust. This point is like a "Window to the Sky" which is an acupuncture point which brings multidimensionality (into the body).[4] Combust is less than one degree and was created in the natal chart to teach oneness. Conjunction indicates a need for the native to learn to sort out the energies, and special counseling is to be given on the energies individually so the native can find a method for perception of each one of the energies separately.

60 DEGREES: SEXTILE

The sextile represents the Star of David in the horoscope and is a crystalline structural dynamic of perfect energy on Earth which is totally powerful, totally balanced, and which can be activated as a resonator with perfect universal form. Sextile formations are not open to negativity; they will function as comfort and balance if just left alone, and they will attune consciousness to the greatest potential if deliberately activated. They also can be visualized as the point where Earth form is crystalline or diaphanous and where galactic resonance can implant. They are a multidimensional interface.

Sextiles to Chiron represent planets which are in perfect relationship to Chiron, as energies in our consciousness which are not blocked from transmutation, of letting go to a more conscious level. As we struggle to bring the consciousness of Chirotic energy into form now, there is no better vehicle than the sextile to Chiron. Conceptually, this indicates that we will have more access to alchemical powers if we explore and develop the fourth and eighth houses. Natally, those planets sextile Chiron are the place to search for our deepest resonance with Chiron. Thus, Venus sextile Chiron would point to potential learning from perfect balance, such as Yoga or Reiki therapy and/or lessons from Tantric Yoga. Chiron sextile the Moon shows that the native can heal with the emotions, and that the moment when the native heals from the heart absolutely phenomenal healing power will manifest.

Activation of the galactic resonance of Chiron sextiles involves consciously attuning the natal sextiles as energy resonators to Enochian levels of mastery vibration. Enoch as well as Elijah is one of the Earth beings who *ascended* in the Hebrew Bible. This level of consciousness is assisted by work with quartz crystals, because quartz crystals are the mineral plane creations which best reflect sextile energy. Of course, quartz crystals are always six-sided, and the angles are sixty degrees. They rarely form a Star of David within a circle because the length of the sides varies according to each individual growth dynamic. Like the astrological chart, we rarely see one with a complete Star of David within. But, like individual crystals, the sextile energy is inherent in one sixty-degree angle, in one sextile.

Enochian mastery vibration is attunement to all dimensions so that we have access to planes that do not presently exist within, such as the fourth dimension. This resonance implies a readiness and willingness to ascend to other planes or dimensions when cosmic holographic attunement occurs in time progression. What on Earth do I mean? I mean that you can use the planets in sextile to Chiron to attune yourself to readiness for ascension to the God plane as Enoch did in the olden times.

For example, one of the most powerful healers I know, who is only 23 years old, connects her clients to the unmanifest or fourth dimension each day, and she has Chiron sextile Jupiter, the home of the masters. In conducting past life sessions, she has the skill to help clients bring in past experiences with the fourth dimension—experiences with the divine—and she helps them reaccess that latent energy into this lifetime. She has developed galactic resonance to Jupiter through Chiron, and she can connect others to the masters as well. She is attuned to her connection to Jupiter, and could ascend to a Jupiterian existence if a new level of attunement on other dimensions occurred in the universe. We are not separate. (See Chart #2.)

90 DEGREES: SQUARE

The square represents the maximum structural tension in the horoscope and in the psyche. Squares to Chiron show the way the native is challenged to *bridge form to higher consciousness*. Squares are your best friend; they represent the *maximum level of growth* in a given incarnation, and squares to Chiron represent the maximum Chirotic *energy points* in the chart. Squares always cause stress and difficulty which often manifest as physical plane problems in the teens and twenties. They represent maximum areas of struggle and work in the thirties, and after forty, represent the areas in our lives where we manifest the most outstanding gifts. Chiron itself is a difficult energy in the horoscope. Squares are difficult growth processes, and so Chiron squares must be examined in light of the three stages of maturation described next.

Before the Saturn return, at age 29 for most of us, structural or square tension is a dreaded experience of confusion and seeming bad results which is loaded with inner past life resonance. When you have a client who has resolved a square early, he or she is usually very developed. Our worst problems are fears we dimly remember from a long time ago. Unevolved indivduals create a wall around their squares— these are the parts of their lives which they feel they cannot handle, and the safest route is avoidance. More evolved individuals are often constantly creating experiences which activate the squares so they can learn from the experience and even burn off karma.

When Chiron is in the square, the issue always signals a potential systemic evolution of the planet that Chiron squares, but this process can only work over time. Also, where Chiron squares exist is usually a place where past life karmic issues are surfacing. This is especially noticeable when Chiron is square Mars, Venus, the Moon or Jupiter natally; and a planet in a parent's, child's, or lover's chart conjuncts either planet. For example, with Chiron square Mars, the male polarized sexual force is extremely over-activated. This native will be having a lot of sexual experiences, causing stress, and this native has chosen this aspect so he or she can learn to use power properly. A parent, child, or lover's planet conjunct Mars or Chiron is past life karmic manifestation. Therefore, what is the evolution? The experiences must be viewed in process. The native needs to learn as much as possible from each experience. Those who are avoiding their squares are projecting the energy of the square on others. The only way they can see this is to help them examine their irrational hostilities toward others. Any time a projection comes up in a reading, an opportunity to deal with great negativity exists.

After the Saturn return, a new way to work with squares develops. In fact, the time between the Saturn return and Uranus opposition is the time to focus on work on squares and oppositions. During the thirties, the native begins to realize that he or she can't avoid the square, and that the tension exists to teach a lesson, that it is within the tension that true growth exists. Those who are unevolved and are projecting the tension on others find that the inner damage is too much, or the object of the projection sends it back to them. For example, sibling relationships are a laboratory of working out our square dynamics. If you envy your sister or brother during your thirties, it is very likely that you are projecting an unresolved childhood need on your brother or sister. We can see much in difficulties with past life karmic relationships, represented by squares, and squares are like vortexes of energy in our lives. Entering the vortex is the Chiron gate—it is the point in place and time where self exists; it is the place where we are forced to relate to our whole environment.

Using Chiron square Venus as an example of those who were more evolved before their Saturn return and allowed themselves experiences with the square, these experiences now are a source of wisdom. This is the person who had extremely unhappy love affairs in the twenties who later develops a really beautiful and full relationship. With Chiron square Uranus, the native will have a very difficult time maintaining mental stability during the teens and twenties. A lot of energy is being expended just being stable. Concurrently, the nervous system is learning to hold tremendous charges of electrical energy. So this native will suddenly begin to manifest extraordinary levels of holographic attunement after the Saturn return which they will perfect in their thirties. Or with Chiron square Saturn the native will have difficulty even wanting to be on planet Earth during their twenties; they will hate the density of this place. But when they come into the body more during the thirties, they will begin to offer wisdom to others.

Those with Chiron square Saturn who did not allow experiences in their twenties for growth on the square are very likely to eventually manifest violence. Chiron square Saturn requires a healing with the father. Frequently, this requires early maturity, taking on a lot of responsibility during the twenties. If this is avoided, the opportunity to heal the father can be aborted, and violence is the result. This is the syndrome of the wounded child.

The Uranus oppostion resolves the structural tension of the square by means of a systemic holographic electrical integration. Squares cause tremendous electrical energy in the body. The electrical energy in the body reaches its maximum power at the exact Uranus opposite Uranus. It is like a power surge in a computer. The body re-organizes itself neurologically, or else short circuits. With this great tension, all the natal squares can resolve into great *awareness*. The squares in general become like massive foundation structures upon which great works can be supported. These squares become the muscle of one's life, the real power bastions of reality. Obviously, if energy is being misused and negative karma is being created, then the squares become vortexes of consciously employed negativity toward self and others. That is what evil is. So, to use examples already given, with Chiron square Mars, a professional killer can result, or it can be an individual who really understands the negativity of unbalanced Mars who enlightens culture about aggression. It is no accident that Chiron's greatest teaching was of high warrior energy. With Chiron square Uranus, this native can become a master of electrical energy and can alter energy patterns in other people, and become a physical healer.

The potential for physical healing is intense with Chiron square Uranus within a grand square. There are many examples. The T-square will be given with the opposition, but the nature of the mature Chiron square is an energetics in the chart of incredible force, which can alter matter to an extreme degree. This energy must be consciously iden-tified so that free will can become a guide. Otherwise, this enormous energy is coming from the subconscious and is potentially destructive. Observing criminal activity, it is amazing how often heinous crimes are committed by people around 42 years old, right after this power is really brought in. And crimes are merely the outward manifestation of energy dynamics in general. What is most powerfully embedded in the psyche will manifest at age 42, and clients need help consciously shaping this energy for good works.

120 DEGREES: TRINE

The trine is an aspect of harmony and creativity, of natural attune-ment with energy, which is a gift from past life mastery of energy and ser-vice. It is knowledge about life which comes after mastery of squares and oppositions. This lovely harmonic attunement is also meaningless unless it is utilized in this lifetime. This incarnaiton is always the one that is important, and past life knowledge is only useful to us if we use it as a teaching tool in this life. Just like squares *evolve* through the twenties and thirties, so do trines *dissolve* in the twenties and thirties if we do not take them to a more significant level. Chiron trining a planet symbolizes great harmonic mastery of that planet, and it is critical to examine the progress with the trine. The question is, is this native ignoring a great cosmic gift that has been evolved into for billions of years? Trines are *magnetic*. They draw the subtle realms into consciousness, but only if we deliberately activate them. They are very Lunar, Neptunian, and Venusian.

As expected, my files yielded many individuals with trines who have extraordinary New Age healing and teaching skills, and the reverse dynamic of the trine was also much in evidence. Generally speaking, each person with Chiron trining a planet evidenced unusual evolution with the issue of that planet. An artist who is also very disciplined (Chart #25) has a grand trine with Chiron, Moon, and Mars. A famous New

Age healing musician (Chart #36) has Chiron trine Moon conjunct Mars. A New Age healing publisher (Chart #3) has Chiron trine the Sun. A symbol teacher (Chart #33) with Chiron trine Venus conjunct Mercury, a great teacher of emotional healing with Chiron conjunct Pluto trine Venus, a New Age physicist (Chart #1) using science to heal the planet has Chiron trine Pluto—the list is literally endless.

The reverse dynamic of unutilized trine power is one of the more depressing reports in this book. Using only individuals over 40 who are undisciplined, unevolved, even neurotic, with Chiron trining another planet, I found that these individuals are showing serious physical disabilities, they are creating negativity around themselves, or they feel frustrated about never bringing through gifts they feel inside. I have found many of them frustrating to work with because they can't hear advice about deliberately activating their greatest potential. They were unusual when young, often way ahead of their peers in consciousness. Since the planet involved is Chiron, often they had unusual psychic attunement. They got used to being way ahead of everybody else. Then during their thirties, people around them caught up, but they didn't notice. In their forties, they are out of touch, but they can't hear the reason because it once was all so easy. This can happen with any planetary trine, but since Chiron is the bridge from body to soul, the results are especially tragic.

We are moving out of a long period in history when men had ample opportunity to develop their potential and women were relatively limited. However, my files revealed a noticeable difference between men and women regarding manifesting the Chiron trine potential. Thirteen clients who were using the trine well were males, none were women. And of eleven clients who had not activated the potential of the Chiron trine, nine were women. There were many more clients with Chiron trine a planet in my files, but I looked carefully at these twenty-four. Two men who were not utilizing their potential to the highest degree are both manifesting negativity at this time, but they are not aware of their actions. One with Chiron trine Sun is involved in developing the Star Wars Defense Initiative. The other, with Chiron trine Moon, is doing great emotional healing work himself, but he is controlled by a teacher who is limiting his own creativity. Both of the men have a natural understanding of the occult, as do all individuals with Chiron trine a major planet, but they did not have to work for that occult knowledge.

One of the women has Chiron retrograde on the IC in Virgo, exactly trining Mercury in Capricorn in the 7th house. She came to me because she was very ill with Epstein Barr virus. I recommended she seek past life regression therapy, and she did some sessions. She was able to instantly regress and go into massive ecstatic past life experiences on a level that often requires many sessions for the average person. She was capable of having consciousness breakthroughs that most people only dream about. And she didn't care! It meant nothing to her. It was all too easy for her, and now she cannot listen to advice even though she is very sick.

No need to give any more examples. Chiron trine a planet is a sign of great gifts for consciousness breakthrough and healing talents from past lives which can be activated into the present life. The native must not take it for granted; he or she must consciously work to activate these skills in a highly disciplined manner. This innate knowledge may save the native's life someday; it may save the life of his or her child, and it may be a skill that will bring planetary healing.

150 DEGREES: THE QUINCUNX AND THE YOD

The quincunx is considered to be a minor aspect by many astrologers, and the Yod, "The Finger of God," is not well understood. In my work, the quincunx represents a dynamic in consciousness which is as critical as the conjunction, sextile, square, trine, and opposition. The trine point in the wheel represents a high level of harmonic attunement, and as the energy moves out of it and into the quincunx, the energy is moving from extreme attunement to another level of stress which activates the consciousness necessary for full manifestation at the opposition. Thus, the quincunx contains all the awareness and attunement of the trine, and it activates that balance even further so that complete visionary awareness and non-avoidance of structural tension is possible at the opposition.

Quincunxes need to be understood as process more than the other aspects, because they are either waxing—moving into opposition, or waning—moving out of the opposition. To determine which planet is waxing or waning in quincunx, identify the heaviest planet in the aspect and then decide whether the other planet is moving *into* or *out of* opposition. Aspecting always moves clockwise. And when this process is understood, then the Yod is easily grasped. (See figure 7) The opposition between Chiron and a planet indicates a high level of structural tension about the issue in question and a high consciousness about it after age 40. The process is the same as described for the square, but the end result with the opposition is full blown polarity awareness. The image for

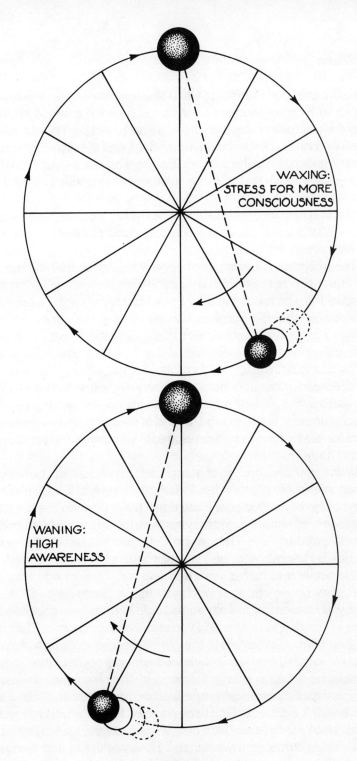

Figure 7
Waxing/Waning Quincunxes

this awareness is the Full Moon, when all issues of the lunar seed planted at the New Moon are resolved. Quincunxes need to be decoded by identifying the opposition they are moving into or out of. The issue of the opposition is the problem being manifested, and the quincunx pushing into it is working to resolve it in this lifetime. This waxing, or 150 degree quincunx, is inherently Chirotic because it is moving trine formation into opposition manifestation. It is moving harmony to at-one-ment. These are the parts of your consciousness which never stop pushing at you for more resolution, and the native often develops highly here due to the incessant pressure.

The quincunx moving out of opposition, or the 210 degree quincunx, represents energy which is pushing toward more realization about an opposition which was highly resolved in a significant life before this one. It merges the subtle realms with this lifetime. This energy is a little unnerving, but it is a safety valve, making sure the native continues to manifest the power of the opposition that he or she worked so hard to develop a long time ago. It is inherently Plutonic, driving full awareness even deeper into the subconscious. Obviously, the quincunxes are fantastic clues about past life information in the natal chart, but that is the subject of another book. This is the kind of energy you have observed in an individual who is really well developed in some area and yet still keeps pushing further.

With the understanding of quincunxes in process, the power of the Yod becomes more obvious. It is, indeed, the Finger of God, and it is also the revelation of the power of Pluto and Chiron working together. Yods are empowered naturally, and they become totally empowered from the following point of view. The waxing quincunx is Chirotic, the waning quincunx is Plutonic, and the Yod point formed from the Chirotic and Plutonic sextile is to be felt like a dowsing rod. If you image it from the sixth/eighth house sextile shooting to the self-knowledge of the first house, you can see the Yod better. You hold Pluto in your right hand and Chiron in your left in sextile, and you shoot all the power of Chiron and Pluto down through the rods to the dowsing end, the planet which is the Finger of God. If Chiron is the planet at the Finger of God in the Yod, then Chiron is the dowsing energy triggered by the two planets in sextile.

This aspect is the most immediately empowered and useful in the natal chart. It is a gift from God to be revealed to the native. However, the Yod can also backfire because it can function like the trine in one's twenties since it is harmonically balanced. However, in the thirties, a native with a Yod to Chiron will become obsessively restless. Unlike the trine, the Yod does not dissolve when not activated. It will finally activate in one's forties. This is a person who is unnoticed until forty and then surprises everyone. Also, looking at Chiron from a point of view of the waxing quincunx reveals Chiron's pushy initiatory nature. And looking at Pluto from the point of view of the waning quincunx offers fresh insight about how Pluto drives us deeper into essence just as soon as we have seen the light of the opposition insight. Chiron rules waxing quincunxes, and Pluto rules waning quincunxes, a major key to utilizing the opposition.

180 DEGREES: THE OPPOSITION

Like the Full Moon, Chiron in opposition to a planet eventually brings the two planets to full manifestation. An opposition always exists in the natal chart in order to bring the two planets to total consciousness. And unlike the square, the growth on the opposition is continually intense. There are no stages; the native just is highly energized. There is some observable tendency to work on one end of the opposition and cancel the other side out, but the normal oppositional teetertottering is not pronounced. Only three clients in my files are under twenty-five who have Chiron opposite a planet. One has Chiron opposite Pluto retrograde, and she is addicted to drugs and sex. She is acting out the low side of Pluto opposite Chiron. Two of the other young people are quite extraordinary and easier to report on. One is a higher consciousness healer (Chart #2) with Chiron conjunct the Sun opposite Pluto retrograde conjunct Mars retrograde. She is manifesting such a high level of the opposition in her work that it is hard to imagine her mastering the energy even more. Another young client (Chart #41) has a stellium of Jupiter/Uranus/Mars exactly opposite Chiron, T-square Venus, and he seems to be not of this Earth.

Of the twenty-six charts I pulled with Chiron opposition, nearly all the natives are very unusual and express high levels of stress with living. The opposite planet to Chiron is activated into an awareness crisis. Of seven with the moon opposite Chiron, all have very complex emotional realities except one. In different ways, all have learned much from mates, but it has been critical learning and stressful. With Chiron opposite the Sun, natives cannot grasp *who they are* without learning about healing. With Chiron opposite Jupiter, they cannot expand until they grasp alchemical consciousness. Chiron opposite Uranus maximizes skill for physical healing, but can disturb the nervous system in childhood. The planet opposite Chiron is tremendously activated and stressed, but the opposite planet will develop to an extreme degree with time.

OTHER 90 DEGREE ASPECTS: T-SQUARE AND GRAND SQUARE

The T-square and grand square are very energized by the presence of Chiron. The planet at the top of a T-square tends to bring the opposition to the center and manifest in the energy of the planet at the top. If Chiron is at the top of a T-square, then it is very energized by the two planets at each end of the T-square, and is very empowered. My young client (Chart #41) who has Chiron in Sagittarius opposite the stellium with Venus T-squaring the opposition is very artistic. He was a developed artist when he was young. A client who has Uranus at the top of a T-square with Chiron opposite the Sun had almost no energy until she activated higher consciousness powers. A cancer healer has Chiron opposite Uranus grand squared by Saturn opposite Sun, but she has no objectivity about herself; she finds it difficult to assess others well. A neurologist who is attempting to measure Kundalini energy in the body has Chiron conjunct Mars opposite Uranus combust Jupiter T-squared by Neptune, and he lacked a strong sense of his real direction until he became conscious of his past lives as a healer.

Figure 6 shows the Wheel Mandala of Astrology. The second half or waning of the aspecting cycle is as significant and complicated as the first half or waxing half. Comments about the waning cycle will be more brief, because the energetics is the same as the waxing cycle, but the process is different. The illustration of the wheel offers the holistic balance of the issue in order to avoid weighing waxing energy over waning energy. Astrology has been heavily involved in problem-solving for clients, which involves the waxing cycle; therefore, there is more to say about it. But Chiron is the bridge to the subtle realms. The ability to work with Chiron is going to literally flood astrology with energy to activate the subtle realms, the waning cycle, and the letting go in life which prepares us for new birth. Also, the waxing cycle is left brain; the waning is right brain.

When we read the chart, we walk through the twelve houses of the Zodiac, and we progress in reverse to the aspecting wheel. The ascendant, where we begin our walk, is located right on the upper square, the maximum tension point in the chart between Earth plane and subtle realms. The IC in the house walk exists at the opposition point of astrological energy, the point of no-self or accessing nothingness in the chart. When we access subconscious with awareness, we get nothingness, pure Neptune, the ultimate mystical state. The fourth house cusp corresponds to the Dark Night of the Soul of the mystics. As we move up to the seventh house cusp, notice that the cusp of the fifth house of creativity is the Chirotic quincunx point. That is why creativity, the child within, and art are the doorway to God. At the seventh house, we are with the first square, in the aspect wheel, in full awareness of the matter at hand. And it is when we can grasp the subtlety of relations that we can begin to understand existence. St. Thomas Aquinas taught that existential questions could only be answered in relations.

At the top of the chart, the tenth house, where we are most energized on the Earth plane, is where we find combust, the perfect fusion of energy. And as we move from the top of the chart through the tenth, eleventh, and twelfth houses, we integrate with knowledge in a given incarnation. This is the full waning energy of the aspecting cycle, the time to let go of the problem, to empty the body to make room for a new creation.

The aspecting wheel in relation to the Zodiac represents the principle of involution as discussed by Richard Wilhelm in *The Secret of the Golden Flower: A Chinese Book of Life.*[5] It teaches circulation of light in reverse in the body to embody the soul. That is how we empty ourselves so that we can experience bliss, ecstasy, or *samadhi*. The aspects of the waning cycle are all about letting go of the experiences we attained in the waxing cycle, the very experience which made a *samadhi* experience possible in the first place.

210 DEGREES: WANING QUINCUNX

Jeff Green's *Pluto: The Evolutionary Journey of the Soul* has ended negativity about Pluto, Scorpio, and the eighth house. To really understand the waning quincunx, it would be helpful to study Green's work with Pluto. The waning quincunx, which is often the left hand path of the Yod, as already explained, is the point when the evolved ecstatic being reenters the wheel; it is when we come back in service. This is an aspect with Chiron where the aspecting planet knows the Earth plane teaching and returns in service. The aspect implies perfect service at the Plutonic level or the maximum bringing in of the energy at the deepest and most powerful level. Quincunxes always push the native until they deliver the energy, and that is why they are so annoying and effective. This native is meant to be a server of the energy of the planet quincunxing Chiron. Thus, a native with Venus waning quincunx Chiron gives him or herself in receptive love. With Mars waning quincunx, the native, Chiron, offers him or herself as high warrior server. With Sun waning quincunx Chiron, the gift of the self is absolute, such as with someone like Mother Teresa. Chiron waning quincunx Venus would mean the native is a teacher of the power of receptive love to others.

The problem of identifying waning and waxing quincunxes is the reason why working with quincunxes has been avoided by most astrologers. However, it is actually quite easy once the concept has been mastered. Figure 7 is offered to assist in the process.

240 DEGREES: WANING TRINE

The waning trine is determined by deciding which planet has the most weight in the aspect and then aspecting the lighter planet to it, moving clockwise around the chart. The waning trine is harmonic fusion with the subtle realms; it is the relaxation point of the journey into letting go; it is dreaminess, bliss, quiet ecstasy. And it is often enjoyed and not utilized. Waning trines need to be utilized on the Earth plane; if they are not used, the native is ignoring a cosmic gift. Ignoring the waning trine is the same thing as ignoring the divine—ignoring mysticism, ignoring the chance to see the subtle realms. The results are not so noticeable on the Earth plane as the results of the waxing trine, which manifest as laziness, but the negative effect on the psyche is just as serious.

The loss from not activating a waning trine to Chiron is especially critical, since Chiron is the experiential bridge to the subtle realms. Following the teaching of the aspect wheel, the waning trine to Chiron indicates a motivating past life behind the present incarnation when the native was a healing server manifesting the work of the planet aspecting Chiron, or he or she was a teacher of that healing. This time, this native is to bring in the full harmony and gift of that healing power if they are evolving. Sometimes I think the waning trine is where many people get lazy and jump off the wheel of learning because they sense the upper or waning square. For example, a native with the Sun waning trine Chiron would have been a master teacher, utilizing his or her life as an example for healing. This time the native is to live a life of exemplifying harmony as a teaching in itself. This might be a Pablo Casals, or a great gardener. But if the chance to radiate harmony is dropped because it is too much trouble, then back to the beginning to find the healing self at the combust point!

270 DEGREES: WANING SQUARE

This is the most subtle and intense crisis of all. The native is called to build a foundation in consciousness, to bring in the subtle realms. The native is given the opportunity to bring in the divine level to Earth. This is the aspect of the prophet, and the life of Isaiah is a good example of the power of this energy. Frequently, a planet waning square to Chiron creates an unhappy life because this is an aspect of extreme service to the higher realms based on extreme consciousness about what this will cause on the Earth plane. Thus, Isaiah knew that his people would be conquered, yet he gave his life in teaching them the moral reasons for their suffering so that they might return many lifetimes later with full understanding of the political consequences of their behavior. This aspect means that an individual must bring in an important teaching from the subtle realms, even though they can see it won't work this time. This is Job's dilemma personified. Only viewing Job in process, as a person living many lives, can resolve the question of his dilemma. Yet, to truly live here on Earth and bring the soul into the body, even this crisis must be met at one time or another, since the upper or waning sextile teaches us that it is possible to live on Earth with the soul in the body.

300 DEGREES: WANING SEXTILE

Comparisons are odious, but this is the most perfect aspect in the cycle. Lying within the psyche are significant past lives of healing when the native has mastered and manifested the Earth plane and subtle realm teachings regarding the planet which is in waning sextile to Chiron. Until the aspect is experienced, there often is great confusion in the mind of the native because the native cannot explain how they know so much about this issue. Eventually, the credentials in relation to the issue create the opportunity to use the aspect, and then a genius emerges.

For example, a native with Chiron waning sextile to the Moon will fully understand human motivation and corresponding motivations as a young child. No one will understand how this child fully comprehends what everyone is doing. The child will tend to try to study philosophy or psychology and will be passed off as "different." The child already knows more than his or her teachers, and education is a frustrating experience. Eventually, credentials will be earned, opportunities to heal emotions will manifest, and this native will emerge as a great healer/

counselor. Still the native will be frustrated because he or she cannot explain why all is known. Eventually, how it is known will be dropped, and a person will emerge who will simply say how it is. And because of the native's astrological vibration, people will listen and be moved by what this native has to say. The same description applies to Mars, which produces a master of warrior energy; Jupiter, a great teacher who expands reality, etc. Astrologers should help to identify such gifts of great karmic attunement, realign the native to his or her own level, and help form a game plan for mastering these gifts as soon as possible.

BACK TO 0 DEGREES: EXTREME WANING CYCLE

Planets in extreme waning aspect to Chiron or planets in conjunction moving into 0 degrees represent healing energies which have been given and now exist as a protection. Soon this energy will cease to exist in its present form in this individual, and will pass back into the cosmos. So this native is free from getting sick from the energies of the aspecting planet, and remains untouched. My files yielded three with Venus extreme waning Chiron which offer some light on the issue. All three are in the middle of long and connected Chirotic love relationships; two of the relationships are happy, one very stressed. In all three there is a curious level of detachment from it which infuriates the partner, yet the partner cannot leave this wise and healing individual. This individual will next let go of learning to heal in love, and the work is almost completed.

Like the extreme waning Moon cycle, the light is diminishing, the energy is waning; soon the subtle seed of the New Moon will plant a new creation.

Chapter Nine

CHIRON IN ASPECT TO SUN, MERCURY, VENUS, MOON, MARS, AND JUPITER

When Chiron aspects a planet in the horoscope, the aspected planet is Chirotic. On the most primary level, the planet aspected by Chiron is similar in feeling to a planet involved in a quincunx, i.e., it is constantly activated and being pushed to a new level of awareness. Specifically, contents in the subconscious mind related to past life struggles which are relevant to emotional responses for this lifetime are activated within the vibration of the planet that is in aspect to Chiron. For example, in a chart with Venus square Chiron, the native would tend to get involved in love affairs with individuals whom they had already experienced trauma with in past lives.[1] On a more subtle level, aspects to Chiron attune the planet in aspect to "Chiros."

Chiros is the realm beyond linear time which is ruled by Saturn. It is the place where events in the here and now relate to the synchronicity principle. The synchronous level is our experience with congruences between this dimension and other non-physical dimensions. It is the place where we can find the interface between realities. It is the place in time where we can attain another plane of awareness by simply moving our focus to another realm. For example, it is the place in the psyche which recognizes significant meaning with another human that you've just met whether you know it is based on a past life contact or not. So, regarding a planet aspected by Chiron, outside events occur which attune this planet to higher consciousness vibrations in attunement with the planet in aspect. For example, natives with Chiron sextile the Sun will draw parents who try to raise the child in a good environment. Those parents also probably knew the child before. Jungians say the synchronicity principle is "acausal." To me that means the cause is not definable on the physical plane; the cause is coming from the universal timeless mind, the emotional and soul body or some other dimension which we haven't even intuited or identified yet. The planets in aspect to Chiron can resonate easily on all those levels. And regarding the "acausal" synchronicity principle, now that Chiron has been sighted, we are beginning to attune to the "unseen" causes. As we attune to them, our bridge to multidimensional realms is stronger.

Planets in aspect to Chiron feel unstable at first; they represent energies which we feel compelled to experience and master. Chiron's role is to *destabilize,* to infuse Saturnian form with Uranian energy. The experiences related to planets aspected by Chiron have only really been pushed into action since November 1977 when Chiron was sighted. Many new consciousness programs, movements, and new paradigms such as I.C.C.S., Asilomar with David Spangler and Dr. Brugh Joy, Jean Houston workshops, and Chris Griscom's work with gold needles started in the fall of 1977, and readers should take a moment to reflect on changes in their behavior since that time. For example, suddenly in 1977 and 1978, people realized they could access emotions by going into places in the body. Your ability to resonate with the planets aspected by Chiron will be enhanced by a moment's reflection on what you were doing in 1977-78, because that is a major power point in the emergence of Chiron.

Aspects to Chiron are subtle because they push us to subtle levels, but Chiron is a knife-like tool you can use to dissect levels of awareness. You can *utilize* Chiron to sensitize yourself to other dimensions. Transits of Chiron are very critical and are *not* subtle, which will be discussed in Chapter Twelve. But, the aspects of Chiron to the planets and Nodes are subtle; like the emergence of a new shoot of a plant above a great root system. That shoot has great energy from the massive root system, and as you allow yourself to attune to Chirotic energy and *eros,* (a life force), or it will infuse your system with a wonderful youthfulness, a sense of great hope. The resonation in the mind is also intense; these aspects are probably the key access point to the large field of consciousness presently not being used. We can only begin to imagine at this time the great potential of working with aspects to Chiron. We will not get this level by thinking, however; it only comes by *experiencing.*

CHIRON IN ASPECT TO THE SUN

When Chiron aspects the sun, the full sense of self, of being who really are, is related to the degree that we experience spirituality, higher consciousness, in our lives. This aspect has to do with identifying one's *dharma,* one's path in life, and then the nature of the aspect shows whether this path has been constant stress or progressive actualization. With stressful aspects such as conjunctions, squares, and oppositions, the years up to forty will be difficult. Natives will feel the destiny they sense inside is not reflected by their reality. Those with sextiles, trines, and even quincunxes, are naturally spiritual beings at an early age. They often stay away from experiences which might confuse their natural spiritualized sense of self. They also may have a superiority complex, a sense of being above others. They have charisma, and others are wary of them, as noted by Zane Stein.[2]

With *Chiron conjunct the Sun,* the innate sense of destiny is so strong that normal patterns are rarely lived out. This native is unique; he or she burns with purpose and creativity. Marc Robertson noticed that most people are at a peak level of success when Saturn transits the natal midheaven, and that most people go into a deep inward search when Saturn crosses the rising.[3] Most people have a success cycle when they experience the Jupiter return. Those with Chiron conjunct the Sun seem to have a different timing going on. Chart #2 is that of a young healer who has been a mystic since early childhood, and is an extraordinary healer at the present time. Her mother is a great mystic and healer, and this native created the correct environment around herself to manifest her power of Chiron conjunct Sun.

Chiron sextile the Sun produces a profound depth at an early age, an environment which offers opportunities to develop high principles, and a great inner need to bring a significant work into the world. Charts #10 and #25 are good examples of the early and deep inner drive to manifest high purpose with Chiron sextile the Sun. The publisher of Chart #10 chose parents of very pure ideals, even though the mother is very difficult, as can be seen with Moon in the top of the T-square formed with Mars opposite Pluto, and difficulties with the father are indicated by Saturn square Chiron. The artist of Chart #25 chose very loving and supportive parents, and she is very disciplined. There is a noticeable steadiness and constant drive in these natives, but they are also rarely satisfied with their accomplishments. Chiron sextile the Sun indicates that the Higher Self will be embodied within this individual during this incarnation, and perhaps the level of dissatisfaction about accomplishments will lessen when the higher self embodies, usually after Uranus opposite Uranus.

Natives with *Chiron square the Sun* show the typical pattern of working with squares: they have a difficult struggle with spirituality before the Saturn return, they work on the real meaning of life intensely during their thirties, and they begin to master the dilemma after Uranus opposite Uranus. These natives have a very difficult time at the Uranus opposition when the Uranian electrical infusion exacerbates the Chiron square Sun and tends to cause neurological stress. This is a tough position; counseling will help greatly, and these natives need affirmation about the progress of their heavy struggle with Saturn. Shoulder massage is a necessity for them. They need to learn to control Saturn and not have Saturn control them. They are hard on themselves, but let go of control. Once they discover their destiny/Sun, they will find themselves in control with working with Uranian imbalance.

Chiron trine the Sun attunes the native to transmutation and encourages a very creative view of the universe. They are naturally aware of the potential fluidity and basic power for change in all structures. My clients with Chiron trine the Sun have shown great sense of purpose at an early age, but they have had difficulty at Uranus opposite Uranus if they were not disciplined before that time. These natives are naturally responsive to spirituality, and they can get addicted to a higher consciousness "fix" of one new experience after another. But they are in trouble at Uranus opposition if they have not developed a Saturnian work vehicle to use as a means to express their creativity.

Chiron aspecting the Sun sets up a dynamic of knowing who we are with the soul in the body, and this spiritual fusion does not develop without service to others. Chart #3 is an example of a publisher who disciplined himself in the early years and created a vehicle for giving his service. Chart #26 is that of a talented woman who did not create a life work as a vehicle for her spirituality by the Uranus opposition. The Uranus opposition has occurred, she is developing her life work at this time, but it is difficult to do it without many prior years of experience. This issue is especially critical in her case because Chiron is also conjunct the North Node of the Moon, and her ability to expand herself to Neptune is in jeopardy, as is also indicated by Jupiter square the Sun.

Chiron quincunxing the Sun creates a double quincunx effect, and these natives are like loaded sticks of dynamite. They simply cannot rest, they are totally driven to bring the higher self into being and to spiritualize the planet in general. Almost every native I've seen with this position is a well-known New Age leader, spiritual teacher, or ecologist; this position truly galvanizes the soul into the body, but it is a tough position. The type of clients I see is reflective of my work in New Age healing circles since 1982. As work with Chiron progresses, many astrologers will see people from all walks of life who have an aspect like Chiron quincunx the Sun. It must be understood that this type of aspect is *critical* now that Chiron has been sighted. No matter what kind of life this native is living, they *must* express this emerging energy. For example, an economically disadvantaged mother with small children might be finding herself by giving powerful healing in her family, church, or job. Back to the type of client I have typically worked with recently, Charts #16, a writer/ecologist, and #17, a theologian, are excellent examples, and both natives have gone through deep personal struggles while they gifted others with their great teachings. The Jungian analyst of Chart #27 is working on the wounded child archetype, but this native has also suffered great personal tragedy that has almost broken him. All three natives are men who have almost not survived personal crises and yet who were driven to bring in their spirituality for the world. Implied is a rigidity about destiny which creates a hard personal life, but enables the native to give great gifts to others.

Chiron opposite the Sun creates a life and death struggle to bring the self into full expression. And the expression the Sun finds must be alchemical and healing. I used my own chart (#28), as an example, because my life was a struggle to find who I was until the Uranus opposition. Then I began expressing my alchemical Sun in works such as *Eye of the Centaur*[4] where my actual journey of self is transmutative for readers who find out who *they* are by journeying with me through many lifetimes. Zane Stein, who founded Associates for Studying Chiron, has Chiron opposite the Sun, and all those who know Zane have been amazed by his selfless and almost fanatical dedication to Chiron research. This book would never have been written if it weren't for the work of Zane Stein. This is a tense dynamic, and the only resolution is to move into maximum self-expression in healing and spiritual practices.

CHIRON IN ASPECT TO THE MOON

Chiron aspecting the Moon means that the native will not be able to have any feelings unless the alchemical or spiritualized dimension is part of the feeling process. The Moon is our emotional vehicle which makes it possible to relate to other people, and the Moon is our way to go deep inside to experience the subconscious mind. All feelings are screened through our Moon and deposited into the subconscious mind. The subconscious mind contains all our experiences since the beginning of time, and we cannot know ourselves without journeying deep within by means of dreams, exploring past lives, or relating our present-day emotional experiences to deep feelings inside. Therefore, the Moon is a critical vehicle for Chiron to connect feelings to the deepest subconscious. If we can't *feel* what our spiritual essence might be, it is hard to get in touch with it. There are other vehicles in the chart for accessing deep feelings, which include the fourth house, Venus and Jupiter, but with aspects between Chiron and the Moon, the native possesses a great vehicle for exploring the subconscious mind and bringing in the Higher Self.

Chiron conjunct the Moon is a difficult position because the natives have such intense emotions that it is difficult for them to understand the effect they have on others. They are extremely sensitive, they are very mystical about emotional bonding, and the day-to-day levels of relationships are almost impossible to bear. The ideal for this native is to master Saturn and to form a solid bond with a mate, because then the power of Uranian transformation can enter his or her life through the relationship. This native will be almost terrified of restrictions because of the Uranian desire for freedom. But if he or she can find the right partner who will help work with Saturn without undue restrictions, then the possibility of kundalini energy will manifest in sexual sharing. This native may be too involved with his or her mother, which can block the opportunity for a relationship. Also, this native will tend to attract intense and transformative partners. The key to actualizing the spiritual beauty of Chiron conjunct the Moon is Saturn grounding and balance, with room for Uranian transformation.

Chiron sextile the Moon creates a perfected vehicle for understanding how emotions can help or hinder spiritual progress. These individuals, once mature, can usually heal other people as soon as they learn they *can* heal, if they can feel the energy of others. Many of the teachings about healing have warned against healers taking on the negative energy of clients, but this native must feel the vibration of a client deeply in order to move energy. This position creates compassion and great balance about the needs of others. In fact, the danger of taking on negativity from others does occur if the healer *pities* the person in need and takes on their karma. With true compassion, one does not take on this karma, that is, pity others. One simply responds to the needs of others from deep inside the heart chakra. You have nothing to fear from anyone if you respond with compassion from the heart. Chart #17 is that of a theologian who deeply understands feelings of others, and Chart #28 belongs to the astrologer who learned to heal by being able to respond to others with deep feelings. Zane Stein said of natives with Chiron sextile the Moon, "They are usually perceptive of the ills and weaknesses of others, their strong points and talents, their needs and wants."[5] It is from this natural perceptual base about the needs of others that deep compassion is born.

Chiron square the Moon creates a crisis over feelings and higher consciousness. In the early years, relationships are very difficult and intense. This position tends to appear in nativities of analysts and astrologers, because the early childhood creates many difficult emotional experiences which are a laboratory for understanding people and their complexes once the native has experienced the Saturn return. The potential with this position is the highest level of awareness about human emotions, and this native may even become an adept at connecting the higher self into the body. This native is usually involved with the occult because the Chirotic awareness factor is so intensified. This position also creates serious perceptual difficulties: these natives are so intense that they have great difficulty learning from outside reality and other people. They will tend to change environments and people so often that they will not develop long-term friendships. Channeling and drugs are very dangerous for these natives, because they will use the drugs to color perceptions about reality, and the channeling will just reflect the opinions they already have about other people and themselves. They need to become more objective about their own perceptions or they will entirely lose their ability to use their experiences with others as material to learn lessons from.

Chiron trine the Moon creates the opportunity for a powerful balance of the emotions and the higher self in consciousness. This native is naturally comfortable with soul attunement and tends to create a beautiful and harmonious environment. This is a great position for an artist or musician. The usual difficulties with laziness and non-activation of the trine are not especially noticeable with Chiron trine the Moon because the trine calms and harmonizes the Moon to Chiron. In general, aspects between the Moon and Chiron function well in the sextile and trine. One of the greatest therapists I know who is an adept at helping people works with the higher self and is given as an example with Chart #19.

Natives with *Chiron quincunx the Moon* are almost always healers.

They are naturally sensitive to emotional intensity. Chiron tends to unbalance and irritate them in the quincunx until they learn to channel powerful healing forces over time. Chiron seems to activate sensitivity about energy and electrical conductivity, and the Moon seems to become their vehicle for understanding how people feel. This is not necessarily an easy position, because the healing energy in the body pushes on the native very hard until the Saturn return. In general, once these natives find out they can heal and create a life in which they can function as healers, they do very well. Until that point, they may seem to be very neurotic because they have exceedingly intense feelings about everything around them. Once Saturn returns and they balance more in the body, the intensity lessens and the power comes in.

Chiron opposite the Moon is the highest manifestation of the alchemized Moon. The moon or perceptual screen is naturally open to all dimensions. The native has difficulty keeping the auric field clear and is open to astral interference. In the terms of traditional psychology, they have "boundary problems." This is a very hard position to live with before the Saturn return, and I have eleven individuals with this position in my files, which is way out of line statistically, indicating that I attract them. These natives tend to have very difficult early childhoods; they tend to have unusual sexual complexes coming from the powerful flow of kundalini energy in their systems. The neurological system is quite activated, which results in electrical healing skills and/or neurological difficulties. These natives possess great power and potential, and if they can balance the emotions they are capable of remarkable achievements. Chart #22 is a good example of Chiron opposite the Moon. This native is a very skilled astrologer who is especially adept at emotional counseling, and yet her own emotional reality is very difficult and complex. The Moon in the fifth house intensifies the sexual dynamism of this position. The charismatic physicist and writer of Chart #1 has Chiron opposite the Moon, with Chiron in the first house—Moon in the seventh, forming a T-square with the Sun and Saturn at the top. The feelings and charisma of this native are so intense that people flock to hear him speak. He has a stable marriage and family life which helps him to manifest the highest potential of his position. Incidentally, he does not seem to respond to transits in the normal fashion; a great deal of his energy seems to be coming from another dimension.

CHIRON IN ASPECT TO MERCURY

Chiron in aspect to Mercury balances right and left brain perceptual

skill and quickens the deeper levels of the mind. This native has potentially great intuitive skills if he or she can begin to trust the thought processes, and this native can read minds easily. He or she knows what to
say and how to respond to people without knowing much about them
and therefore can become an adept at communication skills. The Virgo
rulership of Chiron is very stabilizing to the thought processes, and this
native has the potential to be very precise and still be intuitive at the same
time.

Chiron conjunct Mercury creates a superlative ability to perceive
exactly what is going on in any situation and to understand how people
are thinking in relation to the situation. This is a marvelous aspect for a
negotiator, for a businessperson working with groups, for a teacher, or
for a therapist involved in group counseling. Mercury conjunct Chiron
also indicates great facility with computers. Chiron, ruled by Virgo,
grounds thoughts into exact space and time, and the conjunction extremely enhances this skill when in conjunction with Mercury. Chart #18
of the yoga teacher is an excellent example of the conjunction. This
native is a superb yoga teacher, and her mental skills are phenomenal.
She is finishing her Ph.D. at this time.

Chiron sextile Mercury produces a strong and exacting mind, and
an extraordinary ability to create something and convey the meaning of
the creation to others. This is a great position for a photographer, a
designer, and for almost any field of sales. This is the salesperson who
can sell underwear to people who live in a nudist colony. Also, those with
this position are great counselors and healers because they have an
immediate sense of what technique to use. They are excellent diagnos-
ticians, for example. The artist shown in Chart #25 is a good example of
Mercury sextile Chiron. She has great skill in taking the works of other
people to their maximum potential. Another of my clients with Mercury
sextile Chiron teaches a program called "Superconscious" as developed
by Robert Fritz. Participants present their program for successful living
and how they see themselves in relation to their creation, and this client
tears these carefully laid plans to shreds. Then she proceeds to show
how we create our own reality, and that this is our only *real* power.

When *Chiron squares Mercury,* great mental exactitude exists in
the native, but the mind tends to be so energized by the square that the
native is extreme in his or her opinions. Intuition is high, psychic skills are
second nature, but right brain experiences also unbalance this native.
This is a position which can be extremely enhanced with Chiron counseling. The high side of this square is the potential to employ Virgoan

exactitude as a focal point for a Uranian vortex, and this native can become a magician. The healer and Hermetic teacher shown in Chart #8 is an excellent magician with Chiron opposite Uranus in a grand square with Sun conjunct Mercury opposite Saturn retrograde in Virgo. Her mental faculties are very sharp; she can cause almost anything to happen with her mind. Like all magicians, this skill can be used for good or for evil; it is up to the individual to decide.

   Chiron trine Mercury brings in powerful occult and healing skills. These natives are naturally in tune with the ancient times, and they remember the old healing skills whether they ever actualize them or not; these natives are wise old souls. If they do not discipline themselves and actuate the trine, they will only remain very much in tune with ancient cultures and healing arts and no more. This intuitive knowing will be a source of pleasure for them. These natives love books about Atlantis and Egypt, for example. If they actuate the trine by disciplining them-selves as healers, and occultists, then great skills will manifest with train-ing. Chart #29 is an interesting case with Chiron at the top of a T-square, the opposition between the Moon in the eighth and Jupiter in the second, with Chiron forming the trine with Mercury quincunxing the Moon. He has done well financially, but he came to me shortly after Uranus opposite Uranus because he felt depressed and empty, and his life was meaningless. Due to the power of Chiron in the fifth in Cancer at the top of the T-square, and Pluto retrograde in Leo in the sixth house of healing, I felt he needed to be initiated into one of the healing orders. The appropriate one was Weighing the Heart of the Soul, and now he is a wonderful AIDS counselor, helping suffering gays who are dying. His whole life has meaning now.

   Chiron quincunx Mercury natives think of themselves as servers, and their thought processes are constantly occupied in finding a way to give of themselves in the deepest way. They cannot tolerate trivia; they are driven to find something significant when they are very young. The power of Mercury quincunx Mercury activates once they have dis-covered significant work. These natives are no good at just being ordinary; the awareness of their eventual destiny occupies them almost from birth. This position creates a holistic mind, a mind that works with broad and large cycles and processes, and Uranus tends to be more activated than Saturn by the quincunx. The key to balance is for these natives to learn to use Saturn discipline. Chart #28 of the astrologer has Mercury quincunx Chiron. In the early years, she mastered so much information in so many fields that it was hard to discriminate and focus.

With the focus of Saturn, the Saturn ruled Mercury in Capricorn began to function well after much work on past life information.

Mercury opposite Chiron is a very activated position with the power of Saturn and Uranus balanced so that the mind can function at its optimum. This native is a natural occultist, an initiate, but you may find him or her just plodding along doing their work. However, if you observe carefully, you will notice that phenomenal occult mastery is coming through this work. Chart #30 is that of a jeweler who works with vibrations in gems, and he has had many past lives as an alchemist. The point is, with Mercury opposite Chiron, the Saturn function is perfected, and there is a bridge of awareness to Uranus. Saturn in Virgo forming a T-square to Chiron opposite Mercury galvanizes light into form.

Psychiatrist R.D. Laing, Chart #31, is a healer of schizophrenia. He understood that schizophrenics are just checking out of an intolerable reality for a period of time as they go on a Uranian higher mind journey in order to handle the energy on this planet. If they are supported by others while they journey with the belief that they will return and eventually master Saturn reality, they will have a safe journey. R.D. Laing has Chiron in the first house opposite Mercury in the seventh house, which gives him special understanding about the alchemical journey of the self needing support and understanding from the mirror/our support group. Also, Neptune in the fifth opposite Moon in Aquarius in the eleventh gives him a very special sense of grounding solidly here as we journey to mysticism. He has also given culture a significant insight; he teaches that our left brain scientific culture is insane, and that those who actually go crazy are the sane ones.

CHIRON IN ASPECT TO VENUS

Individuals with aspects between Chiron and Venus are learning the lessons of receptivity, getting in touch with the *anima,* and working on value systems on Earth. Venus rules receptivity, balance, and good values on Earth, and aspects to Chiron signify that the lessons are spiritualized. And, for natives who do not have aspects between the Moon and Chiron, Venus can be an excellent vehicle for connecting the higher self to feelings. This relationship creates intensity and brings kundalini energy into the body once the Saturn bridge has been built, and so this section is one of the more interesting reports in the book. Astrologers need to be *beyond* judgment about human behavior; their calling is to help people transmute karma. It is our function as spiritual teachers to observe the soul dynamic or karmic pathway of *all* lifetimes, and then it is our job as astrologers to help adjust the native within this life, to help him or her better use their natal energies. If a person utilizes natal energy more wisely, they *automatically* transmute karma. Guilt always blocks the opportunity to gain the necessary values from experiences we have undertaken, and our judgment about behavior always inculcates guilt into the client who has graciously opened the soul to the astrologer. Aspects between Chiron and Venus are a sure indicator that a client is having experiences which might be a waste of personal energy and a travesty to society for some, but for this native, these experiences are the necessary vehicle for finding the self.

Chiron conjunct Venus is the beginning of the spiritualization of the value system and of inherent receptivity. This native is idealistic, and he or she must have relationships which bring in the spiritual dimension. Often there is a strong desire to mix sex and religion, and this native experiences an orgasmic fusion with the cosmos. For thousands of years, sexuality was a part of ritual practice in many cultures for fecundating the fields and placating the Gods. Chiron conjunct Venus is a clue that this native is going to try to activate orgasmic response to the universe. The native of Chart #5 has tried to work with ritual as the union of Earth and Sky. Chiron conjunct the North Node in the fifth house indicates that this work is a major lesson, and that there are significant past lives in ancient cultures related to the cosmic orgasmic function. Chart #12 is that of a young initiate who is working in the sacred school of spiritualizing blood and genetic codes and is involved in a deep search for the place of the cosmic orgasm. This native has a very high vibration and is trying to find new pathways into this intense orgasmic level. My personal opinion is that the rituals of the ancient days are meant to end as we move into the Age of Aquarius, that we will simply fuse consciousness with the higher planes without a lot of ritual mumbo jumbo. I do not want to sound negative about ritual. "Mumbo jumbo" occurs when we are stuck in endlessly repeating actions which are *energy-less*. We do them because we think it is our only way to the source, the divine. Ritual is useful if it gives us energy and leads us to the source. But, when we have learned from our rituals, then it is time to let them go. Teilhard de Chardin, Chart #32, has Chiron conjunct Venus/Neptune in the twelfth house, and his writings are a primary guiding light to the future for all of us who are immersed in cosmic orgasm.

Chiron sextile Venus is a red flag that the native may be sacrificing him or herself on the altar of love. At its best, this aspect symbolizes a level of devotion to a partner which is breathtaking, and at its worst, the aspect suggests enslavement and adoration. At whatever level, this native is working out a primary sense of meaning by living out a very important love affair. The love affair in itself is an altar, a place to find a spirituality deep within which can only come in relation. One of the most beautiful virtues any of us will ever attain is true devotion. This native many not seem to be doing much with life, but close analysis will reveal a gift of subtle love which is almost beyond human. The astrologer should help this native to become who he or she is individually, but honor this deep love as a special gift. The artist of Chart #25 has managed to develop and give her artistic skills in the middle of a long and enduring love for a man who needs her very much. This relationship is very demanding, yet because she has mastered devotion, she has great skill as an artist. The AIDS counselor of Chart #29 has given himself selflessly to one partner for many years as they search for mutual unfoldment.

Chiron square Venus sets up the maximum stress between finding a value system which will enhance spirituality, or just giving oneself over to one emotional high after another. Also, Chiron square Venus usually signals heavy duty past life karmic pressure having to do with gender identity. In the esoteric teaching, we are taught that we choose a particular gender identity to balance male/female polarity, *anima/animus* polarity. Life is no more than an opportunity for experience so that we can become more evolved. And part of being able to become developed involves experiencing both sexes. Often when we are moving into a gender we are unused to there is a lot of stress, and Chiron square Venus indicates this type of stress. Thus, a person with many male past lives may be born a female this time or vice versa, and this is often shown in the chart with Chiron square Venus. We also see this frequently when Mars is conjunct Venus in the natal chart. This client may be essentially male trying to cope with being female or vice versa, and astrologers can help the client with in depth Mars/Venus counseling. Often this native will cop out of sexual balancing by becoming gay or lesbian, although he or she might accomplish more by switching genders completely. Or, this native may appear to be gay or lesbian while actually being asexual and adjusting to the situation. In all cases, counseling on Mars/Venus energies in the chart will be most enlightening. The astrologer of Chart #22 has experienced deep emotional conflicts and a great struggle with her powerful *animus* within. The conflict will tend to resolve at the Uranus opposition. It is very likely she has powerful male past lives and that she is learning to use power with female or Venusian means this time.

When *Chiron is trine Venus* difficulties with primary karmic sexual experiences are a major life problem. My files have many examples of very long and demanding love relationships which are very stressful. This native is very alluring to people in general; many people may fall in love with this native during the lifetime, but the native is caught in a stressful love affair which cannot ever be very pleasurable. It is always difficult to know what past-life contents in relationships are unless they have been remembered in regression, but the incidence of relationships coming from much past-life experience is continually coming up in my practice. The theologian of Chart #17 is expressing the trine with a high level of vibration, and his teachings about the true nature of human love and compassion are very beautiful. The channel of Atlantean symbols, Chart #33, has Chiron trine Venus/Mercury in the second house, and she has spent this lifetime in a stressful marriage with a man she has known in many past lives. Natives with Chiron trine Venus can develop the most profound understanding about human love, but that level of understanding usually comes out of very complex and karmic relationships.

Chiron quincunx Venus creates great stress in love affairs which results in keen perception about the motives of other people. With this aspect, it is especially important to determine whether the quincunx is moving in or out of the opposition. When it is moving in, the native is living a life of learning about the greatest possible awareness of a love experience. Chart #4, of a Sanctuary Movement worker, has Chiron moving into the opposition with Venus. She experienced many traumatic love affairs before her Saturn return and now is married to a man who shares her deep intensity about love. Her beautiful and sensitive understanding about love has developed her into a person of deep compassion. Chart #34 is that of Michel de Nostradame, Nostradamus, and he deeply loved a young woman and his three little children, but they all died of the plague. In his chart, Chiron is quincunx Venus, and because of his great tragedy, Nostradamus learned to heal the plague and saved millions. His South Node is advanced in vibration, being 29 degrees of Virgo in the sixth house, and we can see he is a great healer from many past lives who came back to serve the race once more.

Chiron opposite Venus creates a receptivity to the alchemical nature of Venus which is almost overpowering. The native is completely receptive and open to others, and unless great control is indicated in the chart by other planetary positions and aspects, he or she is very nervous.

This native is alluring, often seems to be from another planet, and often has unusual intuitive understanding of the esoteric because of the ancient occult connection with Venus.

The orbit of Chiron is very elliptical, and many researchers, including Velikovsky, have brought forth much evidence of a severe disbalancing of the orbit of Venus around 1500 B.C., when I believe Chiron died. Many of the most hidden teachings are connected to such theories which relate Venus to catastrophic cycles already discussed in Chapter Two. Venus rules *eros*, the feminine receptive power to Uranian kundalini energy. The teachings involve opening ourselves to this energy and the experience *is* chaotic to some degree.

Since receptivity in consciousness is strongly related to the level of fear in the psyche of any individual, many researchers, including myself, believe there is great collective amnesia about a catastrophe involving Venus around 1500 B.C.. This can manifest as a dissociative anxiety complex which attaches itself to any potential fear in the environment. Esoteric mastery training investigates the secrets of Venus eventually, and much of this training has to do with breaking through fear. Now with research on Chiron and the coming work on Nibiru, the awareness of the relation of the 1500 B.C. catastrophe to Venus, Chiron, and Nibiru will grow. And natives with Chiron opposite Venus will have a primary ability to understand this deep level of the occult. Aleister Crowley, master occult wizard, with Chiron opposite Venus, is a great example of this dynamic.

CHIRON IN ASPECT TO MARS

Mars aspecting Chiron natally indicates a deep association with the sacred warrior archetype. Mars is the activation of the *animus*, the male aggressive principle in the natal chart, and aspects to Chiron spiritualize the issue. The sighting of Chiron on November 1, 1977 offers the hope of a successful solution for the nuclear dilemma. As already indicated, Chiron liberated Prometheus from the Underworld, thereby returning the power of fire to the human race. Now, 3600 years later at a synchronous point in the cycle of Nibiru, we have taken fire power to its end point by developing nuclear weaponry. Chiron's natal reading, related to the atom split chart in Chapter Thirteen, indicates a way out of the dilemma. On the most basic level, people don't need to kill each other any more when they have transmuted their consciousness and absorbed their past life karma. But in the Chiron nativity, Chiron square Mars is showing that the sacred warrior has incarnated again! Splitting the atom was a cosmic karmic error, or at least we can say that the consciousness of the scientists was not adequate for the work at the time. The human race will eventually learn not to violate the basic microcosm of the universe; but once Pluto was sighted in 1930 it was inevitable that the human race would have to learn that lesson. But, how do we protect ourselves?

The splitting of the atom was a violation of the holographic galactic essence because of the consciousness of the scientists involved. That is, Earth and all beings here have a molecular sharing relationship to the galaxy. We are the children of the galaxy. We are dangerously playing with fire in the universe when we change the basic unit, the atom, without understanding the whole. It was microcosmic rape by the negative warrior energy here. As individuals participating in a synchronous galactic hologram, we are only allowed to use force to protect ourselves if it is by means of the high consciousness of the sacred warrior. That is, we are to contain our power centered in our solar plexus, and our protection is our own inner strength. Becoming the sacred warrior means becoming the protector of the hearth, of Hestia the goddess of home, balance, and peace. It means entering the Earth with passion, not raping it.

It was low warrior energy when Jason violated Medea, Circe, and Hestia, the three women of the Moon. Low warrior energy is any form of rape and power over women; high warrior energy is protection of the hearth, the women and children. Clearly we have a chance to relearn the sacred arts, to live in balance with Mars and Venus. The collective unconscious already knows that Mars/Venus imbalances result in holocaust and diseases such as AIDS. For example, has anyone considered that just splitting the atom—not even considering the radioactive pollution resulting—has resulted in new disease? All we have to do now is change the dynamic, and those with aspects between Mars and Chiron can teach us the way at this time.

Chiron conjunct Mars is the beginning of knowing the sacred warrior. Of four clients I have who have Chiron conjunct Mars, all but one are using it in an unevolved way. They are amazingly bullheaded; they relate to others as if they were horses wearing blinders, and they are extremely energetic. They find it very difficult to see themselves objectively, but they are good-hearted and care about others. These three are women, and obviously it is hard for a woman to get in touch with the sacred warrior image. However, two of them responded strongly when I suggested that they resonate or attune with Artemis. Chart #15, with

Chiron conjunct Mars, is of a priest working with Native American rituals. He has shared the sacred warrior energy for many years with the Sioux. His Pluto/Sun conjunct in the 12th squaring the Moon in Aries in the ninth house caused him to be very open to the spirituality of the Sioux, and his Chiron conjunct Mars caused the Sioux to recognize his role as sacred warrior for planetary healing.

The *sextile of Chiron and Mars* powerfully births the sacred warrior archetype in consciousness. These natives are naturally courageous and feel like they can do anything. And when they use energy, they are balanced and unceasing. Mr. Miyagi in *The Karate Kid* is a perfect example of Chiron sextile Mars energy in the horoscope. The role Lynn Andrews plays in *Medicine Woman* as sacred female warrior stealing the marriage basket from the rapist male, Red Dog, is a perfect example of the Mars sextile Venus power. Lynn Andrews also has Chiron in the tenth house sextile Uranus/Mars natally, making her the ideal writer to bring the archetype of the sacred woman warrior into consciousness at this time. And cosmic geologian Teilhard de Chardin, Chart #32, has Chiron sextile Mars, and he played the role of sacred warrior within the Roman Church trying to open its doors to new thought.

Chiron square Mars creates a tendency to try to avoid transmutation. The natives are very aware of the power of Chiron because of the square, and they develop all kinds of strategies for avoiding Uranian energy until they experience their Uranus opposition. This position is like the way most of us feel about going to the dentist. Mars is aggressive use of energy, and Chiron is a breakthrough to the other side, so this native is being challenged to develop new and unusual strategies for living. Zane Stein has noted how they tend to get into a rut,[6] and a superb example of this is Jim Jones of the Jonestown massacre, Chart #35. Chiron in the late fourth house conjunct the Sun in the fifth indicates his search for self involved release of creativity, and the square to Mars in the eighth indicates how he got locked into a horrifying necrophiliac pattern which took many lives with him. The artist photographer of Chart #9 has experienced great difficulty with getting into ruts. In fact, he was experiencing paralyzing depressions when Chiron was transiting his Mars/Uranus square Chiron natally. Since the Mars/Uranus is in the seventh and Chiron is in the top of his ninth house, this spiritual crisis put severe stress on his relationships. I can honestly say that I do not think this client would be alive now if it weren't for his work with Chirotic energy. Obviously this effect is radically intensified by the Sun, Venus, and Chiron being in Virgo. The channel of Atlantean symbols, Chart #33, has Mars square Chiron within the grand square of Chiron/North Node in the tenth—Mars in the first—South Node/Part of Fortune in the fourth—Uranus retrograde in the seventh. She learned to activate the Mars opposite Uranus as soon as she found her life path of activating symbols for New Age consciousness.

Natives with *Mars trine Chiron* always seem to be the ones who get all the lucky breaks. Their intuition is superb and aggressive, and they seem to anticipate exactly the right moment to make a breakthrough. The presence of Mars cuts down on the general tendency for trines to be lazy, and the Saturn part of Chiron is activated by Mars, which tends to cause the native to be very adventurous. Sigmund Freud, Chart #51, had Chiron in the third house exact trine Mars, and his ability to communicate his energy is still phenomenal today. Phil Donahue has Chiron trine Mars, and his ability to get all the breaks for himself and then cause consciousness-raising in his work has been admirable. The New Age harpist of Chart #36 has shown the same tendency to get all the breaks and then change consciousness with her work. She specializes in slow tempos in her music which heals people, especially the elderly.

Chiron quincunx Mars creates terrific transmutative force, as do all quincunxes to Chiron. You will find very few natives with this position who are closed to consciousness expansion, but you will find many who yearn for more awareness but do not know how to attain it. As always with quincunxes, the energy never stops pushing toward manifestation. Because of the basic tension involved in aspects between Mars and Chiron, this aspect will mainly result in constant tension with a lot of resolution. Chart #37 is the chart of a priest who has been leading transformative walks to holy sites. He has great charisma, and his drive to bring in great energy is strengthened by the Mars quincunx Chiron. His South Node in Virgo shows he was a healer in past lives who has come to communicate ecstasy (the North Node in Pisces in the third house). Mars quincunx Chiron is a difficult aspect to develop, but there is great potential for continual new levels of awareness.

Chiron opposite Mars is the full potential of the sacred warrior archetype, but since this consciousness is so little understood in culture, there is very little room for expression. Natives with this aspect will have great compassion for the oppressed and be moved to fight injustices. Natives who have been unable to overcome fear and cultivate courage because of the cultural dynamic they've lived in will be honest, trustworthy, and very strong. As more years pass since the sighting of Chiron, more natives will find the power of the sacred warrior growing within. Chart #2 of the young New Age healer shows a younger person who has been able to activate the warrior energy by doing her work, and also participating in firewalks. This young woman is courageous and secure; she is a sign of the future.

CHIRON IN ASPECT TO JUPITER

When Chiron is aspecting Jupiter resonation with multidimensional realities is intense. Now that we are able to name this mastery expansion vibration, a whole new level of creativity and expression will quickly manifest for these natives. Jupiter is the physical home of the masters, the place in our brain centers which enables us to validate the existence of higher levels of vibration. Jupiter is the planet which causes us to feel the presence of the spirit; it is the place in us that perceives "the unmanifest," or that which is not in physical form, as identified by Chris Griscom.[7] But these levels still have existence in some other dimension or form, and Chiron is the bridge between physical form/Saturn and multidimensional thought processes/Uranus. Aspects between Jupiter and Chiron enable us to perceive new levels, because Jupiter helps us to feel them. Saturn makes the form in consciousness, and Uranus activates the mind into perception, activating the neurological system into transmission. If all this sounds like space talk, be aware that we are on the verge of a stupendous consciousness alteration, and often the planetary archetypes are straight and true early indicators of the nature of the shift. The planets help us to put upcoming cycles into words. That is what archetypes are all about.

On a personal level, the connection between Jupiter and Chiron causes the native to react very strongly to transmutative energy forces and to feel great urges to reach other levels of reality. They develop very strong convictions as they mature, and they are very driven to communicate their beliefs. However, with the hard aspects, they may become overbearing and even have difficulties maintaining a firm hold on reality. They know a lot, and they usually encounter many years of being doubted because they cannot explain *how* they know so much. They can easily be overwhelmed by a personified unconscious inflation because the world they perceived from intuition is so much more luminous that they deny outer reality. That is, the contents of the subconscious seem more real than the everyday life and they lose themselves in it. As the Jungians put it, they are swallowed by the unconscious. With this problem it is essential to continue to communicate what is known, because someday it will be valuable in the world, and because inability to com-municate separates the native and opens them to being swallowed by the unconscious.

Chiron conjunct Jupiter is a rather difficult position because the native does not function well with normal patterns. This native is a maverick with a superiority complex who listens very little to others. He or she feels radically different from others. In youth this native fixates on almost anyone who understands this disturbing inner intensity on that contact. As this native moves out into the culture, he or she feels uncom-fortable with the peer group and birth culture and tends to be very attrac-ted to other cultures and previously unknown people. There is so much projection upon these fascinating unknown new contacts that sooner or later the native is always disappointed in the object.

Three of my four clients with Chiron conjunct Jupiter have spent many years working with rituals of native peoples while being fascinated with the individual natives personally. Chart #15 is that of the priest who works with Native American rituals. The writer of Chart #38 is fas-cinated with other cultures, is giving to the world, but has many conflicts with everyday life because he resonates to his inner world so intensely. Writer Elie Wiesel has this position and is a good example of the dynamic. For counseling, it is wise to work with this native on projection issues and personality boundary tension, to help them to recognize the difference between the real world and their own inner contents while acknowledging his or her superior gifts. This complex may appear to be an ego block when in fact it is perceptual.

Chiron sextile Jupiter adds great manifestation powers to the nativity. Jupiter seems to ground powerfully when in sextile to Chiron, and then the avenue for Chiron's questing and guiding force is clear. Readers should note Chapter Thirteen, the natal reading for Chiron's discovery chart. Chiron is in the fourth in Taurus, sextile Jupiter in Cancer in the seventh. Also see Chart #53. Chart #39 is the nativity of a very influential New Age consciousness publisher who has demonstrated great manifestation power coming from Chiron sextile Jupiter. Much of the success of his publishing has come from a key channeled work from a key woman in his life, which is shown with Chiron in the seventh, stimulating his creativity and fortune with Jupiter in the fifth house. The New Age harpist of Chart #36 is an amazing manifestor of her work as a musical healer with Chiron in the second. The spiritual healer of Chart #2 also has a sextile from Chiron/Sun to Jupiter in the third house, which is enhancing her communication skills.

Chiron square Jupiter strengthens the will and the mind, and activates consciousness about social justice and freedom. These natives are revolutionary, but you might not notice it for awhile because they are subtle and refined while they are busy working on a very long-term and radical plan. They will be history makers, but in unique and imaginative ways which often involve magic or art. The consciousness is rather like Chiron conjunct Jupiter, but the square forces the energy into long-term manifestation. I find it especially interesting that both Carlos Castenada and Lynn Andrews have this position. Chart #22, astrologer, has Chiron in the eleventh house squaring Jupiter in the second, showing that her gift is manifesting and grounding astrology. Chart #17, theologian, has Chiron in the second square Jupiter in the eleventh, which is indicating he is a prophet, that he knows how to ground the New Age. The death counselor of Chart #29 is interesting because he was blocked from giving his gift of Jupiter opposite the Moon until he unlocked a creative outlet—counseling people with AIDS—which unleashed his compassionate Chiron in Cancer. Until he found that outlet he wallowed in emotional trivia and boredom.

Chiron trine Jupiter activates nearly perfect perceptual skills from birth which will cause early brilliance and artistic success. This native is irresistible and easily finds a niche for successful operation. The world desires this native, but lurking deep within is a great occult comprehension of reality which may or may not manifest. Around the time of Uranus opposite Uranus, a test situation will occur which will decide whether this native will be just wonderful and successful, or whether he or she will suffer in the cauldron of magic to manifest the gift felt deep inside. If this native manifests the high energy of the trine from Jupiter to Chiron, great powers will come from Jupiter through Chiron. Chart #16, a writer/ecologist, has Chiron in the eleventh exact trine Jupiter in the seventh. He is known as one of the greatest minds of the twentieth century. Brooding and brilliant author Arthur Koestler also has Chiron trine Jupiter.

Natives with *Chiron quincunx Jupiter* have a profound understanding of the many levels of human experience and perception. They feel out of synchronicity during much of their lives because they respond to experiences in a more comprehensive way than their peers. Unless they find a vehicle for this depth, they can become very confused. These natives have difficulty with conventional structures because their own definition of what is possible is outside of structures. Charles Manson has Jupiter quincunx Uranus, for example, and he does not seem to comprehend the reason for conventional structures at all.

Chiron is insidiously calling Jupiterian expansion to a previously unknown level. Like all quincunxes, the only way out is to respond and consciously activate this rich source of stimulation to a new level but, how? Chart #40 is of a Jungian analyst with Jupiter retrograde opposite Uranus with Pluto retrograde forming a T-square in the third, in itself indicating his need for depth expression. It is so intense that he also publishes books on Jungian analytic work. The Jupiter is highly activated in the T-square by Chiron rising in quincunx to Jupiter. He is also very involved in the occult. He has a major stellium in the tenth house, and it is fair to say that Jungian work is a superb vehicle for multifaceted and multidimensional view of reality which otherwise might drive him completely mad.

Chiron opposite Jupiter stimulates occult perception to the maximum. These natives know about the essence of matter, the physical laws of the universe, and their minds are like laser beams into life. In the early years, this opposition creates great difficulties. The perceptions into the very core of existence are so amazing that this native seesaws between being completely ordinary to being a wizard.

Chart #41 is of a young man who has an exact opposition between Chiron and Jupiter forming a T-square to Venus in the twelfth. When he was six through ten years old, he drew astonishing pictures of the destruction of Atlantis with detailed composite beings and technological vehicles never seen before. Then, from ten to seventeen, he tried being completely ordinary, wearing Izod polo shirts, playing football, and being one of the boys. He could not bear to hear about magical conceptions of life, but he secretly drew sketches of beings from other dimensions that would scare even science fiction addicts. Now that the Neptune transit on Venus in Capricorn is finished as of 1985-86, he is beginning to try to manifest his occult brilliance through Jupiter by studying physics.

Chart #27, a Jungian analyst, has Jupiter opposite Chiron forming a T-square to Pluto retrograde in the fifth in Cancer. This native is the specialist in the wounded child field, and his chart indicates this is a fruitful avenue for his search. Chart #21 is that of the physician working on ways to chart the flow of kundalini energy in the body. With Jupiter conjunct Uranus in the twelfth opposite Chiron conjunct Mars in the sixth, there is no doubt he will succeed in this critical research.

Chapter Ten

CHIRON IN ASPECT TO SATURN, URANUS, NEPTUNE, PLUTO, AND THE LUNAR NODES

As we slowly weave our way from the Sun out through the inner planets, we finally approach the outermost of the inner planets—Saturn. Saturn is the last planet visible to the naked eye. It rules linear time, structure, and form in this solar system, and it contains the energies of all the inner planets around the Sun. But with its eventual return to its natal position at around the age of 29, human consciousness is prepared to break through the leaden form of Saturn and experience the outer planets within the essence of the human body. Before 30, Saturn is like a lead shield holding out the galactic resonances radiating through the outer planets. Saturn contains within physical essence the energies of the inner planets and the Earth and Moon to the Sun. We cannot know who we really are without our spirituality, the real meaning of our existence since the beginning of creation. Our spiritual connection happens when the Saturnian lead shield dissipates and the Sun shines through the inner planets out to the outer planets.

It is time to examine Chiron aspects to Saturn and Uranus, and then to Neptune, Pluto and the Lunar Nodes. The trilogy of Saturn/Chiron/ Uranus offers wisdom in itself. Chiron's orbit is very elliptical, moving out to the orbit of Uranus, but not crossing the orbital path. However, Chiron goes *inside* the orbit of Saturn when it moves to its perihelion; that is, Chiron pierces the lead shield of Saturn. As we work with aspects to Saturn it is imperative that we comprehend the meaning of this piercing of the Saturnian lead form. This piercing is what initiation is; this energy expresses the power of Uranus to rearrange the electrical neurological systems. This part of Chiron's path proves that there is no such thing as determinism, fate, or *moira,* as Saturn linear time is pierced by Chiros or spherical time. This is the spiraling of experience, the critical leap of total

151

creativity which affirms that anything is possible.

Natives with aspects between Chiron and Saturn experience break-through from Earth forms and linear time to creativity, but like all breakthroughs, it is hard work. When Chiron affects Saturn by aspect, Saturn has a different dimension than usual. Without aspects between Saturn and Chiron, and also Chiron aspects to Uranus and Uranus to Saturn, the progress of Saturn development is quite predictable, and the native is comfortable with Saturnian growth. When there are aspects to Chiron, the native isn't so confident about predictable patterns. The native has difficulty trusting; he or she usually has serious conflicts with one or both parents, and may project the early home conflicts onto society at large. However, this early and deep distrust of Saturnian fixed form tends to yield openness and creativity after the Saturn return. That is, the psyche is less shielded in lead than usual. At the return the native balances the need for using Saturnian form and structure, and then is more free than most to respond to the outer planets. The aspecting Chiron functions as a constant initiator, moving consciousness out of fixed ruts.

Health is ultimately a question of biological balance, and biological balance has a lot to do with steady and powerful Saturnian growth and Uranian electrical activation of new cellular production and neurological structural reorganization. As we know from science, everything is com-pletely new in the human body every seven years; every cell is new. New birth cannot occur without death. Chiron is in relationship to the seven-year Uranus cycle which contains a Saturn square to Saturn within each seven-year Uranian sign transit. Chiron rules the process of complete letting go of old forms so that new and vital birth can occur. It is the pro-cess of learning to trust, of going forward even when we aren't sure why. Then the new issues have space.

Chiron rules the healing principle, which is a function of both Satur-nian control and Uranian electrical vitalization. Chiron is the key to find-ing that balance. The sighting is a signal that we must begin to know when to heal and when to let go. For example, antibiotics can heal, but they can be used as a control mechanism in the environment. The struggle of the immune system is subverted by overuse of antibiotics. Now after 40 years of antibiotics, we are seeing severe malfunctions, such as AIDS, in the immune system. In my opinion, the physical environment is on the verge of teaching the race that the immune sys-tem itself must be trusted, that total control (or Saturn) by scientists and physicians will never work. Also, medical astrologers should take note of the times when Saturn's lead shield is pierced by Chiron. This cycle will yield clues to cancer radiation cures. Radiation cannot pierce lead. A better piercing mechanism will be coming into medicine with radionics or some other technique which is Uranian.

Now that we can also use Chiron for health research, the true need for trust in the universe or Eros will come into balance with control, or Thanatos. Astrologers interested in health should begin Chiron work immediately so that more information will be available on these critical issues. The aspects between Saturn and Chiron are the key to many of these questions.

CHIRON IN ASPECT TO SATURN

Chiron conjunct Saturn is a very rare aspect. In recent times it has occurred in 20 to 28 degrees of Pisces. The conjunction occurred in 1672, 1820, and 1966, and this conjunction occurs every 147 years during each third Chiron cycle corresponding to five Saturn cycles. I do not have a Chiron program on my computer, and I can't go back before 1672. But, I think it would be fascinating to see if the Chiron conjunct Saturn every 145-150 years has occurred in Pisces during the Age of Pisces. I sense there are some very important great cycles to be revealed by researchers. 1966 was the year of the flower children in Haight-Ashbury, and it was a period of general stress between parents and children in America over the Vietnam War and drug experimentation. It was a year when many people in their twenties completely let go of the "law of the father" or Saturn, or any semblance of trust in the older generation. In 1819-1820, there was a mystical movement for liberation from economic stratification in upstate New York. Later, many of the young individuals who participated in trying to loosen society almost went mad because they lost employment, and severe economic depression had set in by 1835. There are many parallels in the liberation movements of 1820 and 1966.

Zane Stein reported on a recent survey of individuals born during the 1966 conjunction in *Essence and Application: A View from Chiron.*[1] I did three charts of babies with this conjunction who were born to mothers in 1966, and I observed the families from 1966 until 1972 when I moved from the West Coast to the East. As of 1986, these children are obviously only 20. I feel confident about describing their early environment and the logical results from it because my own feelings match the survey reported upon by Zane Stein. Many clients come to me around age 27-29 and then 37-42, and I will not have much data on this group until about 1995. Zane Stein reports, "All seemed to have an extremely low opinion of their fathers, and this included those who lived with stepfathers, and adopted fathers. On the other hand, there was an uncommon feeling of warmth toward their mothers."[2] The three families I observed were exceedingly unstable. 1966-1972 were years of tremendous societal breakdown which damaged young families. The sixties were when the Welfare State system weakened already shaky families in America. Drug and sexual experimentation was the norm rather than the exception, and I strongly doubt that many of these children lived long with their birth fathers. In one family, the mother and father had separated by the time the baby was two. One of the women was unmarried when her daughter was born and thought nothing of sleeping with many different men while her child was in the same bed. I strongly suspect sexual abuse of this child.

On a brighter note, this conjunction is a potentially powerful stabilizing energy for these children. They were born during a time of societal breakdown probably triggered by the conjunction itself. When they have experienced the Saturn return, I believe they will be leaders in creating structures which also contain healing and higher consciousness energies.

Chiron sextile Saturn is a powerful aspect which exemplifies the mature and productive qualities of Saturn and stabilizes Chiron. There is a tendency for Saturn to be stronger than Chiron, as Zane Stein noted,[3] but I believe that is because the Saturn archetype is so well defined in consciousness, and the Chiron archetype is just emerging. Normally, two planets in sextile are balanced. As a result of the absence of a Chiron archetype in the collective, the tendency is toward over-pragmatism, i.e. the native is attuned to Chirotic energy but tries too hard to nail it down. The tendency is toward too much left brain identification and too little intuition.

A well-known and excellent medical astrologer has Chiron in the sixth in Leo sextile Saturn in the fourth in Gemini. She has great healing skills but she tends to shut down her ability to heal intuitively by analyzing her work. Her written work is of great value. Occasionally she is overwhelmed by Chiron funneling into her integrative and communicative Saturn, and she accomplishes remarkable physical healings. I would predict that she will be stimulated by right brain energy at her Chiron return in August 1993 and become a great physical healer, since her

North Node is in Virgo in the sixth house. She will experience her Chiron return and then transiting Chiron conjunct the North Node.

Chiron Square Saturn. Chiron was repeatedly square Saturn from 1935 to 1939, and from 1945 to 1952. Many of my clients were born during those years, and this aspect functions as a generational influence as well as an individual one. That is, many people during those years had a very difficult childhood with intense stress with the dominant parent. Ordinarily Saturn would rule the father, but from 1945-1952 the mothers assumed a very controling and dominant role after WWII, causing Saturn in the natal chart to describe the mother. The early childhood environment was extremely difficult with this aspect, and yet these natives possess uncanny insight about the true nature of the reality around themselves. Many lack essential balancing psychodynamic aspects of character, but if they can heal their lack of balance, they will have keener insight than most. Many of them will have sought out different forms of counseling to heal themselves, and will blossom when they hear about the Chiron archetype. They will have already accomplished some of the work on the squaring tension; and with understanding of Saturn and Chiron they can become adept at grounding Chirotic force.

Chart #5, the guru was born under an earlier series of squares between Saturn and Chiron. He has the Saturn square from the eighth house which intensifies his desire to activate mysticism through the feminine from the North Node conjunction to Venus in the fifth house. From a positive perspective, he can really ground Earth energy in ritual. From a negative perspective, he has become an ego-inflated guru because he has attracted so many followers who need a father substitute and who follow him blindly. He is an interesting case because he is entering old age, and ideally his Saturn in the eighth house squaring Chiron/North Node in the fifth would mature him into a great, wise oldman teacher. Also of interest is the fact that he has experienced great stress with his children, which cut him off from the potential teaching coming from being a parent. He allowed his passion for the occult (the eighth house Saturn, Neptune conjunct the Midheaven, Jupiter conjunct Uranus, and Pluto retrograde in the ninth) to occupy all his time, and he neglected his need for the hearth and children (Sun, Venus and Chiron conjunct the North Node in the fifth house).

The next group with Chiron square Saturn was born between 1935-39. This group is very interesting because some are now close to the Chiron return, and all have experienced Uranus opposition. They are a good predictor of the future energy from this aspect because the intensity of this aspect increases with the number of years of living for these natives after Chiron's sighting. Just like Pluto since 1930, Chiron's impact will greatly intensify as the archetype manifests in the collective. Also, many natives from 1935-36 have a T-square formation with Neptune opposite Saturn squaring Chiron. Neptune opposite Saturn of 1935-36 was a potent introducer of the power of Chiron because Neptune was in Virgo in 1928-1943, and it tended to be an early Chirotic space and time locator of cosmic energies while the collective was assimilating the sighting of Pluto. The stage has been carefully prepared on more levels than many of us comprehend. The universe is unfolding as a great synchronistic creative act.

The native of Chart #42 is a man who went all the way up to his final vows as a Jesuit by the time of his Saturn return, but felt he needed psychoanalysis in order to be a complete person. The Jesuits denied him analysis, and he dropped out of the order rather than become a neurotic and destructive force. His need to ground spirituality is powerfully illustrated by Neptune near the Midheaven opposite Saturn in Pisces in the depths of the fourth house. His father problem was and is acute, and he sought a relationship with a woman (Chiron in the seventh) for healing rather than allow the Church to substitute for his neurotic and cold father. Sun conjunct Jupiter in Capricorn in the second seems to be dominant because he has since been in Freudian analysis for almost twelve years, but at least he avoided the substitution of one neurotic father for another through his potential personal use of the Church. His Chiron return will be the ultimate release of his spiritualtiy, which is locked into Neptune opposite Saturn, and finally mystical breakthrough will be his way.

Chart #14, an author and nun, shows a fascinating similarity in life path with the Jesuit. This time Neptune is in the first, and this author found herself as an artist while she was in the convent (Saturn in Pisces in the seventh—Bride of God) but she left her convent in 1980 when Chiron transited Uranus in the ninth house. Then Chiron manifested in a major book on God as a mother figure at her Chiron return.

As we get closer to Chiron's sighting in 1977, natives with Chiron square Saturn from 1945-52 show an increasing tendency to embody the healing and alchemical side of Chiron. I have always been intrigued by the extreme negativity about Saturn, particularly in Roman and Greek astrology, since I have had such a positive experience with Saturn in my own life. Now I see that I have always been very sensitive to Chiron because it is conjunct my North Node, and Saturn balancing has saved me from possible mental illness. Now that we have the Chiron archetype to bridge Saturn and Uranus, negativity about Saturn has lessened.

Regarding the same cosmic dilation before the birth of Pluto, I attended a lecture in 1981 in which a Jungian analyst said we had really come a long way because the unconscious had only been discovered in 1910 by Jung! Of course, the unconscious has always been there; only a Jungian analyst could come up with such an arrogant remark. But, the point is that the archetype of the unconscious ruled by Pluto flooded the collective as the sighting of Pluto approached. Exactly the same phenomenon is occurring with Chiron, and the group born with Chiron square Saturn are heavy carriers for introducing the qualities of Chirotic force. Many of these natives began New Age healing and bridging movements in the fall of 1977. The theologian of Chart #17 has Saturn/ Jupiter square Chiron/Pluto, and he started a major teaching movement in the fall of 1977. Chart #8, Hermetic teacher, has Saturn in Virgo in a major grand square with Chiron in Capricorn. This native's father abandoned her at a very young age. The priest of Chart #37, who leads transmutative healing walks, has Chiron in the first square Saturn in the tenth, and his father was wrenched out of a normal guiding role for him because this priest grew up in a family of migrant farm workers. Chart #10, a higher consciousness publisher, has Saturn in Virgo close square Chiron in the tenth. He is expressing his healing powers in his publishing work, but his Saturnian mother has her North Node in Virgo close to his Saturn, and she restricts his healing expression. Yet, his work is part of her realization process. In this case, the mother energy is attached to Saturn, and also the father was mostly absent from the family. Chart #43, a healer who specializes in restructuring the hologram of consciousness, has Saturn in Virgo in the eleventh square Chiron retrograde in the third. His Chiron is sextile Jupiter retrograde forming a Yod to Uranus in 29 degrees Gemini in the ninth house. Once this young healer figured out how to focus Chirotic force, his aim was remarkable.

Chiron trine Saturn produces a magnetic and charismatic personality which can result in gross manipulative tendencies in the native, or conversely, the potential for a compassionate heart. This native is never ordinary; he or she will tend to get away with murder because of a natural magical presence. This native usually lives in an auric field isolation much of the time, and it becomes natural to have his or her own way.

The trine tends to ground Chirotic power into the life like a lightning rod striking a transformer. These natives are not always very well liked, and yet they always get what they want. Chart #35, Jim Jones of Jonestown, has Chiron in the fourth, Sun in the fifth trine Saturn in the first. John Kennedy had Chiron in the fifth trine Saturn in the ninth. Chart #11, a physician, has Chiron in Pisces in the eleventh trine Saturn retrograde right at the IC, which generated a great Oedipal complex, but this complex bears a peculiar intensity due to the Chiron trine. When I saw him at age 76, he was still completely obsessed with a fascination for his mother, and his relationships with authority were riddled with father projection.

This aspect bears watching, and astrologers can assist clients by pointing out to them that they possess a magical, alchemical aura so that they can better understand how people respond to their energy. If this magical grounding energy can be contained within the boundaries of the native, then it is a great gift. I have some remarkable child clients with this position, and they are handling it very well now that the archetype is working in the collective. The trine was in effect in 1916-17, 1930-31, and 1978-79.

Chiron quincunx Saturn creates an unavoidable need to ground Chiron to the Earth plane by means of Saturn. It is simply essential to create a vehicle for alchemical change on the Earth plane. R.D. Laing, healer of schizophrenics (Chart #31), has Chiron retrograde in the first quincunx Saturn in the eighth in Sagittarius. He was driven to find a way to free schizophrenics from the ordinary definitions of behavior that were clearly killing them. Chart #15, a priest working with Native American rituals, is another example. This native has Chiron in a stellium in the tenth with Jupiter/Mars/Chiron quincunx Saturn in Sagittarius in the fifth, and he was driven to break through old ritual forms and bring in creativity.

Chiron opposite Saturn creates realization of alchemical wisdom in form—or the native may be a rigid fighter for humanitarian causes. Like the imbalance in the sextile of Chiron to Saturn due to the power of Saturn in the collective and almost no understanding of the Chiron archetype, this group tends to heavily favor Saturn in the opposition. I have been able to carefully observe about ten individuals with this aspect who were born in 1922-24 because one of my close relatives was born then and she has introduced me to her classmates. They are very conservative with Pluto in Cancer and Uranus in Pisces, and I was not in a

position to request their time of birth. As a group they are philan-
thropists yet are very poor parents. They are consumed with saving
society according to their own patterns, and have a remarkably low
ability to learn from their own children. The mother of the publisher with
Chiron square Saturn has this opposition. Almost all of them grew up
with severe and cold fathers which few of them could recover from, and
almost all have experienced severe difficulties with alcoholism. It would
appear that Saturn killed Chiron, that energy died in their system and
they fell into a total Saturn grip.

Saturn has been opposite Chiron in January, February, and March
of 1986, January and March 1987, and will be in January 1988 and
December 1988. So far, the energy has felt like structural breakdown,
like a spinning vortex that will destory as it intensifies unless the energy is
very clear. It seems to signal major shifts in technology as shown by the
automobilization of America in the 1920s and the explosion of Challenger
in late January of 1986. This is an aspect that makes or breaks people.
Columnist Jack Anderson is a good example of the positive power of
this aspect.

The Challenger explosions signaled the end of the unbridled love
affair with technology, since the primary purpose of the launch was
research for the Star Wars Defense Initiative. Space technology should
be carefully observed during the rest of the oppositions because it would
appear that the higher forces are intervening to prevent the militarization
of space. It is, of course, impossible to draw conclusions yet from the
children born during the 1986-88 opposition. But couples are often
much more careful about having children now, and fathers are often
playing a very nurturing role in culture. Parents themselves are potentially the ultimate Chiron figures if they are capable of holding the
highest potential level of consciousness for their children. Perhaps the
children born during the Chiron opposition to Saturn in the late 1980s
will bring in the high side of the opposition with parental support. What
would it be? The ability to bring the soul into the physical body.

CHIRON IN ASPECT TO URANUS

We are beyond the inner planets, and the elliptical fifty-year orbit of
Chiron now becomes our primary center. The orbit of Sirius B around
Sirius A is fifty years. We are letting go of the Sun and beginning to feel
the galactic cosmic ray vibration. "Pentecost" means "the fiftieth" in
Greek, and work with the Chirotic cycle brings the full comprehension of

Pentecost. In the Hebrew ritual cycle, Pentecost is the fiftieth day of the harvest, and the festival carries all the power of the ancient harvest rituals. At the first Pentecost after the Ascension of Christ, the dynamic changed. The fire tongues of the Holy Ghost pierced the physical plane and entered the physical bodies of the Christians. This was a Chirotic event, and the meaning of human evolution was spiritualized into a birthing galactic connection. Now the emergence of the Chiron archetype is the Second Coming of Christos, a name unnervingly close to the name of the Centaur healer. The Second Coming is not a physical plane holocaust, an apocalypse; it is in fact the birth of the Chirotic force in the heart chakra of each healed human being.

Chiron aspects to Uranus need to be examined in light of the Chiron cycle to Uranus in general. As already discussed, Chiron's orbit is highly elliptical, and Chiron is in Aquarius through Taurus for about 28 years, and transits Gemini through Capricorn (8 signs) for about 32 years. It is in Aries for almost eight years, and it is in Virgo and Libra for less than two years each. Uranus spends about seven years in each sign. Therefore, Chiron makes some aspects quickly and then moves rapidly past Uranus. When Chiron is in Aquarius through Taurus, it can synchronize into a long-term aspect. For example, Chiron was square Uranus periodically from 1805 to 1835, and it is in *exact opposition* 41 times from 1952 to 1989. There were *no* aspects between Chiron and Uranus from 1900 to 1939. Therefore, with Chiron aspects to Uranus, often there is no data, and only speculations on historical trends are possible. Generally, aspects between Chiron and Uranus tend to increase the influence of Uranus.

Chiron was conjunct Uranus in 1796 when Chiron was in perihelion and probably within Saturn's orbit. The American Revolution occurred in 1776, the French Revolution in 1789, and Uranus was sighted in 1781—right in the middle. It would seem to me that a conjunction of Chiron and Saturn at the perihelion had a very conservative effect which tended to slow down the violently transformative impact of the discovery of Uranus. Chiron was close to a conjunction with Uranus during 1889 and 1899.

Chiron was sextile Uranus in 1800, 1894, and during November 1939 to July 1941. These natives are very opinionated, energetic, and obsessed with transformation. Chart #44 is of a healer who works with guided imagery in music. Chiron is in Cancer in the twelfth house sextile Uranus in the tenth, and she is extremely nurturing in her work. Uranus is also trine Neptune and sextile Chiron, and she is a powerful meditator and utilizes many forms of artistic expression. Generally speaking, this aspect seems to produce much attunement to art.

Chiron was square Uranus from 1805-1835 when there was much financial speculating in the world economy, and there was a worldwide economic crash in 1835 which caused depression until almost 1850. Chiron was square Uranus again in 1889 to 1891. Again there was much European and American speculation in the 1880s, and there was a currency collapse in America in 1893, with the economy in bad condition until 1897. Chiron was square Uranus again on and off in 1942 to 1944 during the depths of WWII. This aspect produces desperation and conflict in the personality, and an insatiable drive to transform consciousness.

These natives are courageous and cannot be stopped if they believe in something, and they are driven to get to the truth and meaning of any situation. The Chirotic force is intense, and the electrical transmutation of the body at the Uranus opposition is powerful. Chart #33, the channel of Atlantean symbols, has Chiron conjunct the North Node in the tenth house T-square Uranus opposite Mars in the first. When she is actively involved in higher consciousness work and teaching, she is calmed. Reviewing nine clients with Chiron square Uranus, all are unusually attuned to transformation and seem to be relaxed only when they are actively involved in the work. They all seem to be de-energized when involved in ordinary activities.

Chiron was trine Uranus in 1841 and 1842, in 1852 to 1855, and in November 1945 to October 1946. These natives seem to have difficulty finding their places in life; they seem to be confused about identifying the real meaning of their lives. The sanctuary worker, Chart #4, has had a well-organized career, but her work is often not close enough to what she really believes in. Of women clients with Chiron trine Uranus, I have noticed peculiar trends with childbearing. Four of them did not manage to have a child until nearly age 40, whether they were married or not, and now they are having quite a struggle with motherhood. It could be assumed that the upcoming Uranus opposition triggered the pregnancies, possibly to help open the heart chakra.

Chiron was quincunx Uranus a few times in 1844-46, 1848-49, November-December of 1948, and July-September of 1949. This aspect is highly transmutative and creates a great vortex in consciousness for Uranian energy. These natives are extraordinary, and eventually will create something very special with this quincunx. Chart #7 is a weaver who is really struggling to bring in very Chirotic symbols. Her work is very powerful, but it is always an effort for her. Chiron in the seventh is quincunx Uranus in the second.

Chiron was opposite Uranus a few times from 1951 to 1989. This is an aspect of ferocious intensity which either burns the native out or pushes him or her to great transmutative levels. Drugs are a grave danger to this native, especially cocaine or psychedelic substances. Of eleven clients with this aspect, four seem to be hopelessly lost to drug addiction. Chart #8, a Hermetic teacher, has Chiron opposite Uranus, and this woman's skill with electrical body readjustment is great. The spiritual healer of Chart #2 is showing great powers with this aspect at an early age. The physician of Chart #21 is doing research to measure kundalini energy coursing through the body. Chart #41 belongs to a young artist who has been struggling to balance Chiron opposite Jupiter/ Uranus/Mars. He is a person of remarkable awareness at a very early age. Chart #46 is of a glass blower who creates amazing spiraling forms of color within clear glass. It would seem that his fluid Uranian contact transmutes itself into bizarre manipulations of the physical plane.

The oppositions have been having a potent effect for a long time now. Observing the last five or six exact oppositions, I noticed that the accident rate increases, especially for airplanes. As this book gets ready to go to press, the Reagan government is torn apart by the Iran Contra Affair during the November 1986 opposition. The opposition stresses people out, makes them feel like everything is too much. Substance abuse is especially unwise during the opposition. Also, I suspect this aspect intensifies the potency of viral infections and may overstress the immune system. Many of the people dying of AIDS have this aspect natally, and they may weaken when it repeats. Again, we need much research at this time.

CHIRON IN ASPECT TO NEPTUNE

Aspects between Chiron and Neptune are keys to pragmatically utilizing Chiron for bringing the higher self into space and time because of the Chiron/Neptune—sixth/twelfth house polarities. Visualize a funnel of energy with the small end of the funnel located in a specific place, and with the wide end of the funnel swirling out into a wide circle which sucks in timelessness, nothingness, and no separation. In fact, there is no separation in matter, but we exist with identification and specification so that human perception and learning can occur. That is our physical reality. The experience of no separation, of the no-self, of being nothingness within the cosmos is also an essential experience. Until the discovery of Chiron, most mystics had encountered the experience of the no-self quite by accident, and then had tried to describe it. Much of the expression of how to come to it has been of letting go of identifications and specifications. But many, including myself, have found it difficult to "let go" without knowing what one is letting go of. So, it usually happens by accident, and it is always amazing because it feels so wonderful to enter that state.

Some mystics, such as Meister Eckhart, have pointed out that nothing is right under our noses, and that we are looking everywhere for it but right in front of ourselves. Since all matter is one, Eckhart is correct. Now, with the sighting of Chiron, we have a tool in the chart for timing mystical breakthrough which will be explained in the next chapter. And with examination of Chiron aspects to Neptune, we have astrological aspects for tuning into the experience of the no-self, or the self at one with the God force.

When Chiron is aspecting Neptune, the nature of the placements can be used as a meditation path for attunement to that which is right within us at all times, to the divine. It is impossible for us to have access to the divine without also being in service of the divine. The sixth and twelfth houses show the way to compassion and letting go of the small self, which is contained in the ego. The house placement, sign, and nature of influence from Neptune to Chiron is a key to the way to find the funnel to the divine, to Neptune, in a given incarnation. The sighting of Chiron is the Second Coming of Christ, the sign that Christ is incarnating in the heart chakra. As we go into aspects between Chiron and Neptune, ways to locate Neptunian ecstasy in consciousness will be looked at in relation to Chiron.

When *Chiron is conjunct Neptune,* the focalization of the Neptunian vortex exists right at the conjunction. By utilizing the natural pragmatic energy of Chiron by means of a meditation on Saturn form and a deliberate firing of kundalini energy up through the spine clearing the chakras, Neptune can be reached. Natives who are lucky enough to have this placement will succeed with this technique only if they completely understand that they are creating a channel to the divine, that their success has nothing to do with ego identification or personal attachment.

The degree to which they are polarized into attachment to this channel will be in direct proportion to the degree to which they narrow the channel. A meditation on a channel of water with the mud that silts it up as equal to their personal attachment will help those who are ego-attached get the point. Then a second meditation on a tunnel with unrestricted powerful wind blowing through will help them once they really see the limitation of the ego. The second meditation should not be suggested until the individual really sees his or her ego problem. If your client really comprehends the ego attachment and is ready to let go, flower essence remedies which help let go of ego, such as Wild Oats, work really well. The degree to which no attachment exists as this wonderful energy is brought in for compassionate service and love for others is the degree to which the soul is in the body.

I have many clients with this placement. Chart #19 belongs to a highly developed therapist who has made great progress with this aspect. His life has been difficult on the personal level because he has four planetary pairs including Neptune conjunct Chiron. The planetary pairs make it difficult to be objective and make personal progress by learning from others. The ego breakthrough has been very difficult, as a male, with the Sun in Leo. His North Node in Cancer in the ninth house has helped him to learn compassion by nurturing clients with a strong spiritual direction. His Jupiter, very advanced in 29 degrees Virgo also in conjunction to Chiron, caused him to create a pathway for the masters to assist clients and help them to access their higher selves. And, as he sat day after day on a search for letting go with his clients, gradually he balanced the Libran Chiron conjunct Neptune in the twelfth by deliberately acknowledging that the divine energy was not his own. With experience, he began to rearrange his consciousness with the Uranian force of the Moon in Aquarius trine Chiron conjunct Neptune conjunct Jupiter. For someone with this many personal stresses (as seen by the planetary pairs), the Neptunian expansion is a way out of a life of trivial stress. Again, the degree to which he sees that he is merely a channel and learns to expand *beyond* personal blocks is the degree to which he has access to the divine.

Zane Stein noticed that *Chiron sextile Neptune* "creates a real longing in the individual for whatever 'utopia' is described by the sign and house of natal Neptune."[4] This is exactly right. Of nine clients, all have this quality, and some are more successful than others at actualizing this ideal world. Chart #1, a physicist, has Neptune in Libra in the eleventh sextile Chiron in Sagittarius in the first. This person uses his charisma to create a vehicle for bringing his own powerful comprehension of Neptune to others. He is busy balancing the cosmos within his own energy to create a pathway for his great vision of the Aquarian Age, and then he recreates that utopia in the minds of those he teaches. Chart #30, a jeweler, has Chiron right at the Midheaven conjunct Moon sextile Neptune in Libra in the seventh. This native lives in a visionary world of beautiful faceted healing colors, and he projects his inner vision into his clients who are balanced by the Neptune in Libra energy which also connects them to the divine by means of the energy vibration of the gems. Chart #12, an esotericist, is an unusually good example of this aspect, and life did not make sense to this native until he was initiated into his sacred order which is guardian of the genetic heritage and sacred blood. He has Chiron/Venus/Part of Fortune in the twelfth sextile Neptune in Libra in the ninth. The stellium squares the Nodes, and the North Node is at the head of a Yod from Neptune sextile Pluto retrograde. He was clearly an old master wizard who returned to activate Venusian teachings, and his life began to make sense when he could see that. There are many more examples. See Chart #44, and notice that this native is a body therapist with Neptune in the second house. This is a powerful and balancing aspect to be used as fully as possible.

Chiron square Neptune is exceedingly stressful and is a great challenge to any astrologer. In general, the more these natives can activate Chiron and Neptune in their lives and careers, the better off they are. No matter what they do, life will always be very Chirotic and mystical, and this influence means they can never be just ordinary, so why even try? If they can activate the potential of this aspect, their gifts to the race are great. If they cannot find a way to use this energy, they will be confused, prone to substance abuse, and eventually they will suffer nervous disorders. The body cannot handle the force of this energy unless it is channeled by means of higher consciousness serving.

Chart #42 has Neptune in Virgo at the midheaven opposite Saturn in Pisces at the IC forming a T-square to Chiron in Gemini in the seventh. This native began his healing when he left the Jesuits and married at his Saturn return, and he will probably resolve the pressure of the T-square in 1986 with his Chiron return. Chart #47, a student of healing, has Chiron in the third at the head of a Yod from Pluto sextile Jupiter, and Neptune in the eleventh in Libra squaring Chiron. This woman cannot utilize the power of the healing Yod until she resolves the square from Neptune which also squares Uranus. She is going ahead with healing training, which will help her resolve the squares during her thirties. She has much work to do because Uranus in Cancer conjunct the South Node in the eighth squaring Neptune indicates she must burn through a lot of karma connected with magic, sex, and death, in order to activate and ground the North Node in Capricorn in the second. Chart #14, an artist nun, is a great example of resolution of Chiron square Neptune. She funnels the energy of Neptune into her being with the first house placement, and then she creates alchemical art by means of Chiron in the tenth. She never rests, but she is more relaxed when she is creating. Chart #21, a physician, has Chiron/Mars in the sixth opposite Uranus/ Jupiter in the twelfth, T-square Neptune in the fourth. He is working on relating esoteric healing technology to modern medicine. He is very successful and quite balanced with a strong development of his North Node in Capricorn in the sixth house of healing. This chart suggests a very evolved lifetime; the native is young and bears watching. Those with Chiron square Neptune should be very wary of substance abuse and too much fantasy in their lives.

Chiron trine Neptune is a helpful aspect if the rest of the chart shows strength. It seems to really facilitate teaching of small children, and a client who is director and teacher in a private school has this position. I have four other clients with this trine who are really wonderful teachers. They have an innate ability to stimulate the imagination of children because they love fantasy themselves and communicate it well. Chart #2, a spiritual healer, has Chiron/Sun in the second trine Neptune in Scorpio in the ninth. The young teacher of Chart #24 is very empowered by Chiron right on the descendant trine Neptune retrograde in the third. He has much to communicate, is still young, but eventually he will find out who he was as a teacher in past lives so he can focalize the powerful third house Neptune. The artist, Chart #41, is saved by the eleventh house Neptune trine from being overpowered by his ninth house stellium of Moon/Pluto/Jupiter/Uranus/Mars/South Node opposite Chiron. He will be a great artist when he matures.

Chiron quincunx Neptune creates a tendency to try to live a dream. The native creates an ideal, and then tries to live life according to that idea. Chiron was quincunx Neptune periodically from April 1905 through 1907. I have only two relatives who have this position. One became a poet when she was a young girl and spent the rest of her life living the life of a poet by doing commemoratives and belonging to literary groups. She has an odd otherworldly quality that I've always wondered about. The other relative was very wealthy, created a life just the way he wanted it, and didn't seem to notice others very much.

Neptune was opposite Chiron in 1843 and 1900. It will be opposite again in October 1989 when Voyager flies by Neptune in June of 1990. I have no clients with this aspect. It is logical to assume that this position would cause a great deal of confusion when unresolved, but that the native would be very open to divine consciousness if they could balance themselves.

CHIRON IN ASPECT TO PLUTO

Pluto rules evolution of consciousness, which always involves a trip into the Underworld to clear the subconscious mind. Jeff Green calls Pluto "the prime mover, the first cause, or bottom line to which all other planetary factors are linked."[5] That is because Pluto is the bridge to the galactic. Chiron is the bridge between the inner planets ruling the personality dynamic and the outer planets ruling consciousness attunement, and Pluto is the corresponding link to the galactic. Transmutation by means of Chiron will always fail unless the emotions have been cleared and karma has been released.

It would be helpful to read *Pluto: The Evolutionary Journey of the Soul* by Jeff Green because the level of consciousness raising potential with Chiron work is not possible without a corresponding level of work with Pluto. Visualize it: Chiron orbiting and linking the inner and outer planets, and Pluto orbiting and linking our solar system to the galaxy. Sometimes Chiron functions as Saturn, holding and encapsulating the energies and qualities of the inner planets; sometimes Chiron functions as Uranus, linking the electrical apparatus of the physical body to Neptune and the galactic. And similarly, Pluto sometimes functions like Saturn, holding the subconscious energies in check until a vision of ecstasy frees the energy into an erruption; or Pluto functions like the galactic, exploding consciousness into the primordial fireball of the hologram of all matter throughout all time, which implodes into an instant of creation which is the Creator.

In 1978, Pluto's Moon, Charon, was sighted. It would be tempting to view Chiron as the bridge to Pluto work, but the sighting and naming of Charon right after Chiron's discovery is a potent warning not to do so. The Ferryman to the Underworld in Roman mythology is Charon, and Charon is therefore to remain as the Ferryman in Pluto clearing. But Chiron is the catalyst who sears the body with the piercing of the higher self, pointing out that a double process is going on with consciousness raising. To put it simply, we cannot survive the depth analysis of the journey to the Underworld without the synchronous experience of the vibration of the higher self. You can clear yourself and try to clear your emotions all you want, but it will never work without the experience of the rapture of the soul. So Pluto work is a process of evolution, and Chiron is the choreographer until you are ready to be master of the show yourself.

Jeff Green says, "If each person understands what his or her own evolutionary requirements are, and operates in such a way as to actualize those requirements, then the collective evolutionary necessities will be developed in a non-cataclysmic way."[6] Pluto rules volcanoes, and we can have cataclysmic eruptions or slow release of inner Earth energy. Chiron is a primary ruler of ecology, and it has been since 1977 that we have seen that no living thing will survive unless we begin to operate as a wholistic collective. Pluto work makes it possible to identify the evolutionary needs and begin deliberate clearing work in order to trigger slow and progressive growth. And it is the higher self, the glimpse of the divine potential, which offers us the energy to do the work. Chiron rules holographic attunement, which means we attune with the collective as we progress. Actually, we cannot move without this identification of the collective working with the individual, and we only have access to that level with comprehension of Chiron's way of working, or divination.

Chiron rules divination, and divination is the only way to alignment with the collective. So, as we begin work with Pluto, it is critical to see that the relationship of Chiron to Pluto has to do with moving the deepest inner forces in tune with the hologram. Pluto shows us that we cannot even begin to align with Chiron until we have first done the hard work of depth clearing, and we can't make it through the depth clearing without the vision of the higher self. So, as we enter depth clearing, at first we use our intuition as a guide; then once we have learned to trust our intuition, we will find a divination skill which will attune us to the collective. Then finally we will begin to identify the hologram of the individual soul within the larger hologram, and then we can let go of the little self. Aspects between Pluto and Chiron will yield many clues into how to clear the self in attunement with the vision of the higher self.

Before going into aspects between Chiron and Pluto, we need a few words on the potential negativity in aspects between Chiron and Pluto. Chiron is a catalytic planet like Mercury; it is an energy which moves other things. It will cause a catalytic energy with another planet with no judgment about good or bad. Other planets in the chart, like Mercury, have to do with morality, with judgment. In a general sense, Chiron can trigger channeling and divination powers for good or bad. Channeling and divination are just a skill. There is a great big difference between working with a Ouija board, and the healer who sees auras and vibrations and

uses that energy only to heal. There is a big difference between a channel who is overtaken by entities and fascinates his or her audience, and a
channel of divine energies who brings in the information only for healing. The negative side of Pluto is atavism or reversion to primitivism, as
most powerfully exemplified in the Nazis, who surfaced as soon as Pluto
was sighted.

We are moving into the latter stages of the transition into the Age of
Aquarius. Each New Age is meant to be a new energetics. But, there is
much atavism since the sighting of Pluto. As we search for initiation and
energy in our times, many are trying to find the energy in ancient forms.
Chiron rules initiation, and an aspect to Pluto will activate the atavistic
response in consciousness instead of reorganization into a new hologram. If this is your issue, ask yourself whether you really want to activate
some of the highly charged attributes of your subconscious mind. It is
very tempting now to fall back into the old temples, the old ways of finding energy instead of just going into direct infusion of the higher self into
the body. For example, much of the work by non-Indians with Native
American rituals is atavistic. Just as people get close to the creative
power of the higher self, they sheer off into the grasp of a teacher, a guru,
or meditation with an old form. Old forms merely exist to give us clues
abut how to find the energy here and now in the place in this time; their
usage is not actually applicable in modern times. As we examine aspects
between Chiron and Pluto in the natal charts included, we will be looking
especially hard for how to trigger the force in a new and holographic way
and how to avoid falling off into safe and well-known old forms of
ritual.

Chiron conjunct Pluto creates an evolutionary vortex of Chirotic
energy. The house position of the conjunction defines the nature of the
transmutative force, and this energy is so potent that the native's career
of healing work is usually defined by that house. Chart #44, a guided
imagery healer, has a wide conjunction in the 12th house, and this
native's work with art and music is very Neptunian. The New Age
publisher of Chart #39 with the conjunction in the seventh house
brought through his transmutation in a major book which involved a key
seventh house relationship. Chart #17, a theologian, is especially
interesting because the conjunction is in the second house. This teacher
has focused on theories to help his followers get back into the body and
stay in it; he is a powerful grounder. The native of Chart #48 is one of the
most powerful healers practicing in the United States. She is the mother
of the native of Chart #2, and her wide Pluto/Chiron conjunction is in the

second house like the theologian, and she also is a powerful grounder. She found her healing powers when she learned how to bring higher consciousness into the body with acupuncture needles right around 1977-78. This is a strong conjunction and seems to be very active once the native activates the energy of the locating house. Karl Marx had Chiron conjunct Pluto in the first house.

Chiron sextile Pluto creates a very pragmatic dynamic in the chart. The native tends to create a vortex of transmutative power in the location house of Chiron and then shoots the energy to Pluto, locating the power of the aspect in the locating house of Pluto. Chart #35, Jim Jones, shows this dynamic in a negative way. Jones has Chiron in the fourth almost into the fifth, creating energy with a very deep part of himself, and with children, sextile Pluto in the seventh of relationships. Unfortunately, the death archetype of Pluto was triggered, but the power of the aspect is shown by how the people who were massacred all obeyed Jones with his Pluto power in the seventh. The astrological publisher of Chart #3 has Chiron in the third sextile Pluto in the fifth. He gathers all the Chirotic energy of the third house into fifth house of creativity in publishing. The writer of Chart #38 has Chiron/Jupiter in the second sextile Pluto in the twelfth. He is into esotericism, and he grounds the Chirotic force with his pen, and then locates his thought into the esoteric realm of the twelfth.

Chiron square Pluto is a tense, difficult, and powerful aspect. This aspect creates such great stress that the native usually cannot relax and focus until after the Uranus opposite Uranus transit. Once the square is resolved, these natives tend to give their lives to others in service because they feel such deep empathy for the stress of other people. These natives are often misunderstood, even criticized, for their desire to help other people unlock their bonds. Sigmund Freud, Chart #51, had Chiron in the third square Pluto in the sixth. Freud actually healed many people and had a positive impact on the psychoanalytic field, yet you rarely hear praise of his work. The yoga teacher of Chart #20 had a very tense childhood and early adulthood with his family, as seen by Pluto and Saturn in the fourth, but teaching yoga is transmutative for him. Once he began to teach yoga and activate his healing powers, as seen by Chiron in the sixth, he began to relax. Chart #27, a Jungian analyst, has Chiron in the first square Pluto in the fifth. This native is releasing his energy by working on developing a teaching based on the wounded child (fifth house) in relationship to self-emergence (Chiron in Aries in the first house).

Chiron trine Pluto is an aspect which creates an unusual sense of destiny at an early age. This native is responding to a very unusual vibration even as a small child. Pluto causes him or her to work hard from early childhood to find a field of study which can contain this rare sense of destiny, and once the proper channel is found, this native will become a great teacher or researcher. The house placement of Pluto in the chart tends to indicate the field in which the native will influence his or her whole generation, and the location of Chiron shows how he or she expresses this unusual power. The physicist of Chart #1 has become a mystical spokesman for the Pluto in Leo generation (Pluto in the ninth), and his mode of expression is his charismatic teaching energy (Chiron in first). The native of Chart #12, the initiate, has Pluto retrograde in the eighth house indicating work in sacred orders, and Chiron/Venus in the twelfth indicating he is investigating the meaning of the genetic lines in royalty and secret political organizations. I couldn't figure it out at all until he told me he was researching *Holy Blood, Holy Grail,*[7] and that he came to me for some guidance before traveling to Montsegur in France, the primary investigative point for research on a bloodline hypothesized to be coming from Christ and existing in the bloodlines of the royal families in Europe. (This is a Libran or Nibiruan issue, by the way.) For counselors who run into unusual clients like this, a word of advice—I also suggested that he do some sessions with a good past life regression therapist to find out as much as he could about his past life work in secret orders. He did so and got the necessary information before embarking on a very unusual search.

Chiron trine Pluto is an aspect which is working on some level, whether the native knows it or not, because it is such a potent vibration. Astrologers should remember that they have been the primary source of information on secret orders for thousands of years. Now that Chiron has been sighted, again astrologers are needed to be guides to sacred orders.

Chiron quincunx Pluto creates an incessant drive to find the deepest level of meaning in any situation. The nagging prodding of Chiron to Pluto or Pluto to Chiron will either drive the native into imbalance, or push them into developing Chirotic powers with which to explore the Underworld. This seems to be a very karmic aspect which may be blocked until the parent related to the natal Pluto dies or transforms. An interesting example of this dynamic is shown in Chart #47, student of healing. She is very blocked spiritually by her mother (Moon in ninth square Saturn) and in her power by her father (Saturn in the twelfth

square Moon) and mother (Mars quincunx Moon). She has found it difficult to find her path (Uranus conjunct South Node), but the Pluto quincunx Chiron has driven her all her life. Once the parents are gone or
transformed, she will have the power of the Jupiter in the eighth, and she
will be able to activate the Chiron Yod formed by Pluto sextile Jupiter.
There is often a death that releases a native with Chiron quincunx Pluto,
because the parent blocking Pluto must release the tension of the quincunx so that this native is free to join his or her own peer group.

   Chiron opposite Pluto is the full expression of both planets. Pluto is
prodded into the depths of exploring the subconscious mind, and
Chiron continually brings in the higher self to help Pluto keep going.
This dynamic can be seen in Chart #2, the young New Age body healer.
She grounds the Chiron/Sun energy of the second house in her work,
and she drives the force with the depth awareness of Pluto/Mars in the
eighth. This opposition is more comfortable than most oppositions
because Chiron and Pluto like to work together. But this native is also
incapable of living a simple or trivial life.

CHIRON IN ASPECT TO THE LUNAR NODES

   The Lunar Nodes explicate the karmic path in the natal chart. The
North Node of the Moon delineates the chosen purpose of this lifetime,
and the South Node reveals significant past life information for this
lifetime. I've found Martin Schulman's work in *Karmic Astrology: The
Moon's Nodes and Reincarnation* [8] to be the best available source on
the Nodes, but it does not yet contain any information on Chiron. The
Nodes are one of the most critical parts of the astrological reading. I
often start studying a chart by investigating the Nodes first. Since Schulman and many others have not published Chiron interpretations yet, we
are missing some critical parts of astrological interpretation. We are missing the interpretation on Chiron in the North or South Node, the impact
of the North or South Node in the sixth house, and Chiron aspecting the
Nodes. Following the format of Chapter Nine, Chiron aspecting the
Nodes is included here, and other questions on the Nodes and miscellaneous other parts of the reading follow in Chapter Eleven.

   Chiron conjunct the North Node means that the native will create a
way to live a life as a healer, initiator or spiritual teacher. The native will be
completely frustrated until this way of life is found. This aspect always
indicates a life of major importance in the karmic cycle. It is axiomatic:

the degree to which the native is unable to live out the life as a spiritual teacher will equal the level of frustration. Therefore, astrologers are to identify the meaning of the life as teacher by Chiron's sign and house position and give this information to the native.

The astrologer of Chart #28 has Chiron conjunct the North Node in the twelfth opposite the Sun on the South Node in the sixth, telling us that she was a teacher of self-revelation in significant past lives and that she returned to bring in a major esoteric teaching in this lifetime. The effect is doubled because the axis is on the ascendant/descendant. Chart #33, a channel of Atlantean symbols, has Chiron on the North Node in the tenth opposite the Part of Fortune on the South Node in the fourth. The nodal axis is grand squaring Uranus opposite Mars. The South Node shows that the Atlantean symbol system was once her joy and fortune, and the North shows that she will recreate this system in her career in this life. Chart #5, a guru, has Chiron on the North Node in the fifth in Pisces and close to Venus. The South Node in Virgo indicates that he was a healer in a major past life and that he has come back to develop creative forms for initiation. Chart #26, a New Age communicator, has the South Node in Aquarius in the ninth, indicating the native was a teacher in relevant past lives and that she came back to help communicate significant teachings in a very noticeable way (Node in Leo). Chart #49, an astrologer, has Chiron exact conjunct the North Node in the fifth house, showing she needs to work on initiating clients. With Mars in Scorpio conjunct the South Node in the eleventh, she had to burn off manipulative, negative male energy before she could be prepared to initiate others. As Schulman has indicated, a planet on each Node indicates a karmic crisis in this lifetime which must be resolved. The astrologer of Chart #28 could not become a teacher until she un-covered her past life knowledge of the sixth house Sun/South Node, and the native of Chart #49 could not activate learning to initiate until she let go of negative Mars. Bernice Prill Grebner advises that natives with a planet on each Node must eventually learn to "flip the Nodes" or reverse them.[9] I agree with her opinion.

Chart #50 is the chart for the first nuclear chain reaction. I have included it here because Chiron is conjunct the North Node of the atomic splitting which I believe is the most significant event of modern times. Since Chiron let Prometheus out of the Underworld so that man kind could have firepower, it is highly significant that Chiron is conjunct the North Node of the chain reaction. Since Chiron conjuncts the North Node in Leo in the fourth house, our deepest, subconscious, survival self has been disturbed.

Chiron conjunct the South Node indicates the native has come into this incarnation with a strong memory of experiences with Chiron. This native may or may not be slated to use that experience in this life, and the North Node needs to be examined very carefully. Since the polarity is Chiron/Neptune, the native may have lived a life of great healing, and they may be slated to live a life of mystical expression this time. The thing to watch out for is that the native may slide into becoming a healer because they know how to do it easily, but their North Node may indicate they are supposed to do something else now. Or, the North Node may indicate a way to take all that inner healing knowledge and funnel it into the work of the North Node. Chart #20, a yoga teacher, has Chiron on the South Node in the sixth house. The sixth house placement doubles the tendency for him to keep on healing. But the North Node in the twelfth in Taurus indicates that he is to activate teaching himself in some esoteric school, especially since the Node is in Taurus, indicating wide intellectual potential. He has a great background in Hebrew from his childhood as a Jew who was taken to temple, so possibly he should deepen that part of himself. As Schulman has amply demonstrated, we must get off the South Node and activate the North in order to grow. When there is a planet on the South and not on the North Node, as with the yoga teacher, extra care must be taken to see if the North Node is active.

Chiron conjunct the south Node usually means the native will have easy access to past life memory. If this native seems to be stuck on the South Node, it may be advisable to go after the past life contents. But caution is advised because this native may have a strong tendency to get caught in the glamour of past lives. The goal is to work free from the South Node so that the North is activated. When the native is active in living the North Node, then the time will come to pull in the past life memories as a healer or teacher on the South Node and utilize that information for further activation of the talents of the North Node.

There are many other aspects to the South and North Nodes, but the last really significant one is when *Chiron squares the Nodes,* as Schulman has taught.[10] Whenever a planet squares the Nodes, it functions as a significant distraction to the work of developing the life path with the Nodes. So when Chiron squares the Nodes, transmutation energy and higher consciousness functions as a blocking action to progress on the Nodes. That is, the native has a hard time activating the

North and letting go of the South while also funneling in the South Node knowledge to feed the North. However, it is even more complex than that. Ideally, we would activate the North and live it, then funnel in past life memory to further develop the South, and finally the Nodal Axis would develop into a channel of iridescent kundalini energy through the chart with the North Node as a pointer. When Chiron squares the Nodes, it tends to cause all parts of the Nodes to be activated, resulting in a short-term highly activated axis. Most of my clients who have this position had a life of great struggle up to the Uranus opposition, but they are also unusually talented and able to use past life knowledge in this incarnation.

Chapter Eleven

CHIRON MISCELLANEOUS

The sign that Chiron rules (Virgo) and the house that Chiron rules (the sixth) have not been defined until the publication of this book. Therefore, there are many miscellaneous "information holes" in almost all astrology books in print at the present time. It is a tremendous alteration of consciousness to shift awareness to this new dynamic, to let go of the Mercury archetype for the sixth house and Virgo. As shown earlier in the book, Virgo self-definition will move into an entirely new level of consciousness; our ways of resonation with Uranus, Saturn, and Neptune will move to another dimension; and the new role of Chiron as initiator and role leader of the consciousness dance of the higher self in the physical body will transform our senses of what is possible with astrological work. This chapter will attempt to pick up all the loose ends, to fill the information holes in astrology books in print, and then we will move into the most exciting part of this work—experience with Chiron himself now that we know him better.

THE NODES IN THE SIXTH AND TWELFTH HOUSES

The Nodes rule the karmic axis of the natal chart. When the North or South Node is located in the sixth house, it brings in a profound present or past life healing dynamic. We will begin with *the North Node in the sixth house.*

Looking back to the Mercury archetype ruling the sixth house, the interpretation has been that the native is very introspective and lost in a Neptunian inner world. Neptune rules the twelfth house, and therefore the Neptunian influence from past lives remains; but the rulership of Chiron on the North Node creates a whole new sense of potential palpable Neptunian focus which is very empowered. Schulman has noted a latent paranoia in this position, and I agree. But I am finding that this paranoia, coming from problems with boundary definition caused by unplaced Neptunian psychic invasion, can now be worked with by utilizing Chiron on the North.

Regarding Chiron/Neptune polarity, as previously covered, Neptune is to be visualized as an ever-widening funnel to the galactic or multi-dimensional realm which focalizes to an exact point in space and time at Chiron. Schulman says about the North Node in the sixth house, "In areas of work he is an unusually poor organizer, leaving many scattered ends behind him and always chores."[1] This dynamic is correct when the native is defined by Mercury, or when the Uranus side of Chiron is the influence. However, as soon as the native learns to balance Saturn and Uranus and activate Chiron, the energy changes to a focalized electromagnetic power tool. As I said earlier, the sixth house is the last of the lower houses; it is the gateway to the seventh (the other) in the chart. As we move into the zone of the other and relationships, we will never correctly perceive the mirroring teaching that we all require for transformation without the exacting focus of the sixth house. That is, we can never fully relate to another until we know exactly who we are by means of the work and healing we have developed in our life. Natives with the North Node in the sixth are our teachers about the most intense operation of this dynamic.

Schulman noted hypochondriacal tendencies with those who have the North Node in the sixth.[2] I agree, but now we have a new dimension. The native will need to experience various illnesses in order to learn to heal him or herself and develop healing skills. This dynamic can go to a new level if the native can be counseled on learning about electrical polarity (Uranus) by means of experiencing it, learning to hold to the Earth plane but let go of negativity (Saturn), and learning to identify Neptunian sticky stuff or possessions and clear the body so the higher self can reside. To put it simply, the device of the North Node in the sixth house is a perfectly engineered healing tool which can be consciously mastered, validated, and utilized on as many dimensions as possible.

Sigmund Freud, Chart #51, has the North Node in Aries retrograde in the sixth house. First of all, with the North Node in Aries, the native is letting go of lifetimes of balancing (Libra) and needs to aggressively activate singularity and force in this incarnation. Then he needs to funnel in the balancing of the South Node into the forceful energy projection of Aries with maturity. Then this energy projection ruled by Mars is funneled into the sixth house, which is a tremendous healing dynamic.

We have been passing through a long period of putting Freud down in favor of Jung, especially since Freud was not particularly interested in the mystic side. But we can see by examining Freud's chart that he was letting go of mysticism (the South Node in twelfth) in favor of exacting specification of energy. Freud succeeded fully in bringing to the planet the force of his North Node because he broke through the Victorian sexual inhibition block. He made it possible to examine sexuality scientifically, and for all of us to look closely at our childhood sexuality dynamic and examine its effect on us; to view it objectively. Notice that Venus is conjunct the North Node which doubled the effect.

Teilhard de Chardin, #32, has the North Node in the sixth in Sagittarius, and he activated cosmic healing under the Jupiterian quality focused into the sixth. Chart #21, a physician, has the North Node in the sixth in Capricorn which helps him focus the tremendous energy of the Uranus/Jupiter opposite Chiron/Mars in the sixth and twelfth, and then to access the T-square to the Sun/Neptune by crossing the polarity bridge. Without the North Node in the sixth, I believe he would be made almost nonfunctional by the T-square which involves six planets. The North Node focus has steered him in the direction of becoming a great healer. Chart #45, a glassblower, has the North Node in the sixth in Aries with Venus, Saturn, and the Moon in Virgo in the tenth house. This native has taken the great healing force of the North Node in the sixth in Aries and projected the beauty and balance into exquisite and healing glass pieces. Of seven other clients with the North Node in the sixth in Aries, four are exceedingly skilled therapists.

When the *South Node is in the sixth house,* the native must learn to ground the sixth house South Node in order to be able to fly out into the Neptunian funnel. This native is meant to learn to fly in this incarnation, but flying implies knowing what the takeoff point is. This position is unusual because it requires more living on the South Node than is usual in order to activate the Nodal Axis. Normally we like to see people aggressively live on the North Node and gradually funnel in South Node information, but how can anyone aggressively live on Neptune? Schulman notes that, "he must transcend the subconscious past life memories of physical problems that still weigh him down and start to climb the cosmic ladder which leads him to realization of his soul."[3] I agree, and I would go further and say that this native requires past life regression work. This native needs to recover the past life information about illness and healing skills as a ground for Neptune. This native then needs to activate a life skill as a healer, focus the skill perfectly into space and time, and then *samadhi* (being in touch will all dimensions) will flood consciousness. This position is literally the paradigm for comprehending work with Chiron. See Chart #28, an astrologer, as an excellent example of this dynamic. Once she did her past life work as published in *Eye of the Centaur,*⁴ she was freed up to be a teacher-astrologer. Before all the past life sessions, she felt overwhelmed by memories of ancient astrological skills, but she could not identify where they came from. There was no such information in modern books, and her knowledge confused her. The Sun conjunct the South Node in the sixth house and Chiron conjunct the North Node in the twelfth house drove her to find the energy identification in past life work. Neptune is confusion and sticky attachment until we can activate service and giving. Visualize it as a kite with yourself holding the string on Earth and yourself sailing in the sky.

Schulman notes that those with their South Node in the sixth must move through those subconscious places in the soul still harboring memories of past life illness in order to activate the North Node in the twelfth.⁵ My youngest child gave me great teaching on this dynamic. She has the South Node in Pisces in the sixth house. With the first Saturn square at age seven, children come fully into manifestation on the Earth plane. It is always very wise to watch them at the first square, because you can see which parts of themselves they are going to have trouble bringing into form. So, a few months ahead of her square, we had a talk. As I was talking to her about the stresses in school and at home, I was stroking her left leg. She suddenly screamed, "Don't touch my leg, it is wrapped in rags. They are throwing stones at me, I am falling in the street, and I can't walk." Generally, I do not present my esoteric point of view to my children, but she had never said anything like this before. I worked with her to convince her that her leg was fine, I enrolled her in ballet, and I made an appointment with a past life therapist for her. In my opinion, this was a serious indication of future manifestation of an illness in that leg which I decided to circumvent if possible. A few weeks before the scheduled appointment, and at the exact point of her Saturn square, she developed rheumatic fever, was unable to walk for ten days and suffered terrible leg pains. The illness is finished, she is healthy, she will soon do a few sessions with the therapist, but here is the interesting part of it. She has been a very emotional and passionate Scorpio with the usual dark and light attributes. In the middle of the illness she went into a mystical state and her heart chakra opened. She became extremely loving and responsive to all the people in her life and she began a new interest in the protection of animal rights. She has Jupiter conjunct the Moon in Leo in the tenth house, which she had not activated before. Her level of vibration is much higher since this illness, and I feel she managed to release past lives of illness so that she is free to manifest North Node in the twelfth. Also, the rather dramatic heart chakra opening seems to have freed her to bestow her loving healing powers on her family, animals and friends, which will give her more access to Neptune.

Chart #4 has the South Node in the sixth. This sanctuary worker was very confused and exhibited a lot of Neptunian delusion until she found a way to help El Salvadoreans. She considers the people she helps to be her greatest gift. Chart #20, a yoga teacher, has the South Node in Scorpio in the sixth. He is burning off a lot of past life Pluto energy by giving much of his energy as a teacher. He has a great access to Neptune in meditation.

NORTH OR SOUTH NODE IN VIRGO

The Lunar North Node represents growth in this incarnation; the highest evolution in this lifetime. We attain great progress by interpreting the highest level of development of the planetary rulership of it. When the North Node is in Virgo, it is ruled by Chiron, and the meaning of this lifetime is to develop the Rainbow Bridge between the inner and outer planets to the most Chirotic degree. This native is meant to fully actualize healing and alchemical skills; the native will benefit from consciously developing high Saturn attributes such as discipline, efficient use of time, and dedication; and the native will have unusual Uranian potential or powerful flow of early kundalini energy and stong polarity resolution. This native will benefit unusually from Chirotic tools such as divination skills, crystals, and funnel meditations. Any physical or mental meditation work which aims to develop focus in place and time on the Earth plane while letting go of the self to the galactic will be very beneficial. It is axiomatic with this position that the native will feel out of place (as if he or she were dropped here from another planet) until Chirotic skills are developed. Unlike many of us, the native will feel crazy inside until he or she develops a firm and balanced form (Saturn) which can access and hold higher consciousness (Uranus).

We have worked with Chiron in the houses in Chapter Six. The Nodes in the houses are not the subject matter of this work, and I refer all readers to Schulman's *Karmic Astrology* for this information. In my opinnion, it is *the* definitive work.[6] But, since many astrologers find Node interpretation difficult, and since I start the natal study with it, I will work with the house position of the North Node in Virgo placement. In case it is not clear, I do not begin work with the client on the Nodes. But the Nodal Axis is like a compass in the chart, with the vertical ascension needs on the North, the deep subconscious content recovery matter on the South, and the horizontal energy spread on the East and West.

When *the North Node is in Virgo in the first house,* natives exhibit healing power as an attribute of the self. They make everyone feel good just to be near them. The goal is to open the heart chakra completely and radiate Christos power to all encountered. There is danger of heart problems with this position, especially when natives lose someone to whom they are radiating love. Neptune is on the South Node in the seventh, of course, and these natives must love unconditionally and practice Neptunian letting go. Above all, they must trust the universe and simply radiate.

With *the North Node in Virgo in the second house,* it is critical for these natives to actively heal in their environments or professions. They are grounding Chirotic power on the physical plane and in their value system throughout the whole life, as they slowly let go of past life Plutonic karma. If they do not actually ground themselves as healers, they are in grave danger of being swallowed by past life guilt and negativity. As mentioned before, all can be healers—a mother at home with her children, and a janitor who lovingly creates a clean and welcoming environment is just as much of a healer as a great big guru.

The North Node in Virgo in the third house is very strong. The native needs to find a way to develop Chirotic powers in communication. Obviously, someone doing great media work has it all in place, but the key to getting this energy actually has to do with consciousness. In whatever way this native heals he or she must learn to send energy to all sources in place and time. This native possesses remarkable skill at long distance healing. My favorite example of successful work with this position is with an ecologist. He was busy breeding new salmon fry in a fish hatchery. I suggested he try meditating that the breeding power he was working with could be projected to breeding salmon in the various river systems. He did it. There is quite a bit of evidence that the salmon population in the Pacific Northwest is increasing, and he got an incredible Neptunian cosmic charge from doing this. This kind of work is really fun, so why not enjoy it? The New Age musician of Chart #36 has this position, and we can feel the universe resonating when she plays. The healer of Chart #48 has her North Node in Virgo in the third house, and her powers to manifest energy at a distance are amazing. It is important to comment that energy changes to a new dynamic with the kind of changes I am describing. We are moving to a critical mass in a new energy synchronization which is causing a new awareness that we actually change matter according to what we are thinking about. Those with the North Node in the third in Virgo need to spend some time meditating each day on clearing all forms of pollution. They can actually clear radiation and chemical pollution with their minds.

The North Node in Virgo in the fourth house has been a very tough position to live with until now. The North Node in the fourth indicates a movement into nurturing and away from power and control in past lives. With the previous Virgo archetype, we would need to work with the movement into nurturing as partly a being struggle to overcome being too critical and controlling. Schulman almost seems to sense the real presence of Chiron ruling Virgo on the North Node, because he emphasizes the Virgo drive toward health. At any rate, this native must nurture the self and go deep within the subconscious for healing. Once the work on self has reached a certain point, the native will have the skill to become a very good healing therapist, particularly as a Jungian. When this native as therapist travels with clients into the inner journey, he and she will heal their clients just by going along.

The North Node in the fifth house indicates the native possesses special energy to heal children or heal with the creative process. Saturn is strengthened to deal with all the details of children or the creative process, and Uranus frees up the imagination, and then the bridge to Neptune is built.

The North Node in Virgo in the sixth house is very powerful. It is similar to the power of the North Node in Scorpio in the eighth house. It indicates that this being is meant to be a healer in this lifetime, and that he or she will do so with the full planetary energy of Chiron, the planet ruling healing. Balance between Saturn and Uranus plus access to Neptune is critical for this native, so astrologers must examine the planetary rulerships, house positions, and aspects of Saturn, Uranus, and Neptune very carefully. This native will never be free to really live this lifetime without activating and living healing skills.

The North Node in Virgo in the seventh house indicates that the native is a healer of others by means of being in relationship with them. Their whole reason to be in a relationship with others is to *heal* them; therefore, more latitude needs to be given for their behavior. Astrologers can help by assisting them in being realistic about what they are doing, being careful that they are not getting walked all over. These natives begin to blossom when they learn that pity for someone else is always negative, that compassion toward someone else is the level of healing they desire. One of my more interesting clients with this position is a nun who has been the lover of a few priests over the years. She seems to rescue them as they are drying up from lack of nurturance from the feminine in their lives.

   The North Node in Virgo in the eighth house is a difficult position until age forty. This position seems to continually want to take the native on a trip through the Underworld to get to the real essence, or it encourages the native to try to find higher consciousness by means of sex. The only way this position can evolve is with experience, and much of the life experience isn't finished until after Uranus opposition when the higher vibration of Pluto comes into essence. The Pluto square Pluto usually in the forties is a powerful breakthrough for this native. Once the evolutionary nature of Pluto is mastered, this being becomes a vortex of alchemical energy. The occult is very confusing to this native until they have lived a long time. See Chart #39.

   The North Node in Virgo in the ninth house is a wonderful position for a spiritual teacher. Jupiter and Chiron work beautifully together because Chiron is the pathway to Jupiter and then Jupiter benevolently allows full access to Neptune. Neptune should be carefully examined to see if afflictions indicate difficulties with confusion. If there are aspects such as Moon square Neptune, then extra work needs to be done on the nature of Chirotic focus. Some of the funnel meditations for locating Chiron firmly and accessing Neptune will help. This native has something very important to communicate.

   The North Node in Virgo in the tenth is a wonderful position for anyone working with power in healing. But great care should be taken to watch for "power over" in healing. *No one ever heals anyone else;* all we can do is bring in structural balancing energies which can help others to realign themselves, or to be able to advise and direct others. The degree to which we realize we are only channels for the divine and learn to get out of the way is the degree to which we have access to healing energies. This position is a potential gift of high karma to the native, and they will be catapulted into key positions of power to be able to bring in healing forces for others. Misuse of this power will create much negative karma.

   The North Node in Virgo in the eleventh house is an extremely selfless position. The eleventh house is the crisis of whether we will be able to align our truest purpose with the culture in a way that will result in manifestation. I believe that the eleventh house North Node is the nodal position that is most frequently non-actualized at this time, because the culture as a whole is so out of synch with the real needs of people for their spirituality. My clients who have this position are all frustrated. I have made the least progress with them, and I have tried. All I can advise is to work hard on the true purpose and add Chirotic focusing counseling. Crystals may help to unblock this native. I feel the New Age energy coming in will prove to be a great boon to those with this position.

The North Node in Virgo in the twelfth house creates a tremendous crisis in consciousness. As noted at the end of Chapter Ten, these natives will usually experience much illness in early childhood in order to learn how to heal themselves and others. They are meant to become great healers and teachers, but they cannot do that without living through and experiencing much of what they will later help other people deal with. They are deep and thoughtful; they need a lot of time and patience, and the information that their experience is teaching them for future work is very helpful. Past life regression and deep subconscious therapy is recommended whenever these clients are stuck and losing touch with reality.

The Lunar South Node is the indicator of past life experience which is significant for this incarnation. During the first twenty years of life as we are growing up, we will re-experience the past life material which we need at this time, and the childhood environment we have chosen will present various opportunities to resurface that material and have a present life experience with it. That is why conflicts in the psyche exist in the memory bank from previous times *and* early environments. So, as we work with the South Node, we must view all those contents lovingly because they are our most significant library of experience. We must lovingly understand them, be with them until we have sufficient experience, and then empty ourselves of that library. Finally, we can go back to the beginning of the universe so that we can become everything we have chosen in this most significant life, the present.

The Virgo South Node indicates we have brought in significant experience as a healer from before and that we are to be cosmic receptors of the divine in whatever house the North Node in Pisces is located. As said before, this is a very tough position to comprehend because how does one focus on Neptune? There is only one way: you must let go of all need to define and know; you must release all positionality; you must literally walk away from what you have known for twenty billion years; you must empty yourself. Why do it? We are on the verge of synchronization with the galactic vibration; our whole planet going to resonate with the galaxy soon. This new vibration on Earth is unknown to us so far. Old thought forms, energetics, and responses will get in the way. Those with the Virgo South Node are here now to show us the way to clear and open ourselves to the new energy. As Schulman says, they are here to learn faith. It is the kind of faith that can be learned only by jumping off a cliff.

When *the South Node is in Virgo in the first house,* we see the dynamic of letting go the most dramatically. This native must give him or herself with deep compassion to others in various relationships, and he or she is meant to bring through the past life healing skills and give them in relationships. The native must completely let go of personal ego and sense of self. All South Node in Virgo positions are hard to work out. One cannot relate compassionately without a knowledge of the self first, and this native will have worked very hard on knowing the self during the first twenty years. But a feeling of boredom with "just me" will come, because Neptune is calling for expansion and compassion with others. A sense of direction on this position will often relieve much deep anxiety for clients.

When *the South Node is in Virgo in the second house,* the battle to let go of personal needs and karma intensifies. This position may be the toughest one I have ever seen. However, with great difficulty comes great reward. The native is usually heavily involved in relationships with people who have really negative sexual and power difficulties. Finally it gets tiresome as the native begins to mature, and he or she usually discovers that survival is not possible without self-discipline. This is the beginning of evolution. These natives almost always have a significant brush with death which opens their eyes. This is characteristic of the South Node in the second house in general, but it is intensified by Chiron, because Chiron rules the death of an issue so that new birth can occur. Once this native gets the first glimpse of the new energy, the new creation, the potential energy for letting go of the old and allowing the new is the most intense in the zodiac. This is a lifetime of heavy karmic burnoff. Counseling on Neptune will help; advice on empowering Saturn plus sacred initiations such as a warrior may be called for.

When *the South Node is in Virgo in the third house,* the native is freeing him or herself from past life dualities and multifaceted experiences. The native is called to *learn to focus,* but the planetary rulership of the point of focus (Neptune ruling the North Node), seems to be confusing. In fact it is not; once this native focuses on spirituality and the divine, the energy works. The native can funnel in the power of past life healer in the third house like a funnel of information to the focus in the ninth. This is the penultimate position for a mystic.

When *the South Node is in Virgo in the fourth house,* natives must let go of the need to nurture as healers and must empower Neptune and mysticism as much as possible in their careers and in the world around them. They must learn to activate higher consciousness in power situations, to be able to respond and give to many people who depend on them, once they have learned to give unconditionally within their own families. Eventually, they will love being in the center of a lot of demands, and responding to others will cause spiritual expansion and heart chakra opening. This position usually does not mature until after Uranus opposite Uranus.

When *the South Node is in Virgo in the fifth house,* the native must become completely selfless and ask for nothing. This is a very tough position. It usually signals that the native was an egotistical guru or healer before, that he or she used others indiscriminately for personal satisfaction, and now that behavior must be reversed. The divine deals with this need for balancing by placing the native in a very humble position so that the old tricks will no longer work. The beauty of this lifetime is that it ends up being freedom from the dimly remembered past life powerful self-will that was almost consuming. This is a simple and subtle letting go which manifests by giving great inner healing energy without anyone else seeing it. It is critical that this native opens the heart and sees the beauty of his or her life, for any form of skepticism is poisonous to growth.

When *the South Node is in Virgo in the sixth house,* the native has chosen a life of mysticism based upon extreme development of skill as a healer in past lives. As noted before, this position in the polarity is peculiar because this being cannot get to mysticism and Neptune until the extreme progress of the lifetime before is comprehended. First, the consciousness connection with past life skills must be recovered, used for a long time in this lifetime, and then let go with extreme awareness of how we all return to the source in time. This position indicates a wisdom beyond time and space that is a function of the hologram of the divine.

When *the South Node is in Virgo in the seventh house,* the native needs to let go of the needs of others to find cosmic fusion. The native will have much service for others during much of his or her life, will have a tendency to get caught up in giving, but finally the North Node will need to be activated. He or she will enter into contemplation and mysticism after giving healing and care for many years.

When *the South Node is in Virgo in the eighth house,* the native is called to ground Neptune in the second house, but first he or she must let go of much negativity from past life sexual and occult experiences. As always with the second and eighth house paradigm, he or she can only work through the karma experience; therefore, much latitude must be given for behavior up to age forty. As always with Pluto, there is a limit to the experience; something must be learned from it or it will be self-destructive. Finally, this native will burn up with Neptune and Pluto doing a karmic dance, or he or she will transmute to grounded mysticism. Chart #22, an astrologer, can be examined for this position. These natives usually have remarkable gifts of occult skill.

When *the South Node is in Virgo in the ninth house,* the native has created a dynamic for bringing in great skills from past lives as a spiritual teacher and leader in higher consciousness. Neptune in the third will activate strongly into communication and integration in the third and funnel in past lives of healing skills very effectively. These will be some of your favorite clients because they will come to life when they learn there is a spiritual purpose to existence which becomes empowered when we identify it. See Charts #12 and #37 for this dynamic.

When *the South Node is in Virgo in the tenth house,* the native is letting go of power and control as a healer and bringing the force of the energy into nurturing. Success, recognition, and power mean nothing because the native has had it all, remembers it, and is interested in the subtle attributes of healing and nurturing this time. For natives with this position, the healing of a child and/or tender caring for a mate means more than all the fame in the world. Chart #1, a physicist, is a great example of this dynamic from two points of view. He is very well-known and revered, but he would rather be with his family than anyone. But he has also made the world his family because he has his Sun in Virgo and is very ecologically minded. So he teaches about the universe as our home, and he helps people see that we all find life in the midst of our feeling for connection in the universe.

When *the South Node is in Virgo in the eleventh house,* the native was a healer and teacher on a grand scale in past lives and came in to let it go this time. This native has chosen to discover the joy of individual creativity this time and to learn to enjoy children. This native is learning to let go of past life power and recognition and enjoy the small things in life. Ego investment will block the growth of this native from finding the simple child within. See Chart #5, a guru, as an example of a native with this dynamic who could not let go of past life obsession with being a teacher because Chiron and Venus are on the North Node in Pisces in the fifth.

When *the South Node is in Virgo in the twelfth house,* the native was probably a great mystic in past lives and now has come back to bring the skill into the physical plane as a healer. This native will benefit greatly from recovering past life healing skills and activating them on a very pragmatic level in this life. We are letting go of the cosmic dimensions and again choosing experience here for more teaching for our evolution.

THE PART OF FORTUNE IN VIRGO AND THE SIXTH HOUSE

The Part of Fortune is the way of blessing, or joy in the natal chart. It shows what it is that makes the native feel the best on all levels. After doing many years of therapy, I have discovered this in one of the most important elements in the chart because most people will not make progress unless they feel good about the work. It is just basic human nature. Often we need to work hard to help people restructure their personality to enable them to face feelings and realities which actually make them feel bad. But, more often, we are much more successful if we work to create a new dynamic which is in tune with that which they really like, the Part of Fortune. When I read, I do the Ascendant first, the Sun second, the Moon third, and then I see how the basic trilogy of the chart works with the Part of Fortune. I work on the Part of Fortune attunement so that we have something to use as a basic emotional dynamic when we move into the stressful parts of the chart later. As with the Nodes, I recommend Schulman's *Karmic Astrology III* as the definitive book on the Part of Fortune.[7]

When *the Part of Fortune is in Virgo,* the native feels the best when really well located and grounded in the Earth plane so that he or she is free to explore higher consciousness. This native will not really be content until Saturn is mastered so that structure and control are instinctual. Because the rulership is Chiron, the goal is perfect attunement in space and time with healing energies so that the soul can come into the body. The point opposite the Part of Fortune is called the IC, or Point of Impersonal Consciousness, as named by Schulman. This is where the cosmic energy funnels into the chart in order to activate the Part. The dynamic is very much like the Chiron/Neptune polarity. The Part/IC axis may even be the dynamic which Chiron leads just as Chiron rules the Tarot reader. That is, Chiron ruling the Part is the dance point which sucks in the Neptunian/IC energy. For example, the Tarot reader takes all the representations of differing energetics of the spiritual dimensions and focuses them into a card reading dynamic which is accurate according to the degree it reflects the *feelings* of the person being read to. The Part of Fortune is the point which accesses our *feelings* about *all* reality. So the goal of the Virgo Part is the moment in time when the dance of life becomes unconscious; it is the dance of the magician or jester in medieval times. When I teach astrodrama, my personal goal is to be in that state of consciousness as much as possible so that the maximum Neptune energy can suck in and flow through the movements. This client needs help to learn a discipline which will become the tool for the cosmic dance and learn to let go into the synchronous flow of magic. See Chart #1, a physicist; #3, a New Age publisher; #6, a self healer, and #8, a Hermetic teacher.

When the Part of Fortune is in the sixth house, the native finds joy as soon as he or she learns to live in the present moment. The native needs to master Saturnian details and not get caught in them, and to be able to flow with Uranian electrical energy. More than anything else, he or she needs to let go of trying to control reality as soon as the necessary everyday details are being handled well. This is a somewhat difficult dynamic because the Part in the sixth causes a great and early talent development which causes some personal suffering due to jealousy from partners. These natives need help in affirming that they simply have remarkable talents which actually have nothing to do with who they really are. They need to see that any ego attachment they have to these talents will disrupt their personal lives. Once they learn the trick of utilizing the skills effectively in a quiet manner, they can enjoy the fruits of the skills on the Earth plane without being attached and attracting envy. In fact, they can come to the realization that their easy mastery of skills offers them more time for Neptunian mysticism and time for compassion and sharing with partners. When they let it go, they have it all. See Chart #20, a yoga teacher; #25, an artist; and #30, a jeweler.

CHIRON RETROGRADE

Retrograde planets are best understood from a *magnetic perspective,* from an energy point of view, and their activity is best understood conceptually as a time dynamic. Direct planets are electrical, and they cause energy to charge and move; retrograde planets are magnetic and draw energy into the chart. Therefore, when Chiron is retrograde it draws in healing, initiatory, and alchemical powers. Going through my files, I noticed that the clients with Chiron retrograde are more alluring, more fascinated by magic and the occult themselves, and they draw this energy to themselves. The time dynamic refers to the fact that retrograde planets tend to function in the past, present, and future simultaneously. In the short run on the physical plane, this time dynamic is confusing because with direct planets the action just starts at a point in time and goes forward, and it is more easily observed, but this time dynamic lends great subtlety to the psyche.

The outer planets are retrograde more frequently than the inner planets; the Sun and Moon are never retrograde, of course; and it can be asserted that the energies of the outer planets are the most subtle due to the longer retrograde phases. The time dynamic goes to an extremely subtle level with Chiron. The three aspects of the deity in Druidic theology are *Beli* (future destroyer), *Yesu* (present and savior), and *Taran* (past and creator). This triple deity is present for those who have Chiron retrograde. That is, they are worried about the future and meaning of the destructive forces; they feel the essence of the present or savior; they search for the esoteric meaning of the past or creation. That is the tune they dance to, and the sooner they can identify the effect it is having on their consciousness, the sooner they can put it into perspective. This is a deep and intense response to the universe which offers great wisdom and creativity as soon as it is integrated into the psyche. The house position of Chiron retrograde will describe the avenue of perception of this powerful vortex of perceptual sensitivity.

VIRGO/PISCES INTERCEPTED AND CHIRON INTERCEPTED

When Virgo/Pisces is intercepted, the dynamic is a *place dynamic*. Many find retrograde planets and interceptions hard to understand, but great progress is made as soon as it is clear that retrogrades are a *time* dynamic altering perception, and interceptions are a *place* dynamic altering perception. With an interception, the houses intercepted indicate a past and present life karmic dynamic; i.e., they show a past-life karmic failure which will be dealt with in this lifetime no matter what.

Interceptions are very Chirotic because they are always a sign that the soul has set up the dynamic to force the issue in this lifetime. It is as if Uranus is going to electrify and push consciousness until Saturn takes control of the past-life failure, and disciplines the soul into manifesting the issue. Be prepared for a strong statement: I have never yet had a client with an interception who wasn't mastering their karmic failure and giving the gift indicated by the interception. I have puzzled over this for years, and I didn't understand what might be happening until I really experienced the teaching which says that we have the same rising sign degree with each incarnation in a cycle; that the Sabian symbol is a reading of the soul throughout all lifetimes. So when there is an interception the client has created an alteration in the dynamic in order to accomplish something very karmic. And the Virgo/Pisces intercept is the most Chirotic and karmic of all.

The Virgo/Pisces polarity is the polarity of bringing the soul into space and time in the body through ecstatic mystical experiences *or* healing skills. When Virgo/Pisces is intercepted, the native is going to bring the higher self into the body and access Neptune, and this incarnation is directly related to a primary past lifetime where they had the opportunity to bring the soul into the body and refused to do so. Great karma was generated by this refusal; that is, others were deeply damaged through the refusal. Often the damaged ones are all around you now. It might not have been much fun to run into this native the last significant lifetime around, but it sure is great to have him or her walk into your office this time.

Astrologers can help clients handle interceptions perhaps better than any other dynamic in the chart, because one of the few opportunities for this level of identification of esoteric purpose is in an astrological reading. Let's discuss what the interception feels like and then go into how to work on it, while discussing it specifically as Virgo/Pisces. I'm offering extra details here because this issue has not been well covered or understood in the field so far, in my opinion.

The intercepted house polarity is the part of consciousness that the native feels like a complete failure about, when it is in fact the part of themselves that is developing the most. If you ask a native how he or she functions in the area delineated, you will hear a tale of failure or guilt. That is because he or she feels guilty about it, as if it could never be made up, and the native isn't even conscious of the tremendous accomplishment in that area since birth. If you ask other people, they will rave about the contribution of this person in that area. To avoid confusion, a good example is Chart #49, an astrologer. Her interception of Virgo in the ninth and Pisces in the third shows that she was supposed to bring her soul into the body and manifest her energy as a spiritual teacher, and that she once refused. This woman is considered to be a great teacher at the present time by all who know her, she never stops working on the issue, and yet she feels she isn't making it. The interception never stops driving us to bring in that gift that was once asked from us and which we refused to give. Chiron retrograde doubles the energy.

What to do about it? First of all, pointing it out is *very* powerful. The native almost can't resist drawing in a deep breath over having this struggle recognized. Next, you must coach the native to acknowledge very carefully all the progress they have made, because in fact it is always prodigious. The native must go through a series of affirmations of progress in order to placate the past life guilt that is driving him or her into believing the gift cannot be brought in. Guilt is never a healthy dynamic. This is the critical teaching which was highly developed in ancient Egypt. We are supposed to understand this teaching by observing the Sphinx and great pyramids which could not have been constructed by ordinary means. In ancient Egypt, the initiate would lighten a stone with third-eye power, and then move the stone into place. Next, with a priest, the initiate would work on very intense affirmations that the stone had actually moved. The training priest would work with the initiate on the *actuality* of the magical act, that the initiate *did* move that stone.

In a reading the vision can be refocused on the gift being brought in, and it can be consciously given with no reservations. We must stop holding back, we must see that what we *are* is in direct proportion to how we define ourselves. We can, in fact, bring in the most subtle and powerful parts of our natal chart. The time has come, and the universe accepts it. Chart #25, an artist, has Virgo intercept in the eighth and Pisces in the second, meaning she refused to ground and develop a value system of healing and higher consciousness and that she is actively doing that now. Chart #11, a physician, has Virgo intercept in the fifth, meaning he is destined to be a healer with his creativity. He is seventy; he has in fact given much as a creative healer, but he has been unable to acknowledge his progress and let go of the guilt. There is still time.

When Chiron as a planet is intercepted, the Chirotic force was suppressed during a significant past life related to this one, and the native is driven to bring the energy in now. This is a powerful position for alchemical manifestation. These natives need special guidance on activating their inherent healing powers. See Chart #20, a yoga teacher, with Chiron in Scorpio intercepted in the sixth house.

Chapter Twelve

THE CHIROTIC CYCLE AND INITIATING THE CLIENT

The Chirotic cycle in the transit history of the natal chart refers to the cycle of Chiron squaring itself; then in its own opposition to its natal position, its upper square; and the Chiron return about age 50. This book will not cover Chiron transiting the planets and houses in the horoscope because there has been so much completely new material to cover, but readers should be able to understand the effects of Chiron transits easily once they have mastered the archetype of Chiron.

In order to understand Chiron transiting the houses, the basic qualities of each house must be understood as a function of the house cusp, interceptions or sign changes within, any planets contained within that house, and the opposing house and aspecting planets. Once this basic comprehension of the twelve houses in each nativity is attained, as Chiron transits each house, it will create a new form within each house which will create an opportunity for a new awareness in that house. For example, imagine a chart with early Taurus rising with Mercury/Sun/ and the North Node in the first house in Taurus. This native will be very grounded, bringing in much Venusian energy which the ego will identify strongly with. This native will have a difficult time getting out of the body to the other planes and will spend many years developing the ego. But sometime during the first forty-nine years of life, Chiron will transit the first house and break up the ego hold, and this native will suddenly resonate with new consciousness energy which, the native never even imagined existed. There will be a letting go of all the trying for breaking out of the ego egg, and the self will simply shatter. How this dynamic will function will depend upon the age of the person when this transit occurs.

When Chiron transits any natal planet, the energy of that planet is

195

alchemized. The Earth plane form and meaning of that planet is explored and deepened, and as soon as the form and structure of that
energy is fully grasped, Uranus will come in and begin to manifest that
form into higher octaves. In any given lifetime, by age 50, Chiron has
transited every planet in the natal chart, i.e., it has alchemized all the personality dynamics, and it has opened the doors to the outer planets in
consciousness. Later, I will show how you can use this cycle to understand the initiatory cycle of any client, but right now the concept must be
grasped so that you can easily understand the way Chiron alchemizes or
Chiroticizes the planets and natal energy.

For example, imagine a natal chart which has Uranus in the tenth
house. This native has chosen this position to manifest higher consciousness in career issues in outer worldly forms. On the mundane
level, the native might work with electronics; on the more esoteric level
he or she might practice tantric yoga. As soon as Chiron transits the
tenth house Uranus, at whatever age, the physical vehicle will be transmuted so that it can take in and hold electrical energy—the chakras will
clear, for example—and then this native will become a positively charged
magnetic receptor for electrical energy.

In order to avoid sounding outrageous, it needs to be noted that this
energy has only been manifesting fully since Chiron's sighting in 1977.
And you will not understand this chapter well until you have worked with
Chiron yourself already, or if you have been cross checking the Chiron
functions in this book with other charts and your own chart. The Earth
plane was not capable of accepting this force, grounding it and transmit-
ting it into the individual until 1977. But it has been happening since
then, and it is the *only* working explanation for the intensification of
transmutative powers since 1977. We just did not have a guide until
then. I am going to let this go and move into Chiron's special cycle, the
Chirotic cycle, but readers can learn more about Chiron by transit by
consulting Zane Stein's *Essence and Application: A View from Chiron.*[1]
Zane has worked with the various life events which will typically manifest
with Chiron transits, and I agree with his results.

The planets which rule the three major human life transits at this
time are Saturn, Chiron, and Uranus. These life transits are the breakthrough points from physical to emotional to mental to soul bodies. We
are all composed of these four bodies which are each an entity but not
separate; they exist within ourselves, and the natal chart is a hologram or
unifying energy structure which shows how they exist and interrelate.
Ideally, we exist within all four bodies in balance at all times, but in fact,

that is not what really happens. We are actually in and out of the various bodies at different times, and we have varying levels of control over their influence on our behavior and feelings. The natal aspects show how the four bodies function. That is a whole book in itself, and we must focus on Chiron.

The best way to grasp this concept of psychic function is with an example. When I was ready to graduate with my Master's degree, I went to the office to deal with the last details of payments and credits. I was to leave a few days after graduation for a job—based on my degree—two thousand miles away. The person behind the bars informed me that I was two credits short! I felt all my energy suck out of myself as my physical body split in horror. My heart began to pound, and I turned red as my emotional body ran down the stairs. I found myself unable to talk to the person as my mental body flew straight up, and I felt abandoned by my spirit as even my soul left. I was helpless!

Those experiences where you get weak in the knees and feel empty mean that some or all of your bodies have left. This is a human defense mechanism to save us from too much pain, and we know that we jump right out of our body in accidents or death. In order to grasp the Chirotic cycle, we need to understand that the goal of life is to master fear—to *not* jump out of the body—and then all the bodies are balanced in the self, and we can manifest our destiny. The point is that we are always working with these parts of our selves in different ways, but there is a progression of embodiment which is indicated astrologically. If you tune into this progression revealed by the three major transits you will make rapid progress, for this ancient spiritual teaching of the bodies or human organizing principle can now be completed by Chiron. Everything comes in threes, and we only had two parts before—Saturn return and Uranus opposition.

We are meant to finally bring all of ourselves into the body, and that is the goal of each incarnation cycle; it is what happens when we become whole. The best way to image this issue is with Figure 8, which is a triangle showing that the bodies start to vibrate faster as we move from physical into astral or emotional, to mental, to soul. But even that is the ideal, and Chris Griscom has pointed out in *Ecstasy is a New Frequency*[2] that the emotional body actually vibrates more slowly right now than the physical body because of the density of the emotional karma at this point. The emotional body is heavy and pregnant with many unresolved past lives.

The astrological cycle works like this: we work on the physical body

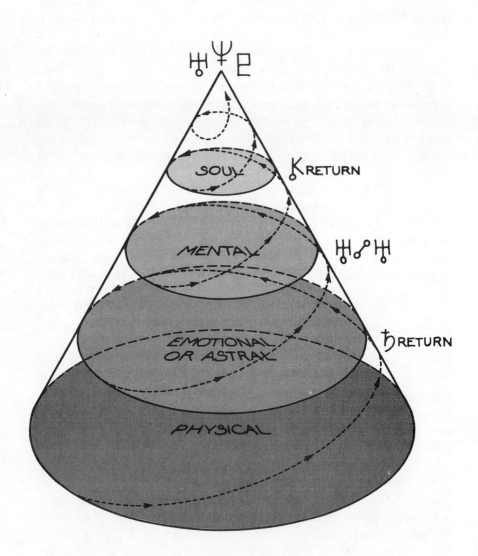

Figure 8
Spiraling Energy Within the Four Planes

issues—work, education, finances, etc.—until age 29 as Saturn transits around the natal chart, working through all the issues of this lifetime. At the Saturn return we experience a physical plane crisis such as job or relationship change which propels us into work on the astral or emotional plane, where we work from age 30 to about 38. Emotional plane issues are the work on our feelings, on our ability to express ourselves. Then as Uranus approaches its opposition, the electrical force surges up the spine and clears through the chakras at Uranus opposite Uranus. It is not that simple, as usually the heart chakra is blocked in males and the throat chakra in women. There may be a heart attack for men, or women may lose their voice in some way. But the energy does its best to blast through the channels. We have an emotional crisis called "mid-life crisis" in conventional circles as we let go of youth and integrate the opposite male or female polarity of self. Then, as we let go of emotional issues, we move onto the mental plane about age forty-two when we develop our purpose for this incarnation. The *real* mid-life crisis sets in at age 42-43 if we have *not* yet done the work of Uranus opposite Uranus.

The last part of the cycle is the Chiron return at age 50-51, when we intensify our vibration again, and we have a mental crisis—a crisis of *meaning.* We are to let go of our ego attachment, of our linear mentality; we are to let go completely now because this transit will empty us so that the soul can come in completely into form. Obviously, few have achieved this transit because it has been getting the full physical plane integration only since 1977. However, the cycle has always been with us and has always been known as the path to enlightenment.

One of my most clear examples of this transit is what happened to St. Thomas Aquinas when he reached age 50. Thomas is a great example, because his mental or left brain development was so intense during his lifetime. But just like everybody else, it was time for the right brain, the mystical response. Thomas' scribe reported that at age 50, Thomas, became blind and dumb and transmitted a last work which is called the *Aurora Consurgens.*[3] The "Aurora" is available in Marie Louise von Franz's book on alchemy, and it is a completely Chirotic alchemical tract. Readers might want to read it as a fine example of a Chirotic breakthrough. After he finished it, Aquinas died. Ideally, we all would have a fourth major life transit at the Uranus return at 84.

The point of our spiritual growth is to *vibrate at an increasingly higher frequency* as we mature and to pass through the gates of the three major life transits with as much force as possible. These three transits are critical because we have great Eros or life force at the point of each transit, which we can utilize to vibrate faster. If we do not move with the energy at each transit point, we can begin death, or Thanatos. So, some people start dying at 30, some at 42, some at 51, and others vibrate faster and faster and move to enlightenment. Also, there are some very negative results if we resist the major life transits and do *not* evolve. For example, one of the most difficult phases for counselors and therapists to cope with is the 42 to 45 year old client who had resisted growth at Uranus opposite Uranus. The client feels empty inside because he or she didn't evolve enough to identify their life's purpose. But, the power of Uranus opposite Uranus has waned, and they lack sufficient electrical energy for transformation. It is sad, but the time is past. There are other ways to work with the problem, especially utilizing Pluto square Pluto. But, it is just so much *easier* to do the work at the time of the transit. This concept cannot be comprehended if you want to get out of your body or out of the incarnational cycle. It is just the opposite: you chose this body, this cycle, *for a reason,* and you are to activate that choice holographically in all parts and cells of your being.

It is my belief that the balance between Eros and Thanatos affects our environment generally, that there is an imbalance at this time of too many waking dead people who have resisted transits, which has knocked our planet out of balance. The film, *Night of the Living Dead* was very prophetic. It is time to see that we are all in *energetic relationship* to each other. If the people around you are sick, you can get sick. As you begin to really understand Chiron, you will begin to feel that sickness as imbalance (even at a distance) which can affect you and the planet as a whole. For example, radiation is not *out there,* it is in the cells of all beings on the planet now that it has been released from its molecular matrix.

It is the sacred duty of astrologers at this time to help people pass through the gates of the three major life transits by helping them attune their dynamic to an increasingly rapidly vibrating frequency which is the life force, Eros. Saturn represents the force of Thanatos when growth stops, and this planet will end up being a dead ball of lead unless we quicken it with Uranus. And so the Chirotic cycle is the cycle which relates and balances Saturn's need for correct form here and Uranus' need to quicken our frequency. It is actually easier to live than to die. Uranus is much more stimulating than Saturn, and so we must gently coax people to let go of Saturn at the appropriate times. The transit times are the appropriate times because they will move us into a new level of organization naturally. So, first we must master the function of these three planetary transits so we can assist in the passages through the gates. And in a more general sense, we must begin to work with the Chirotic cycle itself because it is the only energy we have which seems to have the power to help people choose life over death. We just cannot do it without a guide, yet.

On a general level, sexuality needs to be looked at closely as we deal with the Chirotic cycle and Chiron transits. Now that Chiron has been sighted, we are ready to stop understanding sex *only* on the genital level. Sexuality is the *life force* which charges all the chakras with Eros, so that we can experience fusion with the divine—systemic orgasm—so that we can move *through* ourselves and all matter to the level of true purpose, which is living without a why, as defined by Matthew Fox.[4] Sexuality is meant to be an all-pervasive energizing force and not just a genital focus.

However, astrologers need to prepare themselves for the fact that Chiron actions can be very erotic, and that many people will confuse Eros with genital sex and try to act out the energy in the lower chakras instead of allowing it to flow through the system and clear all the chakras. They need help to not fear this erotic energy and to let it move through the system to clear the chakras. We must realize that we need Uranus in the spine and chakra system, and not Pluto. (See figure 9) Pluto exists in the root chakra as the unfurling snake energy in the body. It is kundalini energy, and people need help to not resist and to not focus only in the genitals.

The Chirotic cycle begins with the first square of Chiron to itself. The first square within the dynamic of any planet is always its first awareness of itself, and so with the first Chiron square, the first experience with transmutation occurs. What does that mean? As explained earlier in the book, Chiron's orbit is extremely elliptical; it is not circular, and it rules spiraling forms of evolution. It rules that helix point in growth where we reorganize structure to create room for new organization. It rules initiation, or death and rebirth. Chiron is the interface energy between the timeless galactic dynamic or spherical time, and the way that we operate within space and time here on Earth. We cannot learn anything here if we do not interface with the larger dynamic. Life here will just be a Saturnian round of Sisyphusian rock pushing up the hill until it rolls back on us again. It is only by quickening to the galactic dynamic or hologram of the universe that we can progress. Our first experience with that happens with our first Chiron square.

The age of the first square is very critical, but we have not been able

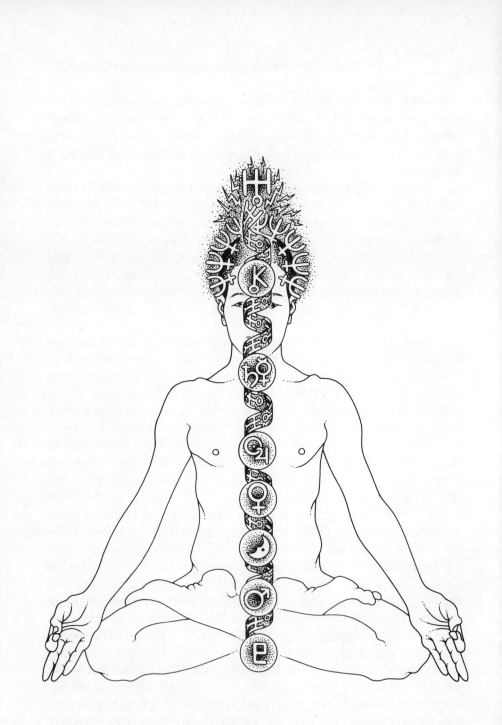

Figure 9
Planetary Energies in the Chakras

to observe this dynamic long enough or with enough astrologers. However, I will offer an early paradigm which we can all work with until we have more data. The Chirotic dynamic involves the process of a) correct development of Saturnian form, b) the ability to allow Uranus to flow in the subtle body systems or chakras, and c) the eventual Saturn/Uranus balance in the body. (See Figure 9) The age of the first Chiron square determines the first experiences with the Saturn-Uranus dynamic. So, if the first square is very early, such as before the first Saturn square at age 7, then the being is blasted with Uranian kundalini energy and has a very powerful and potentially psychotic mystical breakthrough. If the first square occurs around age 14, then the being has experienced the first Saturn square and even opposition and a few Uranus cycles, and it is more balanced.

Do not forget that this first square can trigger all kinds of sexual issues, and if there are some serious sexual issues, check all other planetary aspects at the time of the first square. If the first square occurs very late, then Saturn has gained a grip in consciousness, and the native resists. For example, the whole generation of anti-war radicals and Haight-Ashbury hippies had early squares. The new group of young people in high school and college now are reputed to be very conservative, and they had the first square very late.

For the last four years I have watched people undergo their first Chiron square and opposition, and I have questioned many people about what was going on at the time of their first square. With those I have been able to observe during the first square who were having it very late—people about age sixteen to twenty-five by 1986—there had been significant spiritual crises which separated them from others at first. When they responded spiritually and found the deeper meaning, they found themselves having strong erotic and mystical experiences. Some members of this group have sought the Chirotic wave with cocaine, and the result has been death. The key is the breakdown of the ego, and this transit was very beneficial once they let go of their own separation.

For all ages, if the organization of the self is weak and the native is insecure, this transit can be very dangerous. One client with severe fourth house aspects who had a correspondingly difficult childhood could remember her first Chiron square very graphically. When she was seven, at the time of the square, she felt that the only person who really loved her was her grandmother. She came into a room where her grandmother was sitting, and she saw a newly born sibling on the grandmother's lap. A column of white light (Uranus) formed around the grandmother sitting with the child, then it formed around her, and she stood in the doorway, unwanted, unheld, unloved. She began to believe that no one really loved her at that point.

Rather than get into whether the grandmother or anyone else really loved her, we went into a visualization into the column of white light, and we ascended up into the column to the source of the light. The source was divine, and she began to see that she was supposed to let go of even needing that grandmother because she herself came from the source, and then she could see that it was a misperception that she and that grandmother ever were separate.

This square teaches us that this life will always be one form of separation or another unless we can see that all is one. Some clients let go and allow themselves to shoot up the column of light, and they will have Enochian type ascension experiences. Enoch was the Old Testament or Hebrew Bible Patriarch who ascended and was with God. That is, they will catapult up through all the levels of reality and return to the source which nourishes them. That usually occurs with the very early square, but then the natives have difficulty because they feel so separate, so different from others. If their self-organization is strong and the aspects to the Sun are strong, then they will handle their journey without shattering. But many shatter when the letting go of everyday reality is too intense. Now that we know about this cycle, astrologers should check the time of the first square and check with their clients to see if they are "Chiron sensitive," that is, prone to strong death orientation at the first square. For some, deaths will occur around them.

If they are negatively sensitive, which will usually be indicated by excessive twelfth house activity, stressful aspects between Chiron and other planets, or a difficult sixth house, they will report an attempted suicide, serious illness, or death of a close relative at the time of the first square. It may or may not be indicated astrologically, because the Chiron square is a profound spiritual crisis which can also trigger past life memory and energy. If you suspect your client is Chiron sensitive, then you need to spend more time than usual working on the dynamic and giving the native the dates of the opposition and last square so that they can be dealt with consciously.

I believe Chiron aspects will become a powerful tool for predicting suicide crises for our clients. With a severely depressed client, we all worry about the potential for suicide. First, Chiron aspects will indicate whether they *really* are in danger. And second, difficult Chiron transits are over with eventually. We can tell our clients *when* the pressure will be off and keep them from doing themselves in because they feel like it will *never* end. Chiron rules our struggle over getting into the body, staying in it, and then sucking the higher energetics into this dimension. We have a strong tendency to jump out at the square points. Thus, it would not be wise for anyone to have anesthesia at the time of a Chiron square, and if you have a client talking about suicide and a square is occurring, *take it very seriously.*

The Chiron squares and opposition are the actual times when we can move into another dimension. If the organization of self is strong, we experience our separation resulting from coming into physical form, and then re-merge into a more intense connection with the universe, knowing better who we really are. But, if the self-boundaries are not secure, we may spin dangerously off into depression, being lost, becoming cut off and lonely. People can become very depressed about everything and act like the living dead, or they become shallow and silly, with layers of needless activity and possessions in their lives to cover the inner fear. This crisis must be resolved into a higher level dynamic because it is a spiritual crisis. The only thing that can resolve a Chirotic separation is alignment with our true purpose, because that is the way to our source. So at square time, we can work to enter the column of light and move to the source; and the chart as a whole shows the initiatory dynamic. The Chirotic cycle—as this Hermetic guide transits each house, each planet as it becomes intense at its square and opposition— is set up in the chart to trigger natives into their true purpose. As soon as they *find* it, they will be moving safely on their spiral. That brings us to initiating the client.

The goal with all readings is to communicate and work with the natal energy dynamic as deeply and completely as possible with the client. We need to prepare ourselves beforehand so that we know the nodal axis and anything unusual about purpose, such as an interception. You do need an astrological and intuitive sense of what might be the highest potential dynamic of the chart, but you must not ever have a fixed opinion about the meaning of this nativity or the level on which the native may be functioning. You must know the chart as a whole, having studied it well, and I would never go into a reading without analyzing planetary configurations that had already occurred at the Saturn return and the Uranus opposition. If there is an extremely stressful natal configuration or a powerful positive energy dynamic, it is necessary to find out at what level the client is operating with this dynamic. This is determined by the client's age, and you need to question the client early on in the reading about major configurations. He or she may have recreated a major T-square which was already mastered in a past life, so that it may be used as a power tool this time. You cannot assume anything about your client until you have discussed the chart with the individual. Natal charts are maps of potential, not linear computer programs!

Once you have done your preparation, which includes a study of progressions to determine inner maturity, then it is time for a Horary transit check. If the opportunity to initiate this client in the reading is present, the Horary transit check will tell you. Initiation means to *begin anew,* it means that we perceive that an individual has reached a point where they are on the verge of a new work in life. We can help them by seeing this, showing it to the client, and asking them to agree to bring forth this gift for all. It is an entering into *communion* with clients, an affirmation that they are not separate from us. This *spiritualizes* astrology. The way it is done is to do your transits for the reading by casting them for the exact time the client is going to walk in the door. (Be sure and warn clients to come on time.)

Before you do the Horary work, you will want to note the meaning of transits on the more general level, such as what will be happening this year, what happened recently as seen with inner planet transits, where is Saturn in relation to the rising sign, major outer planet transits, etc.

The Horary analysis involves a form of astrology that is analogous to the I Ching. It is our form of divination, and it was given to us by Horus the falcon who had very sharp vision from high in the sky. When you cast, note any transiting planet, Node, ascendant or midheaven that is *less than one degree to a conjunction to natal or progressed aspects.* Those will tell you why this person is here to see you at this moment. Other aspects or angles cannot be utilized. Remember, less than one degree to a conjunction. Do not violate this rule; it is secret teaching. I recovered it by reliving a lifetime as Ichor, astrologer under Thutmosis III and Amenhotep II during the Eighteenth Dynasty in Egypt.[5] Then, I applied the Egyptian Temple astrological teachings for three years in my practice, and they work. Past life information is of little use unless it is helpful in our present life. This particular teaching reached a high point at Denderah Temple during the Eighteenth Dynasty.

For example, if the transiting ascendant will be fifteen minutes to conjunction to the natal ascendant, you are going to be able to see into the soul of this client. Be sure to utilize the Sabian symbol in a great opportunity like that. If it is the Sun on the ascendant, you are going to be able to determine the essential purpose of this lifetime. If it is the Moon, you will be able to break a significant past life emotional block which is keeping the true purpose from alignment, and so on. Any aspects to Chiron are very significant because if you get any readings which tell you in advance that you are going to be able to move some energy, then you will be working very hard with Chiron to find the way to the most Chirotic level.

Divinatory or Horary astrology is difficult to describe. Like the Tarot, I Ching, or Runes, it can only be learned by doing it. But, divinatory astrology has become a necessity with the sighting of Chiron. Any form of divination is a tool for tapping the synchronicity plane at any given moment. Because Chiron is the ancient initiator, and he was a great astrologer, the sighting tells us that each reading has a special significance which can be understood. We need to know now that each client who comes to us is a great gift to us, for they offer us a window into their soul for the time they are with us. Of course, all astrologers would like to give *the* definitive reading for a client, but divination offers a new message. Horus tells us that we are to see clearly with our well-trained eyes the meaning of that special moment when this special soul comes into our space. And it can only be done with astrological divination. But once you begin to work with it under the guidance of Chiron and Horus, you will be amazed at your results. The universe will tell you what to focus on, what to look at. The Horary guides are the key into the labyrinth of the chart.

The labyrinth that Chiron used for teaching was on Crete, and it no longer exists. But now we are to use this form presented as Horary divination, and we do not need the labyrinth or the way into the issue. The secrets carefully guarded by the priestly orders are now open to us. That is why I didn't mind revealing the valuable information I recovered when I did past life work. Secrecy is nonfunctional at this time. Also, the other Chirotic divinatory tool was astrodrama, which was acted out in the stone circles which have twelve in the middle circle, such as Avebury in Wiltshire, England. You do not need to go to a stone circle for astrodrama. The old forms will be revived without the old ways, because the present time is what matters. One more thing needs to be mentioned regarding what the past can reveal now. When astrodramas were carried out in the stone circles, the stellar synchronistic principle was invoked. You can do it now with astrodrama.

The native of Chart #9, an artist, came to me in 1985. (See figure 10) I will not be giving exact times and dates or too specific information

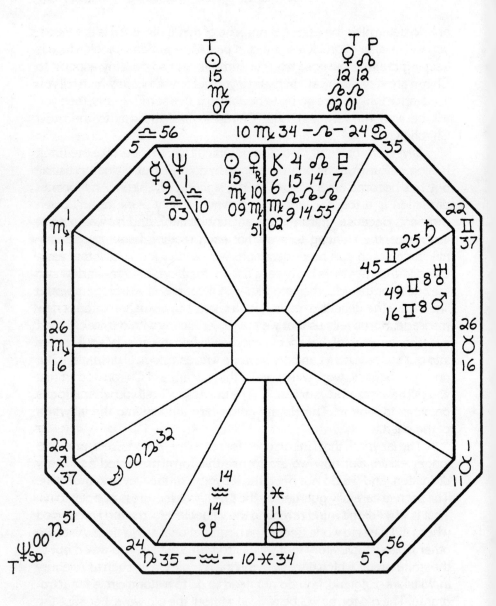

Figure 10
Horary Reading for Chart Number Nine

for reasons of privacy, but I will examine this chart from a Chirotic perspective, leaving out questions of personal life, finances, and health, and give the Horary transiting planets which told me how to initiate. With Chart #9, we have a dynamic which would have looked very different without the aid of Horary transit indications, but first an overview.

The Sabian symbol for Chart #9 is "a military band on the march," telling us that this soul hates trivia, loves excitement, and moves energetically toward a goal. He is likely to benefit from the martial arts, and he will have great capacity to draw matter into focus. I start with the Sabian because it reads the soul, and for initiation, I want to align him with his higher self.

His Virgo Sun close to Venus retrograde in the tenth would indicate a drive for receptivity and a healing career, which would be intensified by the square from Mars/Uranus in the seventh, and this drive would impact strongly on the women in his life. His Moon indicates restriction with Saturn opposite in the eighth, forming a T-square to Neptune in the tenth. The T-square indicates great stress, with confusion about finding outlets on the low side and/or brilliance of emotional focus which would create a channel for other dimensions. That is a case where the level of consciousness about that T-square must be known.

The Part of Fortune tells us he loves to go to the most subtle mystical realms for attunement to his deepest self. The Chiron trine to the Moon intensifies the subtle qualities in this nativity, and its close proximity to Venus retrograde at the Midheaven would tell me to help him find his *animus* within as a key release and assist to the T-square. Jupiter conjunct the North Node in the ninth in Leo indicates a powerful need for ego expansion on a spiritual basis, and a need to bring in and utilize the integrative skills seen with the South Node in Aquarius in the third.

Since Jupiter is on the North Node exact, we do not have to worry about whether he is working out his purpose or not. We can be sure the Uranus/Mars in the seventh has caused him great difficulty in relationship, and the interception of Leo in the ninth has been a problem for sure. He created the intercept because he had great wisdom in an important past life, and he refused to give it. This time he will give it to the planet, and it will be quite a gift, assisted by the Jupiter/North Node.

So, there I am, ready for the reading, and next I do the Horary transits. The Horary transits will tell me what work is needed on his emotional blocks in order to prepare him for initiation. It will reveal any past life history information cues required to find his purpose which are not already visible in the natal search. I also will have studied progressions for inner growth and the transits at the Saturn return and Uranus opposition, but there is no space to report all that. Chapter Thirteen will be a detailed natal and progressed read on Chiron's birth chart in relation to the atom split chart, Enrico Fermi, and a Horary cast, so you can observe that level of detail at that time.

This chart of the artist would be considered a very important chart for an initiation; and if I cast the Horary transits and got no results or no planets less than one degree to a conjunction between the horary cast and the natal chart plus progression, I would reschedule the reading and cast again. There is a lack of significant results in only about 10% of cases, so this is not a difficulty. The rescheduling is never done with transits in mind; I would just set up another reading and cast again. If there are no results three times, I do not read for the person, organization, or business. Oddly, the frequency of blocked readings is higher for businesses and groups than individuals. This indicates a psychic attunement with individuals which many astrologers have also noticed.

In this case, the first results were highly significant. Beginning with the second house: 1) transiting Neptune SD is 19 minutes from his natal Moon, meaning we will be able to access mysticism through his emotional blocks; 2) his progressed North Node is exactly conjuncted by transiting Venus, indicating his *animus* is ready to be integrated so that the feminine side of his being does not block his progress in this lifetime; 3) transiting Sun is exact conjunct natal Sun, showing he is ready to find himself. This reading will be a highly significant one because of the solar transit. He did not come because of his birthday; he came because of deep depression and neurological stress from the recent Chiron transit on the Mars/Uranus in the seventh house.

I cannot go into details about the results, but he was successfully initiated to bring in the subtle realms or Devic spirits into his work, and he is doing it with more power every day. There is a potential difficulty in the life of this client which could only be solved by working with Chiron. Look at his chart and notice that he has Chiron in Virgo, meaning he got his first square in January 1949 when he was 5½, a conjunction to his Moon in February 1951 when he was 8, the opposition when he was only 18, then no more transits until he hit Mars/Uranus just before this reading. That is, he is going to be very Chirotic and very unhinged by the energy. Next he gets Chiron transiting the mid point between Uranus and Saturn (which is the breakthrough point as already indicated by Philip Sedgwick) in the summer of 1986 while the transiting Chiron opposite Uranus is energizing everybody in general. And then he will experience the upper square and the transit of Chiron over eight planets and the North Node next! This is a great example of one of those charts that is a gradually building time bomb of higher consciousness. All he needed was a map to go by.

It was really fun to work with the architect of Chart #52 because I felt I had initiated him thousands of years ago. (See figure 11.) Much of the work I tended to do with him was very intuitive, but finally that time came for initiation in this lifetime. Only the transits would really tell how to go about it. The reading in question was a second reading, and it had already been joyfully discovered earlier that he was in the right profession. He was a sacred architect in the past, which is one of the major orders carrying great energy on the physical plane. His choice of profession showed up natally because he chose the Sun on the South Node in the tenth house, which brought his sacred order right back in, even to the point of having a father who is an architect who wished to pass his firm on to his son. His Sabian is "a deserter from the navy," indicating independence and repudiation of meaningless loyalties. This is an interesting dynamic because he is not especially rebellious, but the Sabian has created an inner soul energy which prevented the common lack of growing with the Sun on the South Node. His Moon further helps him with his Sun because it is opposite Chiron, forming a square to the Ascendant which energizes his inner soul energy.

At the time of the reading, Horary transiting Chiron was conjunct the North Node in the fourth, indicating we could ground the depth of his purpose further and do more work with the difficulties coming from the Sun on the South Node. Transiting Mars was exact cunjunct Venus in Scorpio, giving us special "juice" to work on polarity conflicts. This was very helpful because the reading was scheduled for Uranus opposition exactly. I do not believe we fully comprehend our true purpose until the Uranus opposition, and part of the process has to do with polarity resolution so the electrical energy of Uranus can flow through the chakras unimpeded.

The Mars transit gave us great energetic opportunities for the reading. Furthermore, transiting Saturn was conjuncting progressed Venus, which would help to form the *anima* very powerfully. Then, Mars is opposite Uranus retrograde natally (the big struggle of this incarnation). Therefore, transiting Uranus was conjunct Mars during his Uranus opposition, which further pushed his polarity resolution. And to top it off even further, the transiting Sun was conjunct progressed Mars! I used this chart as an example of how amazing the Horary process can be for

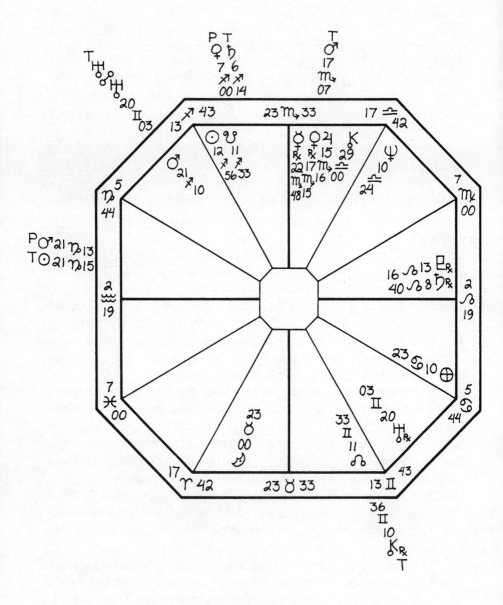

Figure 12
Horary Reading for Chart Number Fifty-Two

astrologers because it is a tap into the synchronicity flow. In general, when you get this many significant conjunctions in the Horary cast, the individual has traveled right to the astrologer through the veils of time for initiation. This architect would have been really confused and blown out by the level of energy at his Uranus opposition, but he *created* a reading at exactly the right moment in order to get the guidance he needed. I cast only once for this reading, which was scheduled months in advance, and it was a taped reading with two thousand miles between us.

These two examples were given as an example of how to tap into the flow of divination now that Chiron has been sighted. I am sure there are many ways which people will discover in coming years. The other form which I love to work with at this time is astrodrama, because Chiron is the leader of astrodrama, just as he leads the Tarot reader. Some have suggested that the card for Chiron may be the Fool, and I have noticed that the energy of the Fool seems to want to rule Chiron in the astro- drama. The point is, we need to stretch ourselves now. We need to let go into the synchronicity flow.

Chapter Thirteen

CHIRON AND THE BOMB

We have come to the end of our odyssey discovering the applications of Chiron. There are also many philosophical reflections throughout this work, and now it is time to tie those elements together. Chiron gave up his immortality to free Prometheus from the Underworld with Zeus's permission. 3600 years later, Chiron has manifested as a force on the physical plane which means all the Chirotic powers are now available to beings on Earth. And, Chiron's sighting is the key to resolving the atomic crisis. We will be trying to see into this crisis with Chart #53, Chiron's birth chart; Chart #50, the atomic split chart; Chart #54, the natal chart of Enrico Fermi, who split the atom; and Chart #55, the Horary chart. The thought behind it is complex, so first let me weave out the issues.

Chiron gave up his immortality so that Prometheus could be freed from the Underworld with Zeus's permission. First of all, as discovered by recovering the life of Aspasia as described in *Eye of the Centaur*[1], this event occurred during the historical search for the Golden Fleece during the time when Santorini-Thera (or Calliste in Aspasia's day) erupted and devastated the Minoan-Atlantean theocracy, also at the time of the Exodus.[2] This destruction was the third recent Earth cataclysm, preceded by one which occurred about 5100 B.C. that revived catastrophic memory of the 10700 B.C. event. This was too much for the psyche to bear. We are now at a fourth catastrophic point, which will occur during the next twenty years, due to the orbital timing of Nibiru which rules/balances/Libra/the Lunar Nodes. This cycle relationship exists in all ancient myth; is being referred to as the destruction of the Fourth World by the Hopis through the prophecies of Thomas Banyaca,[3] and the timing is synchronous with the August

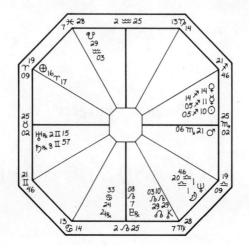

Chart Number Fifty:
Splitting of the Atom
Source: Author's Research
Koch House System

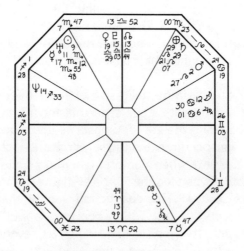

Chart Number Fifty-Three:
Birth of Chiron
Data Source: *The Key,* **#16, January 10, 1981**
Koch House System

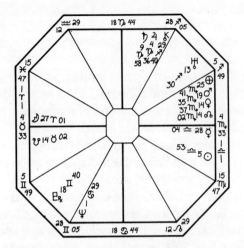

Chart Number Fifty-Four:
Enrico Fermi
Source: Lois Rodden
Placidus House System

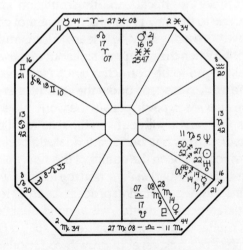

Chart Number Fifty-Five:
Horary for Natal Chiron
Reading
Koch House System

1987 to 2012 date given by Jose Arguelles in *The Mayan Factor: Path Beyond Technology.*[4]

How does all this relate to Chiron giving up his immortality in 1500 B.C.? It means that Chiron asked Zeus/God to let him out of the Earth cycle, that this time in his life was the end of many years of initiating and teaching as a galactic server. He was one of "the Gods" who came here to work for the evolution/Pluto/Underworld journey of humankind, and he was ready to let go, actualizing the fact that creation and destruction are all one. He freed Prometheus, actualizing a new reality which would manifest during the next 3600-year cycle which is ending now. The reality is that "the Gods" no longer control the sacred fire—we control it now, as shown by Prometheus. It is simply power and what we do with it will determine our fate. But, at this point, the scientific application of astrology can *see* a lot. At each synchronous point in the 3500-3600 cycle of Nibiru when it is about 400 years in from its aphelion, we have the opportunity to balance energy. But the 1550 B.C. event and the present time are different, as shown by Arguelles, because we are advanced in the galactic synchronization beam. Our emergency balancing cycle point now is also a galactic harmonic function.[5]

Chiron is the bridging planet between life and death, so now we have a vehicle to make the critical leap. Transmutation is the bridge from the end of this cycle to the new cycle which we cannot conceptualize at this time. We have been actively trying to learn to transmute energy since December 2, 1942, when the atom was split. But we have made a grave error, which has begun to be corrected since November 1, 1977; we have allowed the work to proceed under the control of the scientists, not realizing that we also are to participate in the work. When the atom was split, you were split—as you will see from the reading of the atomic split chart. Our consciousness has been very dualistic during most of the Age of Pisces, which has been the nature of the Age. Polarity resolution will be the nature of the Aquarian Age, and the lessons we have learned during Pisces are part of the growing process. In order to articulate and conceptualize differences in matter, we needed dualities to perceive. But as soon as matter was actually dualized or split, a crises was born which will manifest our next level of growth-consciousness—galactic synchronization or at-one-ment with "the Gods" as co-creators of life— but only if enough of us choose it here.

What am I talking about? It is actually as simple as it is complex. Since December 2, 1942, when the atom was split, we have been duped by our scientists because of their desire to control/Saturn/death/

Atlantean mentality, and it is now time for all of us to observe and monitor their actions. The topic is a book in itself, but it is time to get the news out to as many people as possible so that our natural love of life/Eros can rule our reality again. The fact is that we are all being held hostage by the belief that an atomic war can occur which will destroy the planet, and because we are hostage to that concept, we are ignoring the progress of planetary ecological destruction which in fact *could* destroy our reality. For example, we are not coping with the consequences of releasing radiation into the environment at all. The scientists are perpetrating the karmic lie, and laymen have to expose them if the scientists will not reveal the truth themselves.

The facts are that *atomic war is a virtual impossibility* on this planet because of the unbreakable laws of mathematics and geometry. As proven by Bruce Cathe in *Harmonic 33,* we are all in geometric relationship from the atom, through the solar system with the Sun in the center, to the galactic balances. As Cathe puts it, "To set up a harmonic opposition to physical matter (or atomic explosion) in our solar system, we must pick a spatial point in the system at the instant of time which is geometrically in tune with the particular harmonic opposition..."[6] To put it more simply, he says, "The position they have picked (to explode the bomb) must have a certain geometrical relationship to the solar system as a whole, at an instant of time."[7] The point is, there are only certain places when the bomb can go off when the Sun passes through a certain geometric point. Cathe has published the detonation testing times of different countries and proven his point, and he also believes that the governments of various countries know where it can explode and when. That is, they know that it is almost impossible to have a war.

The situation is remarkably complex because the massive fear complex we are living with is based on previous catastrophes which cloud the mind and emotions, causing us to not know what to really fear.[8] The fear complex from the past is related to the atomic crisis, and Cathe intuited it but did not follow it through. Cathe sees that the eruption of Santorini-Thera is beyond the scope of normal catastrophes as we have understood them from the scientific facts, and I agree. He wonders if it was atomic, looking at it with his brilliant system of geometrical grid coordinates applied to the location of the Island of Santorini. He can't date it exactly to get the solar angle, but I have come pretty close to dating it in *Eye of the Centaur,* and perhaps others can go further in this critical research. Cathe senses the relationship between past catastrophes and the present atomic crisis, which is where we must look for a more scientific understanding.

There is a level on which we already know the answers to these questions, just by searching our hearts. However, we are now going into an initiated reading of the charts, which will shed more light on the atomic split. The sacred fires of creation are lit because Prometheus is free; the waters of life are flowing, and we look forward to the Water Bearer in the midst of our strife. The Earth cries out for us to pay atten-tion to its needs now, as Chiron is the sacred ecologist. As we work with Chiron, let us remember that he created this birth chart with all its qualities as a method for bringing in the work of this incarnation, and that we can read this chart to the best of our ability to comprehend his work during this particular cycle.

First, I needed to cast a Horary chart for the reading. I was planning to begin writing this chapter on December 20, 1986. I thought I'd just cast at 9:00 a.m. that day, but the six o'clock news the night before gave me my Horary cast moment (See Chart #55). The news announced that Ronald Reagan had ordered 50 MX missiles to be put on trains to travel back and forth across America. We know from Cathe's work why he wanted to move them around (so they will be in detonation position) and 50 is the Argonauts again! So, let us begin the reading of Chiron.

The Sabian is 27 degrees of Sagittarius, which is the center point of our galaxy at the present time, which means he is here to center us to the galactic resonance. By the degree of his rising, we know that the infor-mation which we are about to examine is very secret, because his rising is 26 Sagittarius, but his Sabian is 27 degrees. If his rising were 27 degrees, we would have a chart which could not be read, as astrologers are barred from Horary reading of charts with a 27 degree to a 3 degree rising.[9] We can proceed . . . The Sabian image is "sculptor," meaning creative manifestation which makes images of the life force. It is an amazingly synchronistic image for the bridging between Saturn and Uranus because the stone is a rigid Saturnian material made of Uranian crystal parts which manifest as images by means of the Chirotic force or creative artist. As mentioned earlier, Richard Nolle resonates with the Chirotic force as the hand of the artist. The Sabian would indicate that Chiron will use his vision to manifest his dream in this incarnation. The keyword is "Immortalization," which is definitely Chiron's energetics mythologically. The positive use of his energy is "exceptional self-expression through a gift for building all experience into a personal fulfillment."[10] This tells me that creativity is the way out of our present dilemma.

Chiron's Sun is 9 degrees Scorpio in the eleventh house, in close conjunction to Uranus, which tells us that he will manifest his evolutionary being from the depths of Pluto; that he learned about the subconscious during his visit to the seventh rim of Hades. As Horary Pluto is in 9 degrees Scorpio in the fourth, we know that Pluto will clear the radiation if we will clear the issue with our consciousness. Natal Sun with Uranus is in the eleventh, so he will manifest his essence only if he is allowed to give his gift, which will be revealed when we read his interception.

The Sun is trine Jupiter retrograde in the seventh. Jupiter retrograde in Cancer in the seventh means Chiron contains the higher self in this essence—the Ka of the Egyptians—which I would expect of a demigod. He is going to have problems bringing mastery/Jupiter levels into this lifetime because he will remember his past glories when he was the essence of what he thought were the highest qualities of human existence. This aspect is fascinating because I think the most serious emotional addiction is to atavistic rituals instead of just going directly to our own creativity. In his previous incarnation in 1500 B.C., Chiron was master of ritual and initiation. Jupiter trine the Sun tells us that he will bring the self through completely and begin to know himself in this life if he can let go of past glory and technique to find his new and unique way this time. And since Jupiter is in the seventh, we can see that the attachment is to all the people he related to and initiated. His personal experience involves letting go of the old way in order to give his gift this time, but we need to watch out for the fact that he will need to also recover what he knew before in order to go beyond this time.

Before proceeding with the reading, it is necessary to check Chiron's Saturn return, August 26, 2007 (only one hit) to see how he will handle letting go of old ways. At that time, Pluto is 26 degrees 20 minutes Sagittarius, exactly on the natal ascendant, revealing that Chiron is to purify his soul to the depth at his Saturn return. Since Pluto rules evolution, his past life initiatory and healing skills will be in his cellular consciousness but not part of his emotional attachments. He will be free to use what is useful and let go of old stuff for the new ways. This date is also very close to the date of the end of the Mayan Great Cycle as revealed by Jose Arguelles.[11]

Next, we look at the Moon to comprehend Chiron's screen on Earth this time. All that he perceives will move through that screen. His Moon is 12 degrees of Cancer in the seventh house, indicating he is protective and nurturing in relationships, and he will hold on hard and fight strongly for that which he wishes to protect. The Moon is almost exactly trine

Uranus, meaning he easily lets go and sees a higher order, but that skill may not develop until the Uranus opposition in 2021 and 2022. A study of the three Uranus opposition points shows no significant transits regarding this issue, but we can be sure he will not really let go of full Uranian electrical energy until his Uranus opposition because the Moon exactly squares the Nodes natally. We will read that aspect when we do the Nodes, but the full energy of the North Node is never released until the Uranus opposition, when it is squared. At this point, I would say that this aspect means that solar and Tesla forms of energy usage will not be released until 2021.

These energy forms will be the Uranian solution for ceasing to release radiation into the environment for power, and we can possibly predict that mankind will not let go of nuclear power until 2021. This square to the Nodes from the Moon and the nurturing conflicts inherent in it means that Venus may be the key to the nuclear dilemma along with the Moon in the other charts. The atom split chart has the Moon exact conjunct Neptune in the fifth house of the creative solution in Libra. This means that the emotions were highly creative and mystical or deluded when the atom was split. It is an intriguing position, hinting that we may see the way out when we examine the split from the mystical perspective and see what it really shows about our souls. And it says that we are very confused emotionally about what radiation is doing to us.

The Part of Fortune in the Chiron nativity is 29 degrees conjunct Saturn in the eighth house. This reveals that Chiron returned to be in control, to rule, and that he will let go of everything in order to create a new evolutionary dynamic. The Saturn conjunction shows that this will be a powerful formation, that it will be palpable and disciplined. Since Chiron is conjunct the North Node in 29 degrees Leo in the fourth house of the atom split chart, I see the Chiron nativity as the direct solution to the split. The atom split chart shows that we split our home, the Earth, with a Chirotic suicide that also attempts to heal. Enrico Fermi's Chiron is 29 degrees of Sagittarius showing that it was easier to do the test thoughtlessly than to consider the consequences. Also, note that Chiron's natal Chiron is right on Fermi's ascendant. There are no accidents.

Next, we go right into Chiron's chart doing the houses, and we will be watching carefully for the relationships to the other charts. The first house indicates that his search for self-definition involves focus and the ability to be free. And we know from his Sabian that he is the sculptor, that he will create his own reality. His second house with Capricorn tells us he is conservative, that he works hard to establish firm and lasting values, that he will endure. Aquarius is intercepted in his second house. The interception is going to reveal what he was supposed to do in his last lifetime which he refused to do; it will show us what he is going to do in this lifetime, no matter what. As I do in natal readings, we will wait to define the meaning of the interception until the end of the reading.

The third house is very important in this reading because it will indicate to what degree he will integrate and communicate in this life. The cusp is Pisces, hinting that he will bring in his mystical force, that he will integrate the higher self. I don't think there is much doubt about that if you observe all the successful work going on in New Age healing circles bringing in the higher self since November, 1977.

The fourth house is Aries, indicating a forceful grounding, an aggressive deep search into reality. The South Node is exact conjunct the IC, meaning he has brought in the full force of his past life powers, which will activate to the maximum as his North Node is exactly conjunct the midheaven. This greatly activates the square to the Moon and demonstrates unequivocally that the emotions are what is in the way. At the Light Institute in Galisteo, Chris Griscom has pioneered work on the emotional body as an entity; it is the densest part of our perceptual vehicles, and we can only move it and clear it by bringing in the higher self, or a spiritual energy.[12] The North Node is right on the midheaven but still at the very most intense section of the ninth house of integrating the higher self, exactly corroborating the work of Chris. Since Chris is one of the many healers who found their powers in 1977, we have ample demonstration of the power of this nativity. The Moon, the emotional body as an entity, is going to block progress until we learn to activate the power of the balancing North Node right on the midheaven. We must learn to suck in all the power of the Mars-ruled South Node on the IC, activating it with the fusion of the balance/higher self—which is galactically connected because it is ruled by Libra/Nibiru—and shoot the energy into a cleared emotional body/Moon in our relationships. This chart tells us that that is the direction of our healing, that it is the vehicle Chiron created in order to do the work. It also means a dense and blocked emotional body will dull kundalini response energy because the North/South Node axis is the chakra axis, with the Cancer Moon squaring it. The Aries North Node in the Horary chart is solidly in the tenth, showing that Reagan will further exacerbate the bleeding wound of the fourth (see atomic split, Pluto retrograde in fourth and North Node/Chiron) if he gets away with ordering 50 MX missiles to take train rides across America.

Chiron is in the fourth house of the natal chart as well as the atom split chart, indicating the continual difficulties of this house as long as we dare to threaten our home itself—planet Earth. Natal Chiron is conjunct Fermi's ascendant, showing Chiron will heal this scientist's soul in the only possible way—getting rid of the radiation. Chiron is square Mars in the eighth; it is retrograde, indicating Chiron's past life as an initiatory teacher, and this square indicates he will have great stress over letting go of the warrior energy. It was appropriate once, but it is not an appropriate response at this time. The sextile to Jupiter, both planets retrograde, shows that the past life energy will stop impinging on the emotions when the spiritual expansion begins. Chiron undergoes his first square August 17, 1991, when the higher self will move fully into his being. Pluto will be exactly conjunct Chiron's Mercury in Scorpio in the eleventh, showing a great new awareness in the collective.

The fifth house will give us signs of the creative breakthrough potential. The most pronounced characteristic of the nuclear crisis has been the lack of new creative thought because we have been held hostage. The Taurus fifth house with no planets would indicate a slow, balanced, careful, and earthy approach. It also is a sign that Chiron rules ecology this time around, which has been well demonstrated already by Dr. Kenneth Negus.[13] This house again warns us to pay special attention to Venus.

The sixth house is Gemini, indicating flexibility and versatility, and since it is the house that Chiron rules, we must pay special attention to Mercury. As we move into the upper houses, notice that most of the planets are in the upper houses, meaning this is a life of action, a life based on a great deal of well-integrated past life work.

The seventh house is also ruled by Gemini, due to the interception, and it means that the Sagittarius focus and the Gemini integration powers are emphasized in this nativity. Jupiter and the Moon have been discussed, but the Jupiter opposition a little over a degree to Fermi's Jupiter is interesting. It looks like Chiron is Fermi's spiritual foil.

The eighth house is crucial since Pluto and the eighth house rule the bomb, which manifested so quickly after the sighting of Pluto. The Mars in 2 degrees of Leo indicates that Chiron is going to be radical, is going to take chances, that his energy will be very noticeable. The Cancer cusp shows that only nurturance will get to the bottom of it. Mars is intercepted in the eighth, indicating that there will be a lot of male power available once the interception begins to come in. And the Saturn conjunct the Part of Fortune is right on the cusp of the eighth/ninth house and is very powerful due to the conjunction to the atom split Chiron/ North Node. It indicates that Chiron will not only heal the split, but he will enjoy doing it. The situation is so bad that only a few good jokes can break the ice.

The 0 degree Virgo ninth house cusp means the higher self energy is very new, that it will be very focused once we get used to it. The North Node at the very end of the ninth house in Libra is a great balancer, a great energy which is very galactically connected. We are on the verge of finding a new solution on Earth which is related to our galaxy.

As we move into the tenth house, we ask what will be the manifesta-tion of the centaur healer in the world this time? What will he actually *do* to heal the split? Pluto is at the top of the chart, very close to the North Node and Venus, indicating that this is an exceedingly evolutionary natal force which is concerned with feminine power. Jeff Green says about Pluto on the North Node, "The results of the evolutionary transforma-tion can create tremendous growth in this life. Every other contributing factor in the birth chart will be channeled or focused through the North Node conjunct Pluto."[14] The evolutionary and transformative powers of Pluto with Venus will mean that the necessary balancing work will be accomplished this time.

This position even strengthens the solution of the Lunar square to the Nodes because it tips the balance to the North Node, forcing the clearing of the emotional body by means of a Plutonic depth charge. The Neptune sextile means that mysticism accompanies depth. Chiron reaches opposition to itself September 29, 1997, very close to the time many prophets feel we will precess into Aquarius. At that point, the pro-gressed Moon of Chiron is exactly 13 degrees of Aries conjunct the natal South Node, indicating that the inner emotional growth relating to past life material matures at the time of maximum transmutation force in the life. This indicates that September, 1997, will be a time of great emotional clearing on the personal and historic level. Venus is in the tenth in 19 degrees of Libra, close to Pluto, showing the original power of Venus/ *anima*/feminine receptivity in Chiron's essence and its relationship to the Underworld of Pluto. Chiron died in the cataclysmic times when the goddess religion lost power, and many ancient myths, as well as the research of Immanuel Velikovsky, point to the planet Venus as the culprit. The legends about a destructive Venus are particularly common in central and South American mythology.

Venus is 14 degrees Sagittarius in the seventh house in the atom split chart, which is exactly conjunct Neptune in the twelfth house in

Chiron's natal chart. That would indicate that Neptune in Chiron's natal chart brings the soul into the atom split chart, and that Venus conjunct Chiron's Neptunian twelfth house energy offers balance. Then it becomes even more interesting when we note that the 14 degrees Sagittarius point in Fermis' chart is closely conjuncted by Uranus in the eighth house, which is 13 degrees 30 minutes Sagittarius, indicating that Fermi's participation in the bomb birth has some surprise elements.

Then look to the Horary reading of the 50 MX missiles riding the trains to be in position for the exact solar angle for the atomic holocaust, and you will see that the 14 degree Sagittarius point is Saturn exactly conjunct Mercury in the fifth house of creative solutions. This is the kind of 1 degree Horary conjunction which makes this kind of reading fascinating. The Saturn conjunct Mercury in 14 degrees Sagittarius in the fifth house indicates that Reagan responded to this moment in time because it was an energy which could *form* (Saturn) the bomb on Earth and Mercury indicates the idea would work. The conjunction squares the powerful Jupiter/Mars conjunction which is the energy that caused Reagan to recreate the Argonauts. But it won't work again, ever again. The warrior healer, Chiron, will not initiate the missiles. Jason ploughed the fields releasing the monsters of Ares or Aries for the last time.

The eleventh house reveals the gift of Chiron; the cusp is Scorpio, and so his gift is evolution, and his North Node conjunct Pluto leaves no doubt that we will evolve. The Horary chart is clear on the results, with Pluto in 9 degrees Scorpio in the fourth conjunct natal Sun in Chiron's birth chart. Uranus in the eleventh indicates that he will give his gift in some surprising way and the twelfth house ruled by the planet of the masters, Jupiter, with Neptune in 14 degrees of Sagittarius, so close to Fermi's Uranus in the eighth, indicates a big surprise for Fermi which is revealed in the atom split chart. Venus is 14 degrees of Sagittarius in the seventh house in the atom split chart which tells us that Fermi's splitting of the atom unleashed the *anima,* the feminine chaos force. The female will tolerate pollution, radiation, and male control over the elements only for a while: Fifty phallic MX's riding around on little boys' train sets is going too far. The Sabian for 14 degrees Sagittarius is "The Pyramids and the Sphinx."[15]

The interception of Aquarius in the second and Leo in the eighth reveals that Chiron failed to assume leadership in search for truth in his previous life, that he had an ego investment in being an authority. He failed to reflect truth last time, and he returned now to do it right. He will bring in the truth this time, and ground it in the second house as seen with Aquarius intercept in the second house. He is the harbinger of the Aquarian Age of brotherhood; he remembers all too well how we lost the battle before. This time we will find true values by learning his teaching of making Saturn form here and bringing in Uranian kundalini energy and life force. Leo intercepted in the eighth house shows Chiron will lead in ways to open the heart chakra in the face of death. He remembers losing, and this time he will transmute. And now we can use the tool of transmutation consciously. It is time for astrologers to teach with Chiron about how to live on Earth in harmony with wisdom and the higher self.

Chapter Fourteen

SEARCH FOR
THE GOLDEN FLEECE

Initiate, stand waiting for your vision of the Tree of Life to be grounded in your body. Listen to my story of Jason and the Argonauts. See with your inner eye so you may know that what you've been told for a long time is a lie. You have been barred from listening to your own inner mind. You have been taught there is only one lifetime. But you existed when the eternal search for the Golden energy happened. We all did. I, Chiron, have returned so you can see and hear again.

What we have been told is a lie from the Ancient Ones, the stealers of our hearts, the priests. As long as we think we only come here once and there is a final judgment at the end of our time, we will miss the Chirotic point. It is very simple when you realize you have always existed and you always will. As you exist right now, you can see and resonate with all time and all places. Come with me, with Jason and Medea, and see with the eyes of timelessness. Let us round the large bend on the spiral together.

This is a story of a quest for survival of the most intense level of attunement. Whenever the vital number is fifty, the survival of a people or species is at stake. Do not forget that. A people is like a last jaguar: all that matters is the seed, the genetic pool and its survival within the environment. For if you cannot reincarnate because you have destroyed Earth, you truly are in Hades, wandering endlessly through the timeless void of your own aborted growth. So, I, Chiron, have returned as a teacher to give you the secrets of the elders. I have returned to free you to find your inner self which ties you to all beings, because ecology only works if you feel your connections with all living things. I have decided to teach the Jaguar Way again because enough of you have now prayed for my return. You are the generation being killed by your own parents. Your elders say that you are spoiled and lazy consumers, and that you are not producers as they were. But in fact, you are killers of yourselves at the hands of the products they sold to you as babes. You are the labeled ones, but notice that you are not being watched. You have nothing to fear if

---

Note: This chapter was set in a different typeface to indicate that the mythological characters are speaking directly.

you just resonate with the Jaguar within. Your inner spirit will save you.

My temple is on Mt. Peleus; my deep Earth energies come from within the cave and call to the sky from the mountain. I, Chiron, am chosen as elder to initiate each warrior onto the right path, to lead each brother and sister on the way to their greatest fulfillment. You wonder why I am different now than I was when I initiated the sacred warriors of the olden times?

I am different now in the way Uranus, Neptune, and Pluto are different since they have been sighted in the sky. Now, my energy is in form on Earth. We were once gods on Earth; we came long ago and planted our sacred male seed into mother Earth and human females. Then we went away when the women ceased being cosmic vessels. We became planets way beyond the planets which rule inner earth energies—Mercury, Venus, Mars, Jupiter and Saturn; and we orbited with you as you evolved your consciousness with our level of attunement.

We orbit in the sky spiraling energy, and for thousands of years initiates of the sacred orders knew our presence and attuned to us. Finally two hundred years ago human sight developed and saw us, and our energetics became a cultural dynamic instead of the work of the esoteric orders. First, with Uranus you manifested free will; with Neptune you learned that you could see and know the divine yourselves; and with Pluto you knew you were ready to learn courage, to know your own inner darkness. Now you have seen me, Chiron, and you are ready for the path of the sacred warrior, you are ready to heal yourself and the planet simultaneously. I rule the simultaneity of the hologram. And you must absorb my energy so quickly, quickly now . . . For Nibiru comes next behind me.

This vision is revealed in the path you walk and the choices you make along the way. I am process. You don't need alchemy any more; you are process itself. The only way to know it is to unfold with it. For example, there is no such thing as fate; each result is created by the action before it. The goddess is your universal muse; this time, she is Medea. She is present for you as mediator to teach you process as meditation of your body in this life. The gods or collective unconscious chose to link Medea up with Jason to solve the crisis over the Golden Fleece during the last polarity balancing cycle. The Golden Fleece represents sympathetic magic—the power within a sacral culture to create its own reality by being in touch with the natural law and manifest rituals that tell the gods what is needed for Earth community. The Golden Fleece saved Phrixius from his death as sacred king in atonement to the goddess. The event encapsulates the point when the Ram/Aries becomes the solution for the problem instead of eternal trust in the Goddess/Earth which had been the cultural dynamic for two thousand years during the Age of Taurus. The dynamic became control/violence instead of trust/peace, and we've suffered ever since. Evolution must have its way. The dynamic had to change. Growth is hard. Now is time to hear again the true story from Medea/ Goddess within. Listen . . .

You missed your chance when you lost your courage. The violence of the Earth in my times was beautiful like the wild, wild wind. The Earth crunched and groaned so that rocks became molten liquid. The water rose so high that Deucalion entered the sacred ship and sought the stars. The volcano was of such violence, the earthquakes shook all that was left in your soul; and then men decided to never trust again. Pluto actually split matter. But all women know that if she fears ugliness and weakness her fetus will be deformed and twisted. Women know that all things around them weaken and die when her thoughts are murderous. Women do not require chemicals to poison; she knows how to poison with her thoughts. Witch/priestess you say I am? You fear me because you know I know who you are, Man: You are warrior, murderer, rapist, destroyer, instead of hearth keeper. I know how to take life force in the plants, rocks, fire and water and transfer it into the body/soul. Look what has happened to Earth since my power was wrenched from me!

> *So now it is, when she carries a fetus within,*
> *You invade the womb with thin knives like a wolf in*
>   *the night.*
> *You vibrate life essence with low sound like a soul-*
>   *quake.*
> *When you violate my canyons and soil with your foul*
>   *pollution.*

You alienated yourselves from your place, Earth, and you began then to kill your place. Your murderous power has made you into instruments for the monsters from the other side who love death, violence, and the void which always is looming in front of you when you no longer trust. And now you have created monstrous weapons of destruction that you have lost control of because you fear me, Medea/chaos/lack of control/passion/Eros/essence. My planets revolve around my Sun in the middle of my galaxies, and if you continue to not trust in my powers, I will let go of my radiant hold, and I will disperse all to infinity in a grand cosmic orgasm.

> *So now it is, when she carries a fetus within,*
> *You invade the womb with thin knives like a wolf in*
>   *the night.*
> *You vibrate life essence with low sound like a soul-*
>   *quake*
> *When you violate my canyons and soil with your foul*
>   *pollution.*

I, Medea, joined the mighty warrior, Jason, because he carried the mantle of the fifty Moon Men, the Minyae. Jason was raised in open fields under Io, the Moon Goddess. None can question Io, the Jupiterian magic cave of the gods. But I should have known he was a woman soul-stealer, for it was Jason who yoked fire-breathing bulls, thus ending the Age of Taurus when gods and goddeses walked on planet Earth. But Jason worshipped Poseidon, god of metal power. Initially, the potential return to the old ways, Poseidea, lured me, and I listened when Jason brought the New Fire from Delos and said he trusted Aphrodite. But this time, Eros cheated virility, and Aphrodite persuaded Eros to pierce my heart with the arrow of love. Jason enlivened my passion with a live wryneck spread-eagled on a flywheel, and the cosmos for me became a mad search for this earth union. I let go of myself and plunged into the deep of merging with the other side.

So now it is, when she carries a fetus within,
You invade the womb with thin knives like a wolf in
   the night.
You vibrate life essence with low sound like a soul-
quake
When you violate my canyons and soil with your
   foul pollution.

So Jason challenged the dominion of the other side, the secret place we all travel to when we let go of self. My father, Aeetes, had no choice but to take on the challenge, and he gave Jason impossible tasks to accomplish for the Golden Fleece. If Jason could do as he said, then Jason would learn the atomic secret: anything is possible if we just image the end result. First, Jason was to yoke two iron bulls/rockets/shems, then he was to plough the field of Ares/the last remaining germs of the Ancient Ones/ Nibiruans. He was to sow the field of Ares with serpents' teeth/the last pods of the sacred seeds of the Ancient Ones.

I, Medea, agreed to help you, Jason, with your impossible heroic deeds in exchange for a bargain with Hera: Your heroism would make me your wife, and you swore by the Olympian Gods to keep your troth forever. I made you the flower potion from the saffron crocus first sprang from the blood of Prometheus-bound, and thus you learned from the flower essence to image courage. So it was that only you yoked the rockets, and ploughed the fields of the gods, Ares, and planted the pods of the Ancient Ones. Up they sprang to life, always they wait to break into our reality, up they sprouted. Jason provoked them into a furious battle among themselves. He was very clever, as Cadmus was when he slayed the Canaanite autochthons. Next, Jason faced the dragon, Typhon/eternal chaos/destroyer/ madness. I, great Medea/goddess power, tricked the dragon, and we stole the Fleece.

So now it is, when she carries a fetus within,
You invade the womb with thin knives like a wolf in
   the night.
You vibrate life essence with low sound like a soul-
quake
When you violate my canyons and soil with your foul
   pollution.

We sailed—Jason, Medea, and the fifty Moon Men, away into the Black Sea with our Golden Fleece in hand. From afar over the sacred channels of the inner psychic mind, Cheiron our Master Teacher reveled in that moment of recapture. But, my father, my Aeetes/old ways/control/ being a virgin forever, overtook us with his fleet near the Danube mouth as we fled with our booty. Legend has it that I, Medea, killed my own brother, Apsyrtus, and cut his limbs off one by one, thus forcing my father to fall behind as he stopped to pick up each piece. In fact, Apsyrtus is Phaethon who shot the Sun with his golden arrow; then Earth went into a spasm, and our passage on our sacred ship/sky sailor was ended. Those of you who put off nurturing your planet by watering your tree of life, please hear me when I tell you that woe is the man or woman who lives in a time when mothers eat their own offspring and fathers mate with their daughters to keep the species alive. The truth is that when my brother came to me, Jason killed him and cut off his limbs and drank his blood and spat it on the ground three times, asking forgiveness of the Moon Goddess, Io.

Oh! woe is me, my karma has come, my soul is cut from my body, and such is the fate of anyone who tries to keep the balance in these dire times. In deep gloom we sailed up the Danube for the ancient Atlantean theocracy, Poseidea. Woe is me! for the Earth shakes, the rocks grind, the skies rain fire! We have stolen the Fleece and unleashed the Ancient Ones, but alas, fratricide is the way of these doleful times. The blood of my brother reddened my silver moon dress like Venus reddened the sunless sky. These are the times of brother against brother, sister against sister, and son against father. And, alas, our vehicle will no longer fly because the sacred trust was broken. To Circe/sorceress, my father/sister, we go for purging.

> *Night threw her shadows on the world.*
> *Sailors out at sea looked up to the*
>   *circling Bear*
>   *and stars of Orion.*
> *Travelers and watchmen longed*
>   *for sleep,*
> *And oblivion came at last to*
>   *mothers mourning for their*
>   *children's death.*

Oh, what a strange land we crossed as we wandered for the cave of Circe. We see the pit where Phaethon struck the Earth; it boils with such metallic force no bird can fly above its surface. Tears of amber fall from the sky into the sand like manna from the gods. I, Cheiron, am mourned by Poseidon at this time because I released Prometheus from the Underworld, and I went to the Underworld giving up my immortality. Everywhere the rocks groan, the waters boil, the sky is strange, and where it is usually hot, it snows, and where it is usually cool, it burns. Finally we passed through the world in chaos and arrived at Aea, and we tied the Argo at the shore.

Circe had seen in a dream the destruction of all civilization that we had feared for three generations, just as you do now. She washed her hair in the salt sea as she wondered how she had saved her own oracle. Just like the blood of the gates of Passover, she protected her oracle against the fire by washing herself in the powerful ichor of a murdered man. But

Circe, revealer of male energy, knew she sucked his spirit, and so now she washed away his blood in the healing sea as the dolphins swam the pain to the stars. Circe, shepherdess of the animal kingdom, you are surrounded by composite beings, sphinxes and griffins, unicorns and pegasuses; and you know the still secret myth of Cheiron. As we arrived, Circe was calling creation to order as the Sun rose. We went to Hestia/hearth with Circe, and Jason pierced her Earth floor with his fratricidal sword. Circe knew they were supplicants of Zeus.

> Night threw her shadows on the world.
> Sailors out at sea looked up to the
>   circling Bear
>   and stars of Orion.
> Travelers and watchmen longed
>   for sleep,
> And oblivion came at last to
>   mothers mourning for their
>   children's death.

Circe propitiated Zeus with blood offering for the supplicant wanderers. In the human realm, the killing of a man is anathema, and yet all must eventually befriend the killer for community. Circe stayed by Hestia/hearth even when her ablutions were complete, as she wished to calm the chaos monsters. Then Circe sat with Jason and Medea by the hearth wanting to know all about the source of her horrible dream, as her land experienced distant echoes of the groaning. Circe lived on a coast off Vulscii that was spared the wrath of the sky gods and earth groaning. Medea told the story of the Argo's journey with the fifty Moon Men, her flight from her father Aeetes. Circe listened, then Circe banished her from her hearth with the foreigner, Jason. Circe circled her hearth with water from her sacred pot made by her own hands. Circe asked Zeus that she herself return never again to Earth until the star sign of the Water Bearer would come.

As they went on their journey, agents of Medea's father, the Colchians, pursued the Argo. The dolphins guided the Argo to Drepane Island near Dodona, and the fifty Argonauts were granted hospitality from the king. Then a fleet of Colchians from Aeetes appeared and asked the king of Drepane Island for Medea's return to her father. The king decided to return her only if she was a virgin. Now ruled only by Saturn/Necessity, Jason married Medea in the sacred marriage cave of Macris, an ancient Atlantean Bee Goddess. Bees are the sacred carrier of polarity energy from Mars to Venus, and this sacred marriage of the sky and Earth was made on top of the Golden Fleece/trust symbolizing balance of polarities.

> Night threw her shadows on the world.
> Sailors out at sea looked up to the
>   circling Bear
>   and stars of Orion.
> Travelers and watchmen longed

> *for sleep,*
> *And oblivion came at last to*
> *mothers mourning for their*
> *children's death.*

The Argo was driven across the Mediterranean by a fierce north wind engendered by another fierce catastrophic blast, and the good ship was marooned in Lake Tritonis near the seashore of Libya. A horrible snake from Gorgon's head bit the seer Mopsus in the heel and killed him, and the Argonauts lost their prophet, the one who knew the meaning of the journey. Mopsus asked to return again as a child in Libya under the sign of the Water Bearer. Their voice was gone, he died in agony, and the Minyae/ Jason/Medea were lost to the fortunes of the wind. As all stood by the edge of the sea overland from Lake Triton where the Argo was marooned, a great horse of Poseidon magically came to the beach and then all knew Poseidon's fury had subsided. The Triton horse carried Argo and the Argonauts back to the sea. The groaning was finished, and all could return home. Then Lord Triton, still elder guardian of the Atlantean kingdom, here for all to warn of causes of Earth upheavals of the Ancient days, gave us a clod of Earth for a shield.

He is eternal protector of shields. He blessed the fifty Moon Men, and taught them that their only shield was the Earth. Lord Triton taught that the erotic and conscious return to Earth by all creatures someday would end the imbalance. His lake would be filled again by the rising waters under the Water Bearer.

> *Night threw her shadows on the world.*
> *Sailors out at sea looked up to the*
> *circling Bear*
> *and stars of Orion.*
> *Travelers and watchmen longed*
> *for sleep,*
> *And oblivion came at last to*
> *mothers mourning for their*
> *children's death.*

As we entered the Aegean we encountered a thick pall of gloom and we knew it was a sign of great evil, evil too great to be comprehended by inhabitants of Earth. Nearby was a great void in the waters from a recent eruption of a giant volcano, a vent from Pluto to the angry sky. Volcanoes are the emotions of the mother disturbed by bad blood of no trust, but we had returned, bearing the Golden Fleece. One of the Minyae tossed the Earth clod from Lord Triton into the void, and the new growth of Thera began on the salt wound on the ocean floor vent into the deep. For there are three gods at all times: the god of creation, of destruction, and the god of being here and now in time. But we all knew that we would find death on every island and shore awaiting us.

We journeyed in faraway lands away from the heart of the destruction and we escaped for the time being. Eventually we came home to Jason's rightful kingdom, Pagasae, still ruled by Pelias. Medea disguised herself as the Moon Goddess/Crone to reenter Pagasae to take the throne back for Jason whose parents had been killed by Pelias. Jason's father had even mercifully bashed a younger brother, Promachis, to death—a younger brother Jason had never known. Medea cried out that the great goddess, Artemis, had come in a divine chariot drawn by flying serpents. Medea charmed Pelias to sleep as she saw the nature of the death around herself, and she commanded his daughters to cut him up after she had boiled him in the regeneration cauldron.

> *Medea, guardian of life, sometimes forced*
> > *to kill;*
> *She saw that only the children mattered now.*
> *Like a mother who kills her young when*
> > *there is no life on Earth,*
> *Medea ravaged all but future life for us all.*

Pelias was boiled in the cauldron, a secret desire of all women who hate destroyers of life/children, but one daughter, Alcestis, refused to assist. Pelias was the brother/murderer of Jason's father, Aeson, and Medea had no compassion left after Jason had murdered her own brother, Apsyrtus. Next, Jason feared the revenge of his brother, and he gave up the throne and home that Medea coveted. Again, the sacrifice of the sacred king for the goddess religion was foregone, the Earth was again not blessed, and there could be no sacred kingdom again. Thus, Medea/Moon Queen came in a chariot for Sun King/Jason, and again Jason refused his role as guardian. Jason wished for a better throne and was banished by the moon priestesses.

> *Medea, guardian of life, sometimes forced*
> > *to kill;*
> *She saw that only the children mattered now.*
> *Like a mother who kills her young when*
> > *there is no life on Earth,*
> *Medea ravaged all but future life for us all.*

Jason and Medea secured the throne of Corinth because the king was dead, and Medea's father was the rightful king of Corinth. After ten years, Jason came to believe that Medea had poisoned the king of Corinth, and Jason wished to divorce Medea to marry Glauce, daughter of King Creon of Thebes. Medea burned Glauce up, and Zeus was so impressed with Medea's deed that he fell in love with her. Medea, true to other women/wives, refused his advances, and the wife of Zeus, Hera, made the children of Medea immortal. Medea fled in the winged serpent chariot from Helios, and she gave the kingdom to Sisyphus in disgust, condemning it to eternal struggle and no reward. Medea was witness to an age of chaos and healing, an age we need to remember now as we face similar issues and times.

> *Medea, guardian of life, sometimes forced*

to kill;
She saw that only the children mattered now.
Like a mother who kills her young when
there is no life on Earth,
Medea ravaged all but future life for us all.

Divorce me! screamed Medea. Her voice shook the galaxies and the supernovas. Divorce me! the woman who bore your children, left her father for the sacred marriage, and who is sky queen Aphrodite who never wavered in her trust of the universe. And then I am even coveted by Zeus when my only loyalty is to women/wife/Hera. I am the mother of fourteen sacred children, seven daughters and seven sons. What greater proof will there ever be that I am sought when you desired me and used by you only as a vessel for the sacred seed? You, Jason, swore that you would be my husband if I used my female powers to protect civilization by helping you recover the Fleece/Ark/Source. It seems it was easy for you to make promises when you were terrified of universal destruction, and it is easy for you to return to your short-sighted awareness of Earth once the danger is over. You are as low as a man who has just sodomized a young boy, and then you snivel for your life when caught!

Sorry—you say you are sorry after you ended life for thousands of years with nuclear power and chemical plants? Many of the scientists who participated in creating the Bomb at Los Alamos later said they were sorry. Beware all you males who think you control me and my energy; with all your devices you think you create yourselves. You still think I will allow starfuckers called Challenger or Centaur or Atlas? I am the life-force itself, and I can kill in more ways than you will ever imagine. For I am fire, and each time you create imbalance I will purify Earth until you learn. Do not forget that even though later ages say I murdered my own children, do not forget that all of them are immortal by Hera's command. And seven boys and seven girls each year spend a year in Hera's temple for all eternity. That is why you must see with the eyes of children in order to gain the kingdom.

Medea, guardian of life, sometimes forced
to kill;
She saw that only the children mattered now.
Like a mother who kills her young when
there is no life on Earth,
Medea ravaged all but future life for us all.

I, Chiron, have manifested on the physical plane for the first time as a planet. Medea just told you her story of the most important journey-search during the last transmutation crisis. These times exist every 3600 years when Nibiru has orbited out to its farthest point and is moving back toward Earth. At these times of heightened imbalance, the hologram can be altered so that Earthlings can finally understand their relationship to everything in the universe. Humans are now invited into galactic communion if they will learn the ways of Earth initiation. If you will just seek pleasure and Uranian electrical excitement instead of Saturn/control, you will make the right turn. If you will just see that immortality cannot be found by controlling planet Earth—it can only be found by letting go completely into the present time and space. If you could just see that ecstasy and one-ness with the divine is only known by forgetting oneself.

Stop struggling to get to a place or have a feeling that you think you need. Just respond to your world as it is. Every time you try to alter your world, you move from your place; instead, change yourself by being present right where you are. My orbit, my energy, is eccentric. I have appeared because you are ready now to let go of all habits and ideas about reality and just be present. Yes the old part of you must die; that is what initiation is. But the outer is a reflection of your inner self. Surely your hideous, polluted, monstrous world will tell you that your inner self is ready to die and be reborn in Medea's cauldron of regeneration.

I do not want you to forget that the higher and deeper essence of my energy is understood without words by people born since 1942, and that few of the older generation will know it because they are afraid of death. The last few generations have destroyed so much Earth life-force that they fear their own death. They fear Hades, but the young do not understand this place. Many of the older people know it well and they are going to Hades themselves from their fear. If they would just decide to live for one second, that would be enough. I tell you that my way is to break Saturn control, and now that I was sighted November 1, 1977, I will do so if enough people just assist me now. Each individual who transmutes the ego so that the universal peace and love can channel through—each one of them heals the Earth. I have returned to tell you how. I have told you Medea's story because I lived on your planet at that time. If all of you only understood that the Earth is the cosmic training school.

Listen well and do not forget this: Medea's fate was the death of the goddess religion and the fate of your times will be terracide, death of the Earth. Now the greening life-force shield, ozone, is disappearing above the polar ice caps. Only this crisis could bring me back, and you are like me. Only danger of this degree will make it possible for you to give up everything and become essence. You are now to focus on planetary orgasm instead of terracide. The last baptizer used water and my element is Earth.

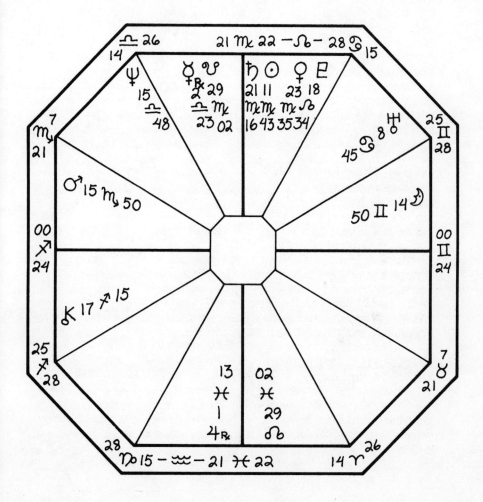

Chart Number One:
Physicist
Koch House System

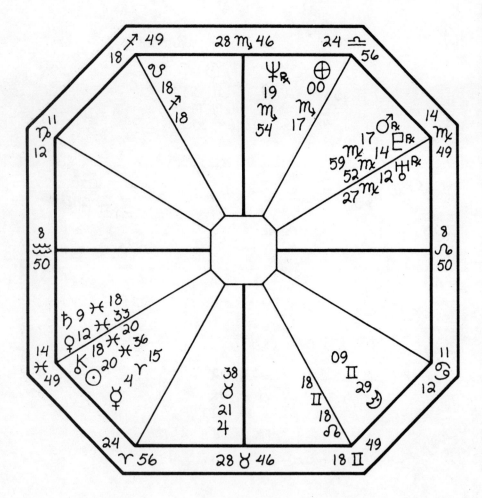

Chart Number Two:
Spiritual Healer
Koch House System

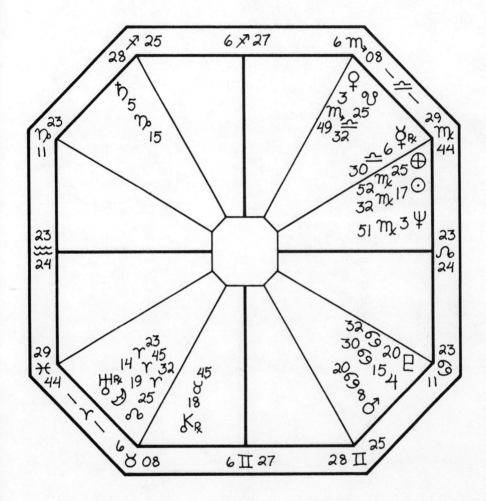

Chart Number Three:
Astrological Publisher
Koch House System

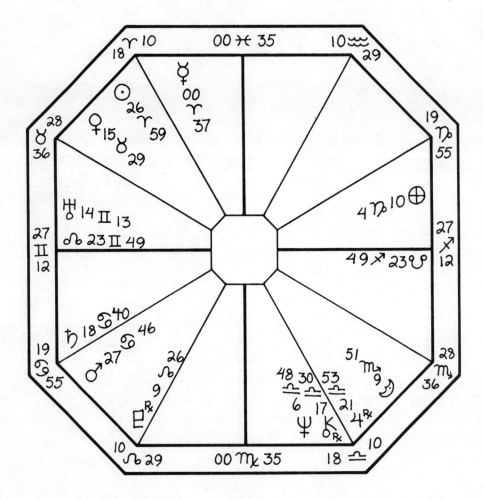

Chart Number Four:
Sanctuary Worker
Koch House System

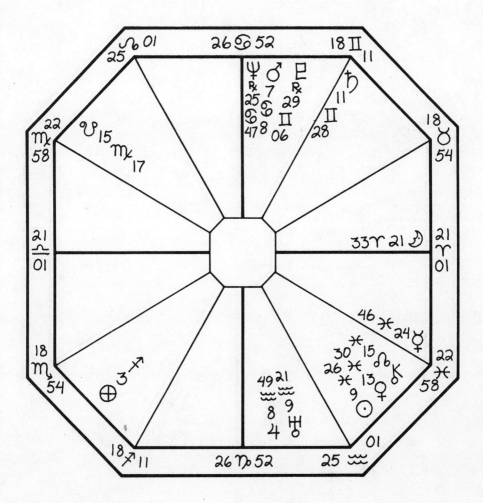

Chart Number Five:
Guru
Koch House System

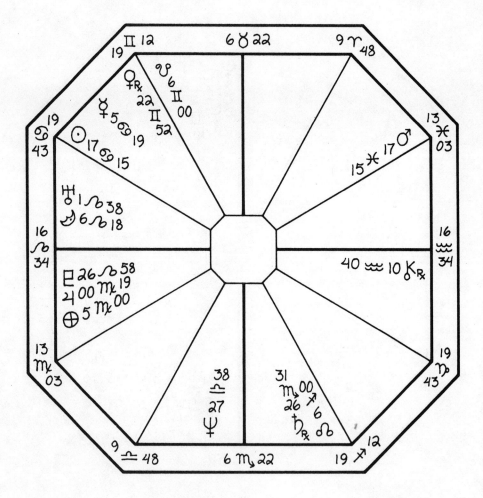

Chart Number Six:
Self-Healer
Koch House System

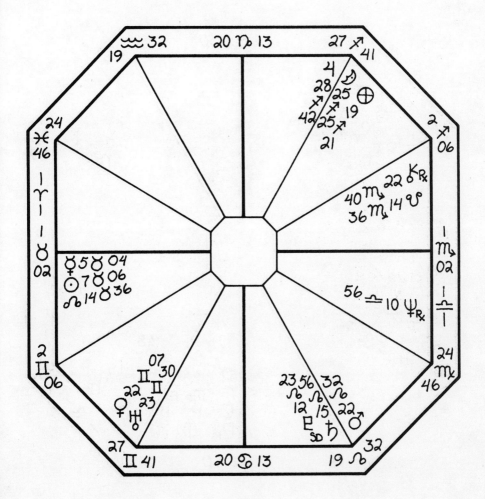

Chart Number Seven:
Weaver
Koch House System

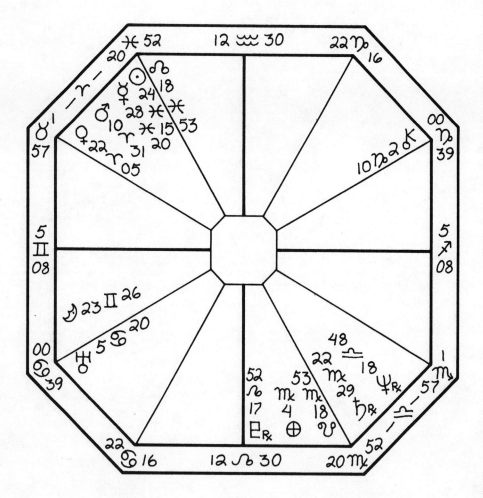

Chart Number Eight:
Hermetic Teacher
Koch House System

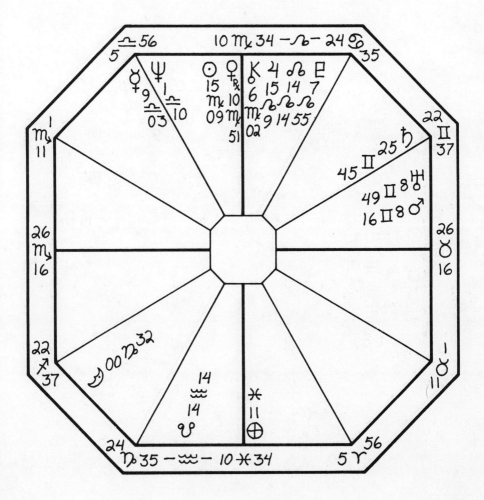

Chart Number Nine:
Artist Photographer
Koch House System

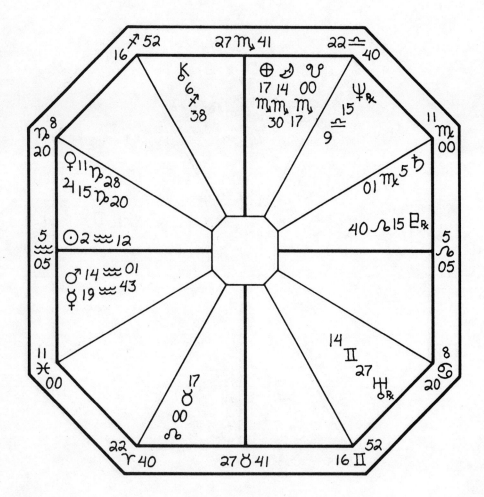

Chart Number Ten:
Publisher
Koch House System

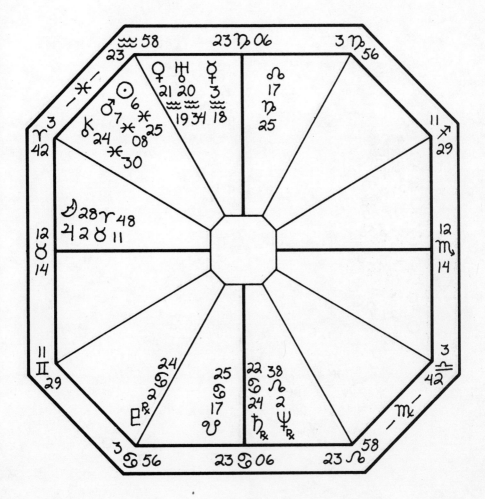

Chart Number Eleven:
Physician
Koch House System

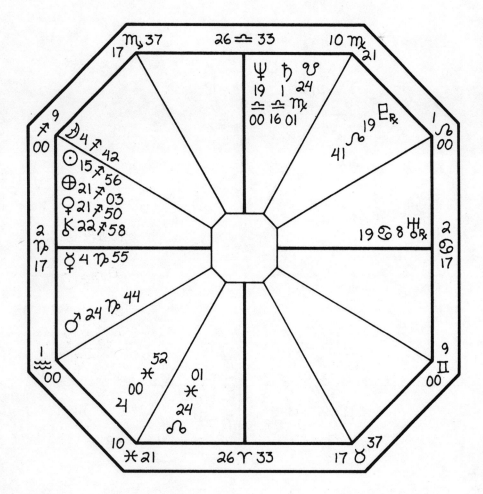

Chart Number Twelve:
Initiate
Koch House System

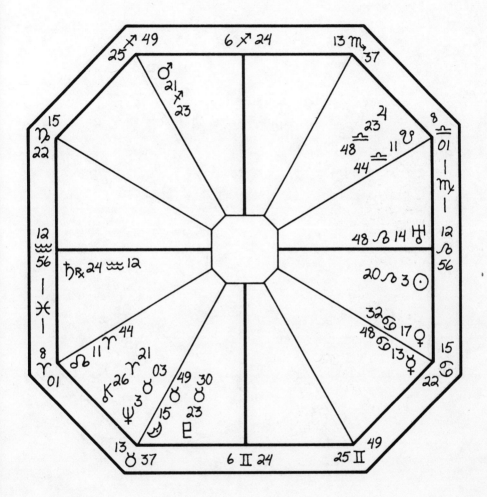

Chart Number Thirteen:
Carl Jung
Placidus House System

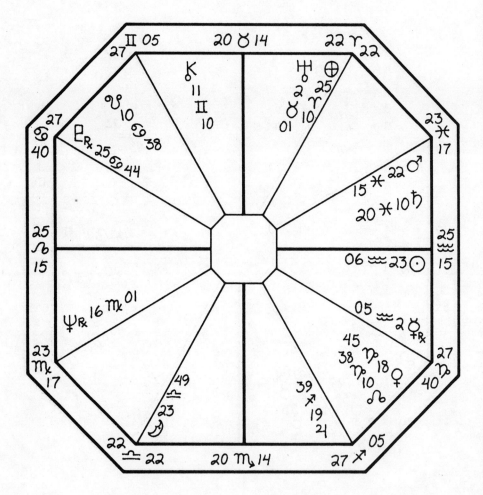

Chart Number Fourteen
Artist & Nun
Koch House System

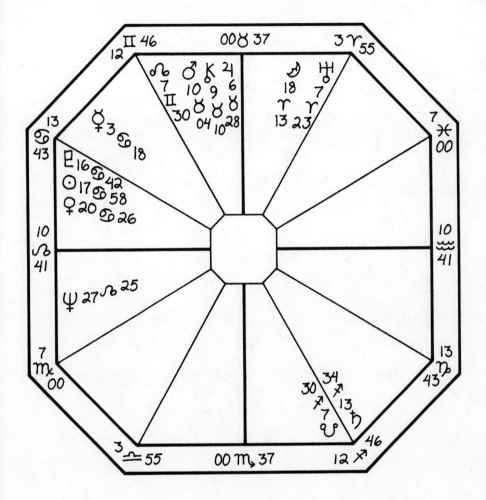

Chart Number Fifteen
Priest
Koch House System

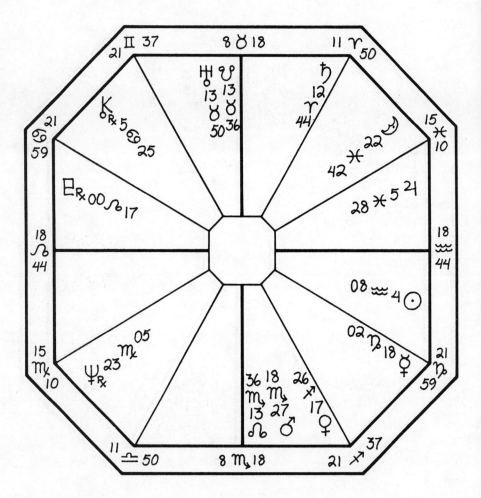

Chart Number Sixteen:
Futurist Writer
Koch House System

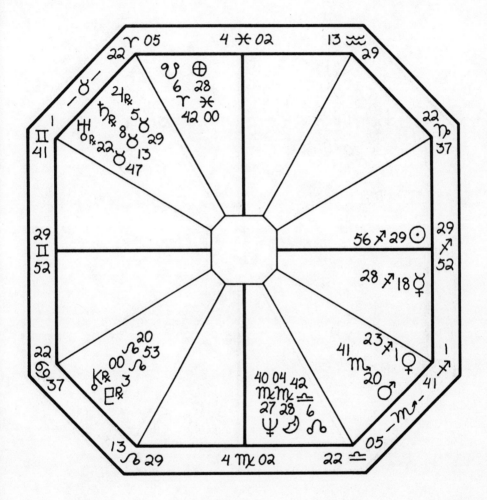

Chart Number Seventeen:
Theologian
Koch House System

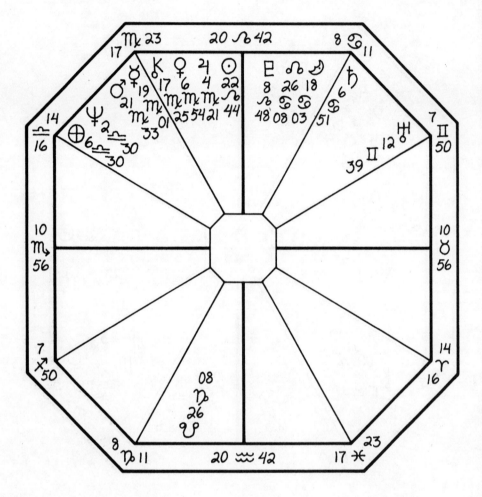

Chart Number Eighteen:
Yoga Teacher
Koch House System

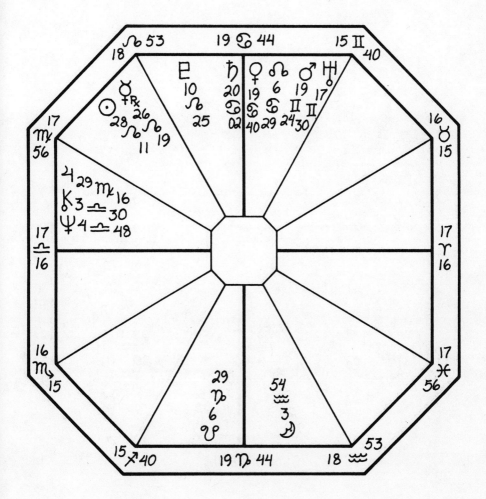

Chart Number Nineteen:
Therapist
Koch House System

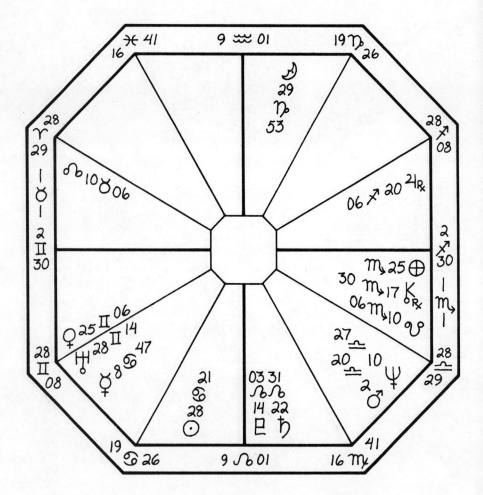

Chart Number Twenty:
Yoga Teacher
Koch House System

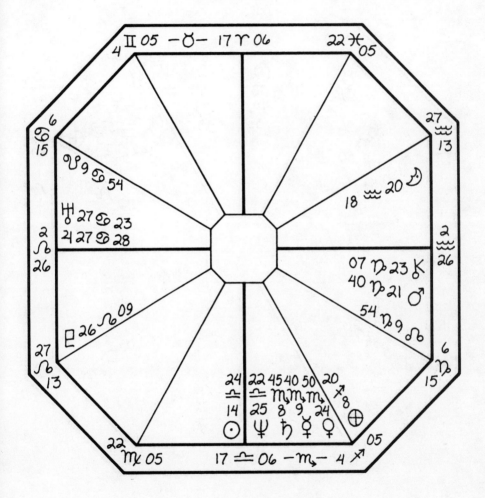

Chart Number Twenty-One:
Physician
Koch House System

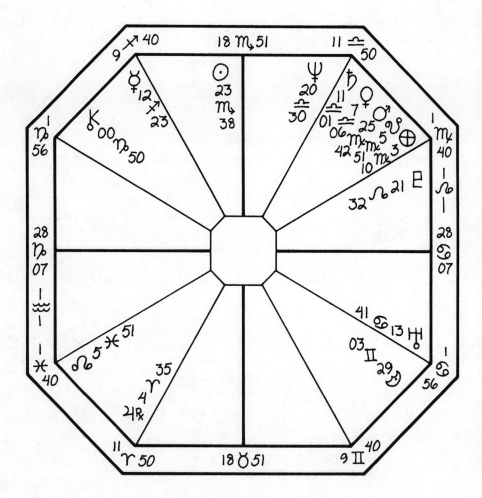

Chart Number Twenty-Two:
Astrologer
Koch House System

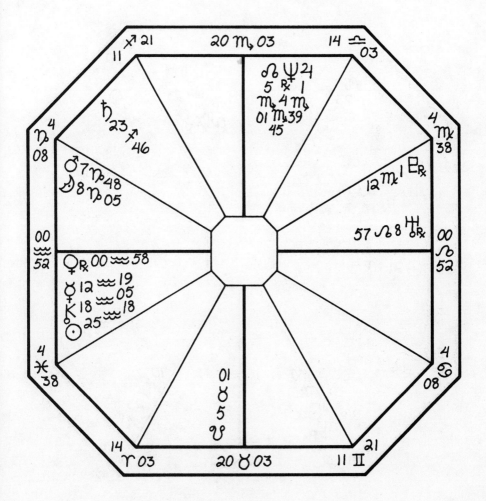

Chart Number Twenty-Three:
Native American Political Leader
Koch House System

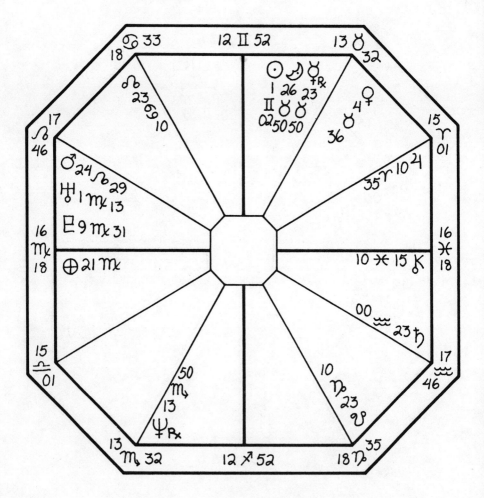

Chart Number Twenty-Four:
Young Teacher
Koch House System

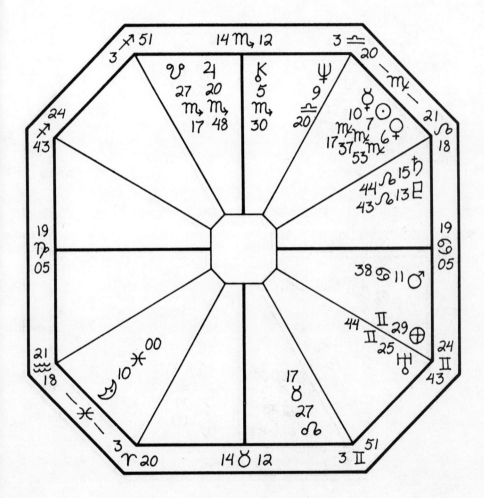

Chart Number Twenty-Five:
Artist
Koch House System

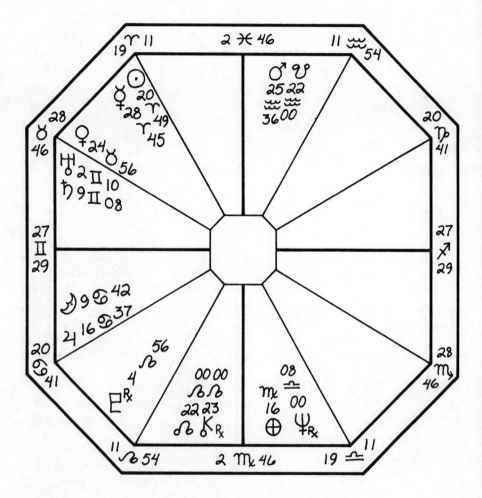

Chart Number Twenty-Six:
New Age Communicator
Koch House System

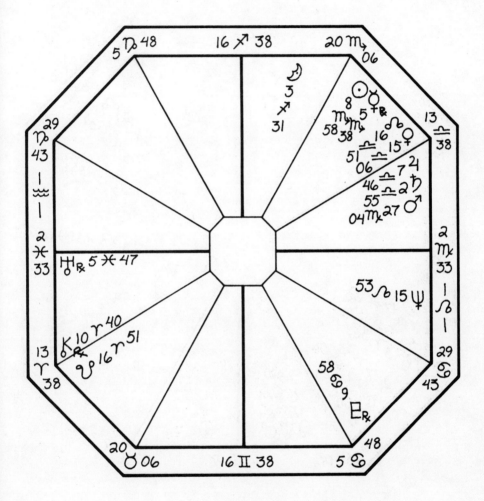

Chart Number Twenty-Seven:
Jungian Analyst
Koch House System

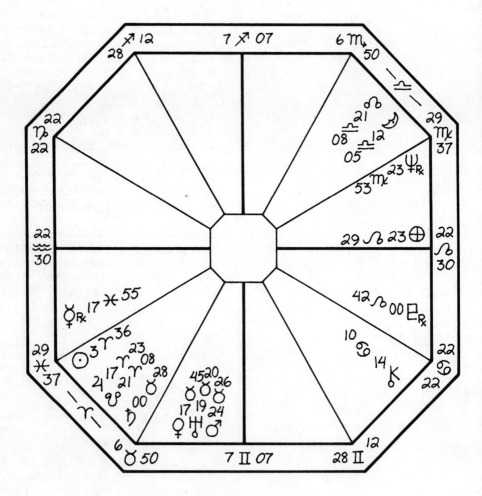

Chart Number Twenty-Nine:
AIDS Counselor
Koch House System

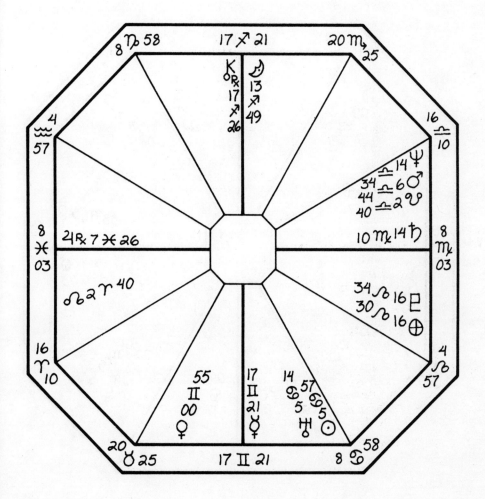

Chart Number Thirty:
Jeweller
Koch House System

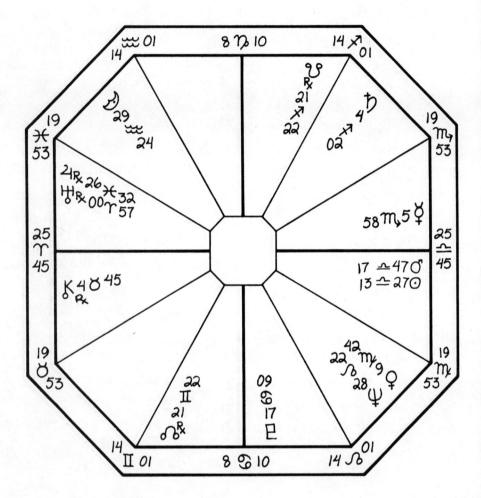

Chart Number Thirty-One:
Psychiatrist R.D. Laing
Source: Lois Rodden
Koch House System

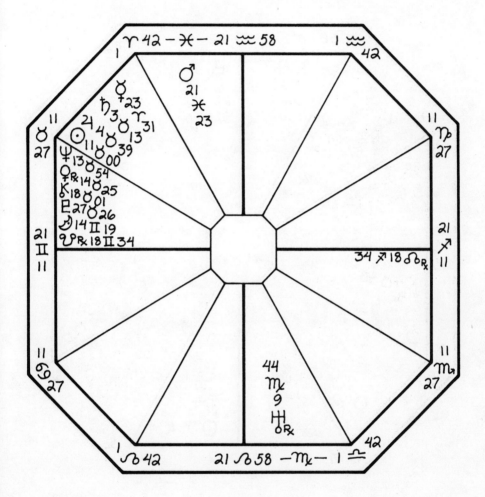

Chart Number Thirty-Two:
Chardin
Source: Lois Rodden
Placidus House System

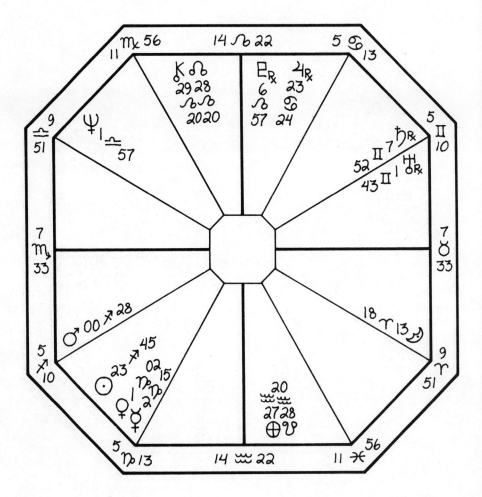

Chart Number Thirty-Three:
Channel of Atlantean Symbols
Koch House System

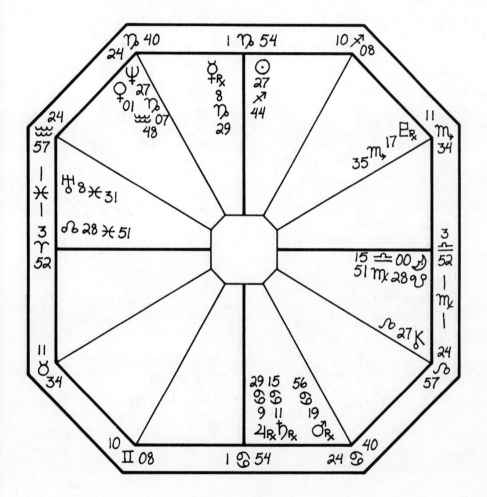

Chart Number Thirty-Four:
Nostradamus
Source: Author's Research
Koch House System

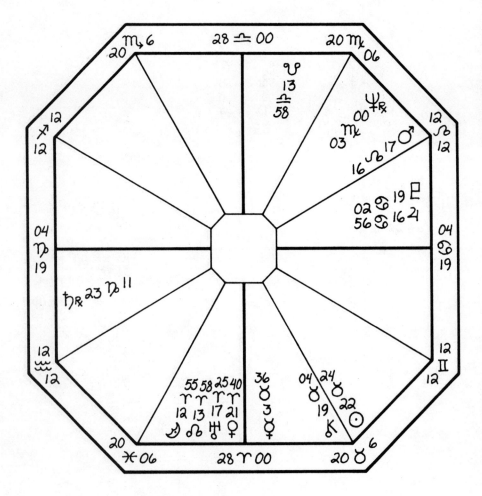

Chart Number Thirty-Five:
Jim Jones
Source: Lois Rodden
Placidus House System

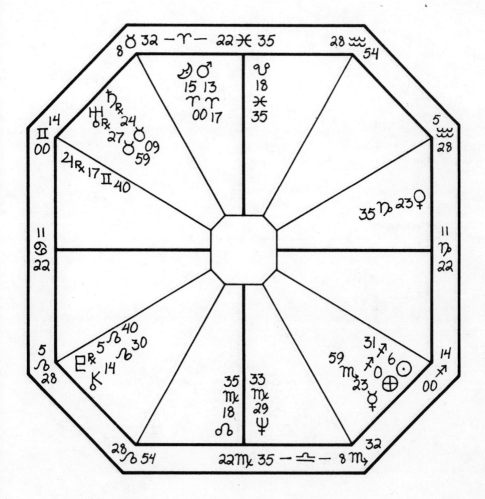

Chart Number Thirty-Six:
Musician
Koch House System

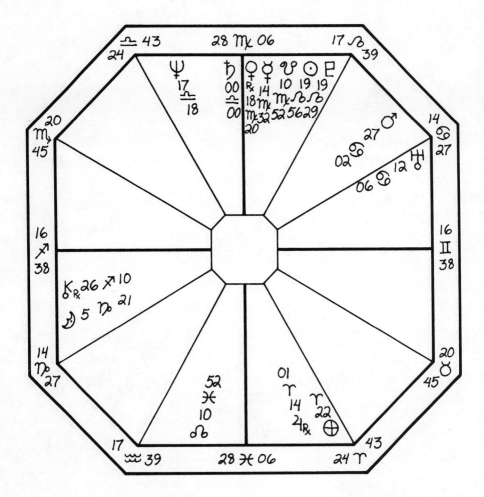

Chart Number Thirty-Seven:
Priest
Koch House System

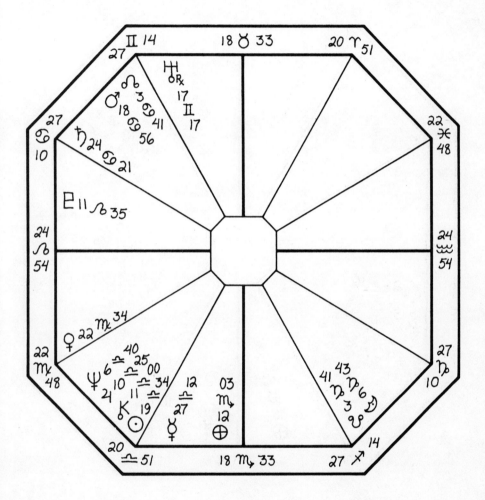

Chart Number Thirty-Eight:
Writer
Koch House System

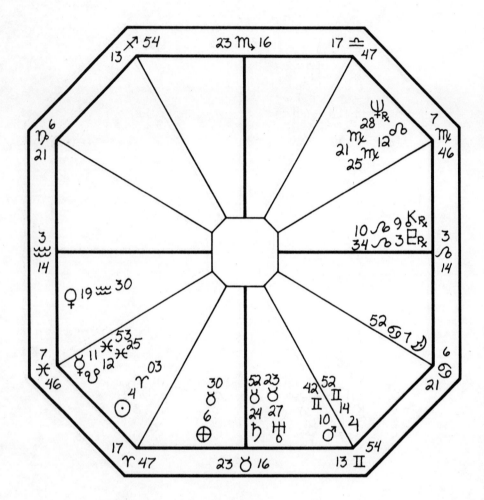

Chart Number Thirty-Nine:
New Age Publisher
Koch House System

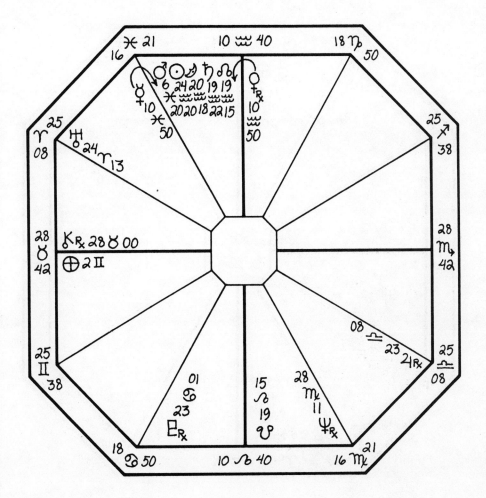

Chart Number Forty:
Jungian Analyst
Koch House System

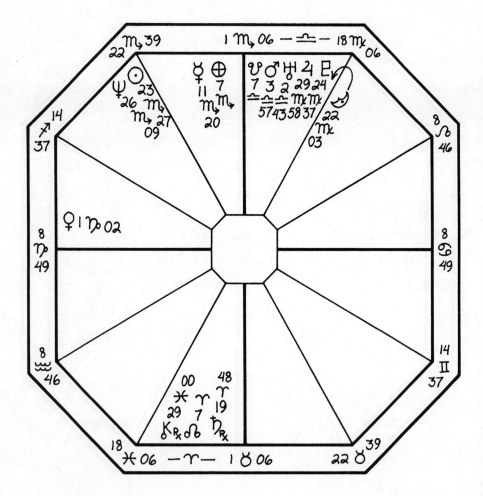

Chart Number Forty-One:
Artist
Koch House System

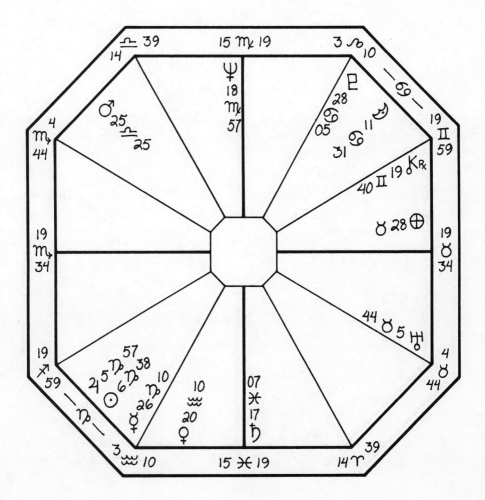

Chart Number Forty-Two:
Priest
Koch House System

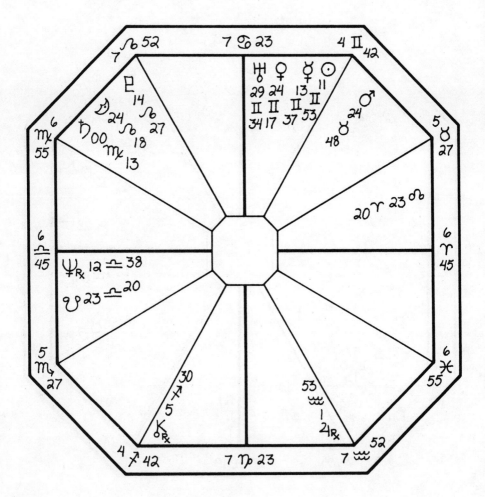

Chart Number Forty-Three:
Healer
Koch House System

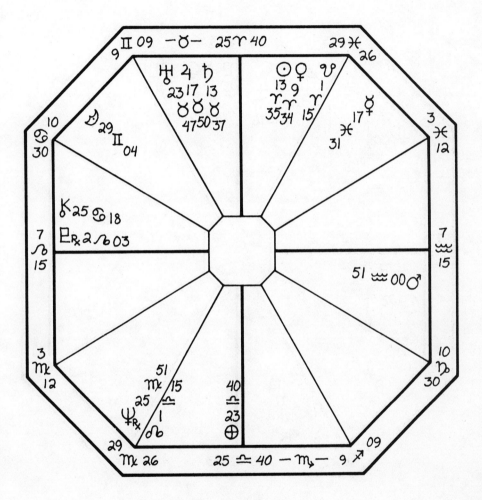

Chart Number Forty-Four:
Guided Imagery Healer
Koch House System

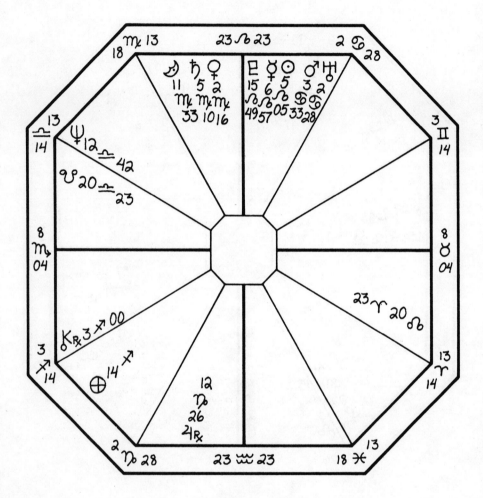

Chart Number Forty-Five:
Glass Blower
Koch House System

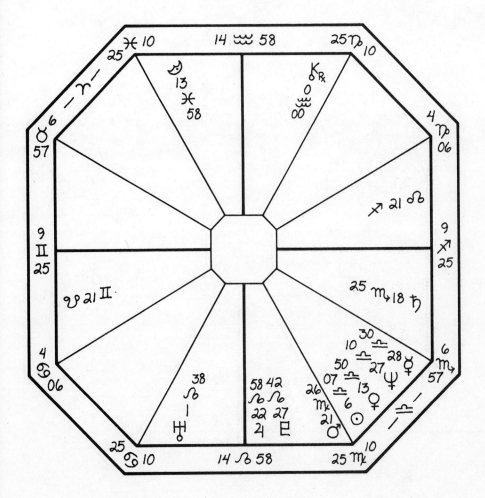

Chart Number Forty-Six:
Healer
Koch House System

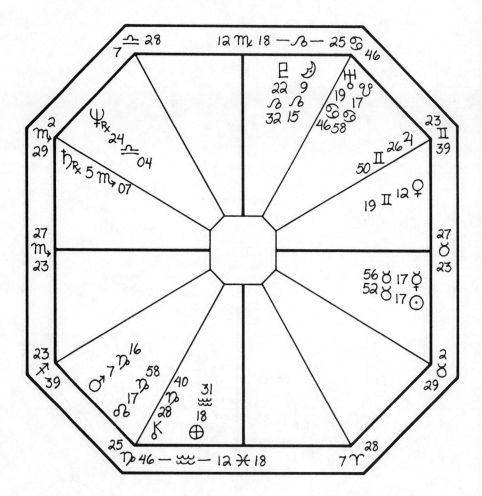

Chart Number Forty-Seven:
Student-Healer
Koch House System

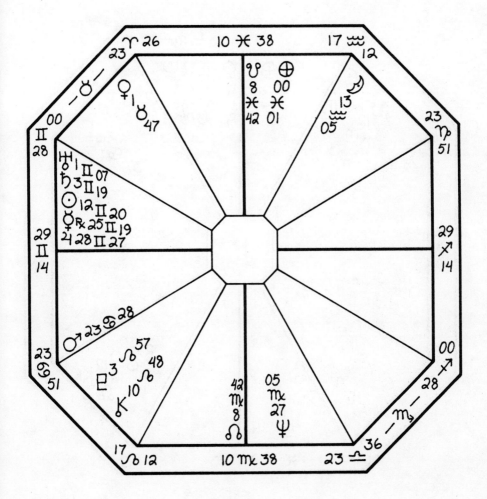

Chart Number Forty-Eight:
Teacher-Healer
Koch House System

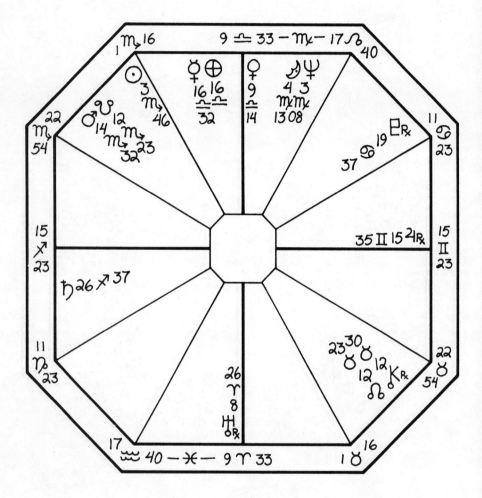

Chart Number Forty-Nine:
Astrologer
Koch House System

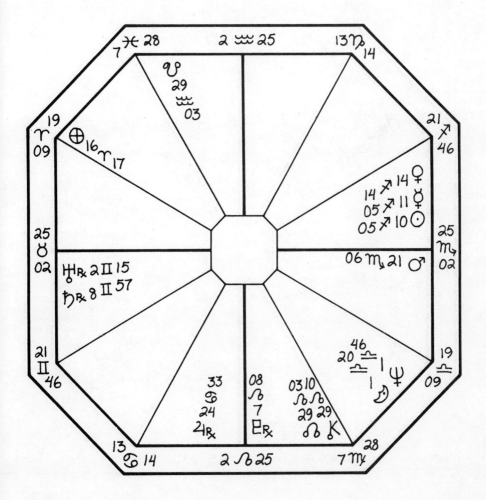

Chart Number Fifty:
Splitting of the Atom
Source: Author's Research
Koch House System

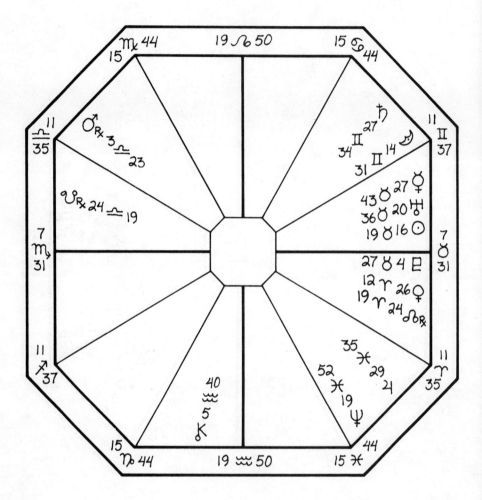

Chart Number Fifty-One:
Sigmund Freud
Source: Lois Rodden
Placidus House System

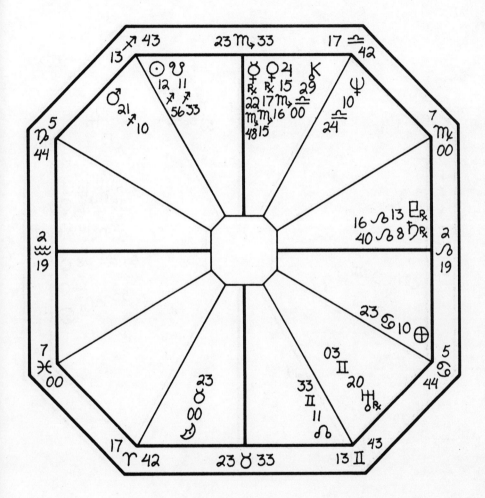

Chart Number Fifty-Two:
Architect
Koch House System

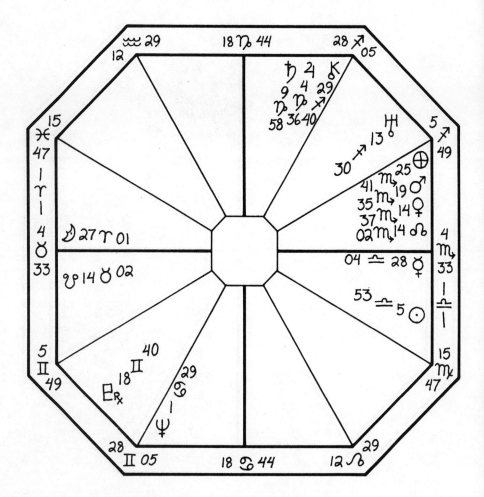

Chart Number Fifty-Four:
Enrico Fermi
Source: Lois Rodden
Placidus House System

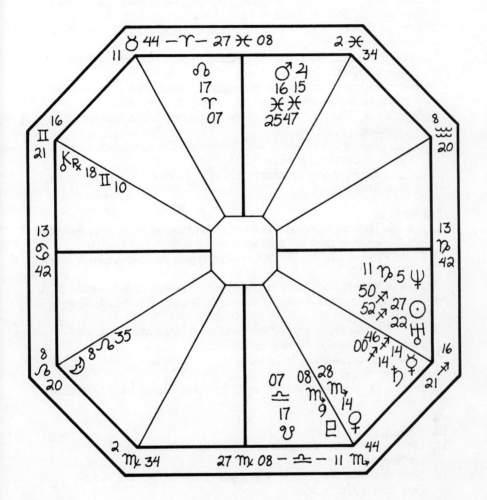

Chart Number Fifty-Five:
Horary for Natal Chiron
Reading
Koch House System

NOTES

Introduction:

1. Green, Jeff, *Pluto: The Evolutionary Journey of the Soul,* Vol. 1, Llewellyn Publications, St. Paul, 1986.
2. Lantero, Erminie, *The Continuing Discovery of Chiron,* Samuel Weiser, York Beach, 1983.
   Nolle, Richard, *Chiron: The New Planet in your Horoscope,* AFA, Tempe, 1983.
   Joseph, Thomas Anthony, *The Archetypal Universe: Myths and Symbols of the Heavens,* privately published by the author, 1984.
   Stein, Zane, "The Key: Journal of the Associates for the Study of Chiron," Lansdale, 1978-1986.
   _____, *Interpreting Chiron,* ASC (hereafter, The Associates for the Study of Chiron), Lansdale, 1983.
   _____, *Essence and Application: A View From Chiron,* CAO Times, New York, 1986.

Chapter One:

1. Joseph, Thomas Anthony, *The Archetypal Universe: Myths and Symbols of the Heavens,* privately published by the author, 1984, p. 161.
2. Nolle, Richard, *Chiron: The New Planet in your Horoscope,* AFA, Tempe, 1983, p. 9.
3. Graves, Robert, *The Greek Myths,* Pelican, England, 1982, section 50;5.
4. Cory, Isaac Preston, *Ancient Fragments,* Wizards Bookshelf, Savage, 1975, p. 18.
5. Clow, Barbara Hand, *Eye of the Centaur: A Visionary Guide into Past Lives,* Llewellyn Publications, 1986.
6. Graves, *op cit.,* section 56 *passim.*
7. Nolle, *op cit.,* p. 10.
8. Negus, Dr. Kenneth, lecture on Chiron and ecologists, AFA Chicago, 1981.
9. *Ibid.*
10. Joseph, *op cit.,* p. 165.
11. Lerner, Gerda, *The Creation of Patriarchy,* Oxford University Press, London, 1986.
12. Spence, Lewis, *The Occult Sciences in Atlantis,* Samuel Weiser, New York, 1978, p. 56.
13. Lantero, Erminie, *The Continuing Discovery of Chiron,* Samuel Weiser, York Beach, 1983, p. 26.
14. Graves, *op cit.,* p. 96.
15. *Ibid.,* p. 11.
16. Clow, *op cit.*
17. Anonymous: Translation by Robert A. Powell, *Meditations on the Tarot: A Journey into Christian Hermeticism,* Amity House, Amity, 1985.
18. Nolle, *op cit.,* p. 15.
19. Joseph, *op cit.,* p. 165.

Chapter Two:
1. Graves, Robert, *The Greek Myths,* Pelican, London, section 70 passim.
2. Joransen, Phil, and Ken Butigan, *Cry of the Environment: Rebuilding the Christian Creation Tradition,* Bear & Company, Sante Fe, 1985.
3. Gallanopoulos, A.G., and Edward Bacon, *Atlantis: The Truth Behind the Legend,* Bobbs-Merrill, New York, 1969.
4. Fontenrose, Joseph, *Python: A Study of Delphic Myth and Its Origins,* University of California Press, Berkeley, 1959, p. 414.
5. IRAS sighting of new planet in San Francisco Chronicle, Dec. 27, 1983.
6. Sitchin, Zecharia, *The Twelfth Planet,* Avon, New York, 1976.
   _____,*The Stairway to Heaven,* Avon, New York, 1980.
   _____,*The Wars of Gods and Men,* Avon, New York, 1985.
7. Clow, Barbara Hand, *Eye of the Centaur: A Visionary Guide into Past Lives,* Llewellyn Publications, St. Paul, 1986.
8. Arguelles, Jose, *The Mayan Factor: Path Beyond Technology,* Bear & Company, Sante Fe, 1987.
9. Nolle, Richard, *Chiron: The New Planet in Your Horoscope,* AFA Tempe, 1983, p. 6.

Chapter Three:
1. Clow, Barbara Hand, *Eye of the Centaur: A Visionary Guide into Past Lives,* Llewellyn Publications, St. Paul, 1986, p. 100.
2. Sedgewick, Philip, "The Matter of Soul and Spirit," *The Chiron Booklet #2,* edited by Zane Stein, ASC, no date, p. 23.
3. Ibid., p. 30.
4. Ibid., p. 27.
5. Robertson, Marc, *Critical Ages in Adult Life: The Transit of Saturn,* Marc Robertson, 1976.
6. Sanella, Lee, *Kundalini: Psychosis or Transcendence,* privately printed, 1975.

Chapter Four:
1. Green, Jeff, *Pluto: The Evolutionary Journey of the Soul,* Llewellyn Publications, St. Paul, 1986.

Chapter Five:
1. Nolle, Richard, *Chiron: The New Planet in Your Horoscope,* AFA. Tempe, 1983, p. 113.
2. *Ibid.,* p. 115.
3. Heard in a lecture by Chris Griscom at the Light Institute, Galisteo, New Mexico, August, 1985.

Chapter Six:
1. Arguelles, Jose, *Earth Ascending: An Illustrated Treatise on the Law Governing Whole Systems,* Shambhalla, Berkeley, 1984, p. 16.
2. Griscom, Chris, *Ecstasy is a New Frequency: Teachings of the Light Institute,* Bear & Company, Sante Fe, 1987.
3. Baigent, Michael, Richard Leigh and Henry Lincoln, *Holy Blood, Holy Grail,* Dell, New York, 1982.

Chapter Seven:
1. Nolle, Richard, *Chiron: The New Planet in Your Horoscope*, AFA, Tempe, 1983, p. 77.
2. *Ibid.*, p. 76.
3. Clow, Barbara Hand, *Eye of the Centaur: A Visionary Guide into Past Lives*, Llewellyn Publications, St. Paul, 1986.
4. Sitchin, Zecharia, *Stairway to Heaven*, Avon, New York, 1980, p. 95.
5. Joseph, Thomas Anthony, *The Archetypal Universe, Myths and Symbols of Heaven*, privately published by the Author, 1984.
6. Nolle, *op cit.*, p. 88.
7. Stein, Zane, *Interpreting Chiron*, ASC, Lansdale, 1983, p. 13.
8. Nolle, *op. cit.*, pp. 103-105.
9. Green, Jeff, *Pluto: The Evolutionary Journey of the Soul*, Llewellyn Publications, St. Paul, 1986.
10. Nolle, *op cit.*, p. 108.

Chapter Eight:
1. Green, Jeff, *Pluto: The Evolutionary Journey of the Soul*, Llewellyn Publications, St. Paul, 1986, p. 168.
2. Dorland, Frank, *The Mystery of the Crystal Skull*, Wisdom Books, Inc., Taos, 1984, tape, side 2.
3. Tierney, Bil, *Dynamics of Aspect Analysis: New Perceptions in Astrology*, CRCS Publications, Reno, 1983.
4. Griscom, Chris, *Ecstasy is a New Frequency: Teachings of the Light Institute*, Bear & Company, Sante Fe, 1987.

Chapter Nine:
1. Various aspects in the natal chart may indicate past lives such as Lunar Nodes, retrograde planets, interceptions, etc., and transits and progressions in natal comparison work. However, the contents can only be obtained by consulting a reader of the akashic records or doing past life work.
2. Stein, Zane, *Essence and Application: A View From Chiron*, CAO Times, New York, 1986, p. 88.
3. Robertson, Marc, *Critical Ages in Adult Life: The Transit of Saturn*, Marc Robertson, 1976.
4. Clow, Barbara Hand, *Eye of the Centaur: A Visionary Guide into Past Lives*, Llewellyn Publications, St. Paul, 1986.
5. Stein, *op cit.*, p. 97.
6. *Ibid.*, p. 125.
7. Griscom, Chris, *Ecstasy is a New Frequency: Teachings of the Light Institute*, Bear & Company, Sante Fe, 1987.

Chapter Ten:
1. Stein, Zane, *Essence and Application: A View From Chiron*, CAO Times, New York, 1986, p. 141.
2. *Ibid.*
3. *Ibid.*, p. 142.

4. *Ibid.,* p. 159.
5. Green, Jeff, *Pluto: Evolutionary Journey of the Soul,* Llewellyn Publications, St. Paul, p. xviii.
6. *Ibid.*
7. Baigent, Michael, and Richard Leigh and Henry Lincoln, *Holy Blood, Holy Grail,* Dell, New York, 1982.
8. Schulman, Martin, *Karmic Astrology: The Moon's Nodes and Reincarnation,* Samuel Weiser, New York, 1975.
9. Grebner, Bernice Prill, *Everything Has a Phase,* AFA, Tempe, 1982.
10. Schulman, *op cit.*

Chapter Eleven:
1. Schulman, Martin, *Karmic Astrology: The Moon's Nodes and Reincarnation,* Samuel Weiser, New York, 1975, p. 77.
2. Ibid., p. 78.
3. Ibid., p. 97.
4. Clow, Barbara Hand, *Eye of the Centaur: A Visionary Guide into Past Lives,* Llewellyn Publications, St. Paul, 1986.
5. Schulman, *op cit.,* p. 97.
6. *Ibid.,* general reference.
7. Schulman, Martin, *Karmic Astrology, Joy and the Part of Fortune,* Samuel Weiser, New York, 1978.

Chapter Twelve:
1. Stein, Zane, *Essence and Application: A View From Chiron,* CAO Times, New York, 1986.
2. Griscom, Chris, *Ecstasy is a New Frequency: Teachings of the Light Institute,* Bear & Company, 1987.
3. von Franz, Marie-Louise, *Alchemy: An Introduction to the Symbolism and the Psychology,* Inner City Books, Toronto, 1980.
4. Fox, Matthew, *Original Blessing: A Primer in Creation Spirituality,* Bear & Company, Sante Fe, 1984.
5. Clow, Barbara Hand, *Eye of the Centaur: A Visionary Guide into Past Lives,* Llewellyn Publications, St. Paul, 1986.

Chapter Thirteen:
1. Clow, Barbara Hand, *Eye of the Centaur: A Visionary Guide into Past Lives,* Llewellyn Publications, St. Paul, 1986.
2. Gallanopoulos, A.G., and Edward Bacon, *Atlantis: The Truth Behind the Legend,* Bobbs-Merrill, New York, 1969.
3. Heard at a lecture by Thomas Banyaca, "The Hopi Prophecy," in July, 1984, Santa Fe, New Mexico.
4. Arguelles, Jose, *The Mayan Factor: Path Beyond Technology,* Bear & Company, Santa Fe, New Mexico, 1987
5. *Ibid.*
6. Cathie, Captain Bruce, *Harmonic 33,* AH and AW Reed, Auckland, undated, p. 73.
7. *Ibid.,* p. 74.
8. Velikovsky, Immanuel, *Mankind in Amnesia,* Doubleday, NY, 1982.

9. Watters, Barbara, *Horary Astrology and the Judgement of Events,* Valhalla, Washington, D.C., 1973, p. 15.
10. Jones, Marc Edmund, *The Sabian Symbols in Astrology,* Shambhala, Boulder, 1978, p. 237.
11. Arguelles, op. cit.,
12. Green, Jeff, *Pluto: The Evolutionary Journey of the Soul,* Llewellyn Publications, St. Paul, 1986, p. 19.
13. Jones, op. cit., p. 223.

EYE OF THE CENTAUR
by Barbara Hand Clow

This remarkable book functions on two levels. First, it tells an exciting story of personal and spiritual evolution via a new approach to the practice of Past Life Regression. Rather than being limited to our personal remembrance of past lives, Clow shows how to have a direct *collaboration* with our Higher Self. The result is that past experiences of high spiritual development and initiation are drawn into the mind and body of the present self! This allows for quicker transformation and spiritual growth than would normally be the case.

While this alone is well worth the price of the book, the second level makes this book a minor miracle. For *The Eye of the Centaur* is written in a style which actually *includes* past life experiences! It allows each reader to experience his or her own past lives while reading about the author's experience in the times of the ancient Celts, Greeks, Egyptians, and even back to Atlantis!

Unlike other books on Past Life Regression, this is not a set of instructions which will only work for a few people. Nor is it another listing of a group of people who have remembered their past lives in an attempt to prove that reincarnation is a fact. Rather, it is as exciting as a well written novel of adventure, pride, love, lust, passion and spiritual advancement. This book will do far more than just affect you, It will change your life!

0-87542-095-8, 264 pages, 6 x 9, illus., softcover.   **$9.95**

PLUTO: The Evolutionary Journey of the Soul
by Jeff Green

If you have ever asked "Why am I here?" or "What are my lessons?" then this book will help you to objectively learn the answers from an astrological point of view. Green shows you how the planet Pluto relates to the evolutionary and karmic lessons in this life and how past lives can be understood through the position of Pluto in your chart.

Beyond presenting key principles and ideas about the nature of the evolutionary journey of the Soul, this book supplies practical, concise and specific astrological methods and techniques that pinpoint the answers to the above questions. If you are a professional counselor or astrologer, this book is indispensible to your practice. The reader who studies this material carefully and applies it to his or her own chart will discover an objective vehicle to uncover the essence of his or her own state of being. The understanding that this promotes can help you cooperate with, instead of resist, the evolutionary and karmic lessons in your life.

Green describes the position of Pluto through all of the signs and houses, explains the aspects and transits of Pluto, discusses Pluto in aspect to the Moon's Nodes, and gives sample charts and readings. It is the most complete look at this "new" planet ever.

0-87542-296-9, 6 x 9, 360 pages, softcover.   **$12.95**

Please write for our catalog (see previous page) for a list of our astrological services and other products.